Brass Singers

The Teaching of Arnold Jacobs

Luis E. Loubriel, D.M.A.

SCHOLAR PUBLICATIONS

CHICAGO

COPYRIGHT © 2011 BY LUIS E. LOUBRIEL
PUBLISHED BY SCHOLAR PUBLICATIONS

First Printing, April 2011

This book is a publication of:
Scholar Publications
P.O. Box 428335
Evergreen Park, IL
60805-9998
U.S.A.

All rights reserved. No part of this book may be reproduced in any form or by any means, electronic or mechanical, including photocopying, recording, or by any information storage or retrieval system, without permission in writing from the publisher.

Library of Congress Cataloguing-in publication data

Loubriel, Luis E.
Brass Singers: The Teaching of Arnold Jacobs
ISBN 978-0-9828935-1-7

Printed in the U.S.A.

To Eunjin.

Brass Singers

The Teaching of Arnold Jacobs

In your mind, you have to be a master musician. You have to be a master interpreter of style and phrase as well as one who communicates a message to someone else. The rest is just minor stuff.

The basis of my teaching has been finding out what we are in life and transferring that to our work in music.

Arnold Jacobs

Contents

Acknowledgements	ix
Introduction	xii

1. ARNOLD JACOBS'S PEDAGOGICAL APPROACH ... 1
    Preview ... 2
    Introduction ... 2
    Song and Wind ... 3
    The Art Form of Music ... 9
    Mind Over Matter ... 10
    Having One Voice in Your Head and One Out the Bell ... 12
    Summary ... 13

2. THE EVOLUTION OF ARNOLD JACOBS'S TEACHING ... 14
    Preview ... 15
    Arnold Jacobs's Evolution ... 15
    Teaching with Simplicity ... 19
    Adolph Herseth's Influence ... 21
    Summary ... 23

3. ARNOLD JACOBS IN THE TWENTIETH CENTURY ... 25
    Preview ... 25
    Brass Pedagogy in the Twentieth Century ... 25
    Playing with Freedom ... 25
    The Process ... 27
    Jacobs's Continuous Development ... 28
    The Difference Between Teaching and Performing ... 29
    Summary ... 30

4. SKILLS AND DRILLS ... 31
    Preview ... 33
    Skills and Drills ... 34
        The Study of *Solfège* to Improve Pitch Recall ... 34
        Entry Notes ... 37
        The Mental Signal for Each Note: Sensory and Motor Nerves ... 38
    Breath ... 40
        Physiology ... 40
        The Shallow Breather ... 41
        Common Breathing Misapplications ... 43
        Breathing Exercises ... 46
        The Aging Process ... 48
        Refinements of Breath Control ... 50
        Breath Modifications ... 50
    Buzz ... 52
        Embouchure ... 52
        Embouchure Formation ... 54

Rim Buzzing	54
The Embouchure that Wants to Vibrate	56
The Singing Brain	58
Mouthpiece Buzzing	58
Embouchure Development	60
High Range Development	62
Lipping Up and Down	63
The Damaged Embouchure	64
Bell's Palsy	65
The Warm Up	65
Endurance Development	66
Brass Playing Acoustics	69
Musical Amplifiers	69
Instrument Makers - Concept of Sound	70
Importance of Equipment	70
Mouthpieces	71
Vibrato	72
Dynamics	73
Tongue	76
Thick Wind	77
Air and Embouchure	77
The Study of Vowels	78
High Air Pressures	79
The Use of the Rim	79
Tongue and Articulation	81
Multiple Tonguing	82
High Register Tonguing	83
The Aging Process	84
Summary	85

5. ARTISTIC CONCEPTS — 86

Preview	87
Artistic Concepts	87
The Use of Imitation	88
Imitate a Better Player	89
The Use of Imagination	89
The Voice Singing in the Head	90
Round Sounds	91
Show Business	93
Playing with Authority	94
The Art of Phrasing	95
Storytelling in Music	97
Summary	97

REFERENCE LIST — 101

APPENDIX A: EDITED LECTURES	103
APPENDIX B: MENTAL ASPECTS	146
APPENDIX C: MUSICIANSHIP AND INTERPRETATION	178
APPENDIX D: PRACTICING	195
APPENDIX E: BREATH	221
APPENDIX F: EMBOUCHURE	236
APPENDIX G: TONGUE AND VOWEL FORMS	255
INDEX	270
BIOGRAPHICAL INFORMATION	277

A NOTE ON THE TEXT

Arnold Jacobs's speech was characterized by a colloquial, humorous, and idiosyncratic style that was part of his charismatic and polite professional demeanor. Therefore, during the transcription process, the author left some aspects of Jacobs's speech intact while rearranging the text to facilitate its reading, sense of cohesion, and narrative style.

ACKNOWLEDGEMENTS

Writing books is no walk in the park except when the readers find the walk stimulating and the conversation with the author informative. The author hopes that his readers find knowledge and enjoyment in reading this book. Yet, preparing for the walk is no walk in the park either, and in this case the author owes many thanks to a number of contributors who helped in the research, editing process, and in the final review of this book.

The author is grateful for the contributions of former Jacobs's colleagues and students who gave interviews and facilitated access to recorded materials. First, to the late Vincent Cichowicz who gave of his time to explain important concepts and narrated some of the developmental aspects in Jacobs's teaching; William Scarlett, who found the simplest of ways to explain Jacobs's concept of *Song and Wind*; John Cvejanovich who, as a former student and Jacobs's driver to and from the Fine Arts Building in Chicago, had a front row seat to Jacobs's teaching; Ronald Hasselmann who narrated his experiences of studying with Jacobs in the 1950's; and finally, Manny Laureano, who, besides serving as an interviewee, encouraged and helped the author in bringing this book to print.

The author also thanks Jacobs's former students who made available the recorded lessons that contained some of the most insightful information used in this book. Those recorded lessons dated from 1971 to 1998. In the same vein, a number of individuals granted the author access to the recorded lectures Jacobs gave in a number of locations. The author owes a special thanks to the Northwestern University Library for granting access to the *Arnold Jacobs Master Classes* (1987 to 1998).

Individually, the author is indebted to his gifted peers who gave of their time to review this book. In particular, the author wants to thank: Allen Pekar (Former student of Arnold Jacobs from 1967 to 1998), Dr. Bruce C. Briney (Professor of Music, Western Illinois University); Michael D. Grose (Associate Professor of Tuba and Euphonium, University of Oregon, School of of Music and Dance), Alex Wilson (Former

Principal Trumpet, Buffalo (NY) Philharmonic Orchestra), and Galindo Rodriguez (Assistant Professor of Music, Northwestern State University).

Finally, the author extends sincere thanks to his family, friends, and colleagues who have been patient and supportive during the research and writing process, including—but not limited to—his wife Eunjin Lee, Milagros Martinez, Gregory Denardo, Ph.D., and the late Michael Ewald, D.M.A.

INTRODUCTION

Arnold Jacobs began teaching in the mid-1930s, but it was during his years in Chicago, IL—serving from 1944 to 1988 as Principal Tuba with the Chicago Symphony Orchestra and teaching in his private studio until 1998—that he developed his remarkable pedagogical approach.

Today, most brass players appreciate the positive changes Jacobs brought to the performance and teaching of brass instruments. These positive changes include the development of an efficient and effective *process* for rectifying brass players' artistic and technical deficiencies, the importance of playing with freedom while avoiding isometric contractions, and an emphasis on the artistic aspects of brass playing as a platform for teaching.

At the foundation of Jacobs's *process* was his students' ability to recall pitch and to create mental images of sound in tandem with the necessary conditioned reflexes—as well as the muscular development—to convert those mental images into physical sounds. Jacobs stressed the development of aural skills—preferring the study of *solfège*, but worked with various sight-singing systems—and insisted that "there is no way or reason to do the advanced technical work on a brass instrument before doing the ear training work."

Jacobs proposed that brass players improve their playing when they focus—without intruding thoughts, sensations of discomfort, or feelings of insecurity—on the artistic message they want to convey to their audience. He said that "instead of thinking of music, some players pay attention to how their embouchures feel." He added, "This is what the so called naturals avoid all the time." Thinking of music first was of utmost importance because ultimately, as Jacobs often reminded his students, "We must be in an art form where we work for audiences."

Jacobs emphasized the artistic aspects of brass playing when teaching his students new concepts or when helping them overcome performance problems. For example, he did not base his approach to embouchure change and development on the study of specific musculatures, but instead he based it on the correct choice and artistic interpretation of musical materials—e.g., solos, orchestral excerpts, etudes, and drills.

As a way of bringing his pedagogical approach together—once he corrected any hindering physical deficiencies—Jacobs encouraged his students to *sing*—as if pretending to be singers—as he believed that "up to the moment of buzzing, great brass players are close to singers." This is especially true when players allow their lips to function as vocal chords. "Players must *sing* perfect notes into their instruments. *Sing* with your lips!" Jacobs would often say.

This book emphasizes the *singing* aspects of brass playing paying particular attention to the concepts Jacobs taught in private lessons and master classes between 1967 to 1998. The author transcribed those concepts from 420 hours of recorded lessons, interviews, and master classes and structured the information to be accessible and useful to all brass players. In addition, the author interviewed former Jacobs's students and colleagues—including the late Vincent Cichowicz, William Scarlett, John Cvejanovich, Ronald Hasselmann, and Manny Laureano—to gain insights from their experiences with Jacobs.

Chapter one, *Arnold Jacobs's Pedagogical Approach*, introduces the reader to selected concepts found in Jacobs's teaching. The concepts include Jacobs's most popular mottos: *Song and Wind*; *The Art Form of Music*; *Mind Over Matter*; and *Having One Voice in the Head and One Out the Bell*.

Chapter two, *The Evolution of Arnold Jacobs's Teaching*, provides insights about Jacobs's development as a teacher through the comments and observations of some of his former colleagues and students.

Chapter three, *Arnold Jacobs in the Twentieth Century*, presents four distinctive characteristics that set Jacobs's pedagogical approach apart from other pedagogical approaches of the Twentieth Century. (In particular, his emphasis on playing with a sense of freedom; the development of an efficient and effective *process* for learning the performance of brass instruments; his continuous development as a teacher; and his belief that teaching and performing—although allied in the music profession—conflicted in actual practice).

Chapter four, *Skills and Drills*, delivers information related to the development of skills, rectification of deficiencies and negative habits, and the application of performance concepts.

Chapter five, *Artistic Concepts*, discusses the artistic concepts Jacobs used in his teaching. In particular, the concepts of imitation; the use of imagination; singing in the head; round sounds; show business; the art of phrasing; and storytelling in music.

The reader will find the appendices particularly helpful in understanding specific content areas found in Jacobs's pedagogical approach. The author took special care in organizing the information from lessons and master classes to create an easy-to-read narrative. As such, the appendices stand alone and could be studied separately from the main text of this book.

Brass Singers

Chapter One

Arnold Jacobs's Pedagogical Approach

Contents

Preview	2
Introduction	2
Song and Wind	3
The Art Form of Music	9
Mind Over Matter	10
Having One Voice in Your Head and One Out the Bell	12
Summary	13

Preview

• *Jacobs based his pedagogical approach on the concept of Song and Wind. Song represents the mental aspects of playing while Wind represents the physical aspects of playing.*
• *Jacobs insisted that brass players need to conceptualize their music as good singers—by thinking of each note before they play it. He called this way of thinking mentalization.*
• *Similar to the vocal chords of a good singer—actively moving toward the direction of the wind while changing length, thickness, and tension to achieve various pitches and tone qualities—a brass player's lip changes shape according the player's artistic thoughts.*
• *Jacobs did not want his students to focus on the series of scientific procedures he had just explained as a recipe for good playing. Instead, he wanted his students to play by putting perfect notes into their instruments.*
• *Jacobs explained the relationship between mind and body by saying that players have to communicate with their body by using honest simple thoughts and not rationalizations or peripheral thinking.*
• *To maintain the seamless communication between mind and body, brass players need to concentrate on the one thought that will produce the best results. This thought is the sound of the their instrument—or a human voice—loud and clear resonating like a bell inside their heads.*

Introduction

Once a century comes along a brass master whose teaching and performance concepts represent that century's collective approach. Often, that master's influence remains latent for generations after the master's passing. Whereas Jean Baptiste Arban is arguably the representative figure of the Nineteenth Century, many brass players regard Arnold Jacobs to be the representative brass pedagogue of the Twentieth Century.

Jacobs based his teaching on brass performance concepts—most notably the brass player's ability to hear a perfect note (with all its pitch and tonal qualities) in his mind's ear. He insisted that, as naturally as a good singer sings a beautiful tune, a brass player should *sing* his notes into his instrument.

In transcribing 420 hours of Jacobs's recorded master classes and private lessons, the author found that Jacobs used key concepts repeatedly. Jacobs returned to the same concepts, rearranging them in countless forms and variations—similar to how Wolfgang Amadeus Mozart or Ludwig van Beethoven transformed thematic motifs in their symphonies. For example, the concept of holding a mental image of an ideal brass sound could take the form of "having an instrument in your head and another one in your hand" or be varied and be called mentalization.[i] Those key concepts functioned as "three by five" cards that Jacobs had stored in his arsenal of teaching tools to use at applicable times.

Jacobs used his key concepts while teaching brass performance skills to his students—skills such as the free and uninterrupted release of the breath or the ability to buzz instantly were among the most common—and to encourage them to play artistically.

In this book, these key concepts will serve as the descriptive landmarks of Jacobs's pedagogical approach. The author carefully transcribed Jacobs's recorded master classes and private lessons with the goal of finding those quotes that would most vividly and clearly describe his pedagogical approach. The author also took special care during the transcription process to write Jacobs's quotes in a style geared toward ease of reading while maintaining the meaning of his message and his speech mannerisms. The concept of *Song and Wind* will open a narrative that will take the reader through essential technical and artistic aspects of brass performance.

Song and Wind

Today, most brass players refer to Arnold Jacobs's pedagogical approach as *Song and Wind*. Although *Song and Wind* is Jacobs's most popular motto, not all brass players comprehend its applications. By *Song*, Jacobs meant the player's ability to hear—or conceptualize sound—in the player's mind. The concept of *Song* also included the player's potential to execute, as if it were a command to speak or to sing that mental conception of sound. *Wind* signifies all the physical aspects involved in providing a motor force—or active wind column—necessary to propel the player's lips into constant vibration.

The following—from a lesson Jacobs gave a trumpet student in 1995—is an example of the deeper meaning of *Song and Wind*:

> You are a musician and things have to be always worked out based on music. The final arbiter in everything is sound, phrase, and style. Now, the words *Song and Wind* are very important. *Song* has to do with the biocomputer and *Wind* is your motor force. Just like the bow is the motor force for the string family. The bow is just a bow without a string. Our string is our lips. You can't associate your lips with the reed family because it's a different principle. Theirs is a piece of wood. The lips are part of you, and they are tied into your nervous system. The woodwind reed is not. As a result, you have to associate your lips with your vocal chords. Then you get the picture. You *sing* with your lips!

Jacobs emphasized the quality of *singing*—in terms of pitch, tone, tempo, articulation, and dynamics—brass players mentalized while playing. However, a description of what Jacobs meant by the word mentalization will facilitate the understanding of its application.

Jacobs used the word mentalization to describe the mental images of sound players create in their minds. Similarly to poets or novelists—who posses a rich linguistic inner mind—musicians must have a mind full of sounds. Musicians develop their mentalizations through a lifetime of varied listening and performing experiences. Their minds are then capable of creating—or mentalizing—vivid mental images of sound.

Although psychologists use the concept of mentalization in the study of overt behavior, Jacobs coined the word mentalization to be used in his brass performance lessons and master classes. Hence, the word mentalization cannot be found in standard English dictionaries. Concerning his unique use of the word, Jacobs said to a student:

> I coined the word mentalization because I don't think it exists in the English language. Nonetheless, the idea is that you should always play as a singer by mentalizing what you are about to play. The vocal chords receive the message from the brain based on what the singer is communicating to someone else. The embouchure must act like the vocal chords. As long as you are in the music profession, make sure of your mentalizations and not of your physicalizations.

It could therefore be established that the mentalizations brass players use while performing are, according to Jacobs, similar to the mentalizations good singers use. The benefits gained from studying the artistic interpretations of vocalists are remarkable. Yet, Jacobs warned not to imitate other physical functions or specialized techniques singers use. He explained:

> I'm impressed by the closeness of singing and brass playing. The quality of vocal teaching is sometimes terrible. The average vocal teacher doesn't know which way is up so I can't send a student to a singer because they might acquire bad habits from bad teaching. However, the training for the brain in terms of interpretations of music and styles is marvelous. Mentally, a brass player is much closer to a singer than any other instrument. The more vocal your brass playing becomes, the better you'll sound.

These mentalizations, once conceived by the player, are channeled through "the buzzing of the lips." Similar to the vocal chords of a good singer—actively moving toward the direction of the wind while changing length, thickness, and tension to achieve various pitches and tone qualities—a brass player's lip changes its shape according the player's artistic thoughts. Jacobs helped his students achieve a level of performance where they would play by *singing* with their lips—almost as if purposely transferring the function of the singing vocal chords to the lips.[ii] However, many students had deficiencies that impeded them from "*singing* with their lips."[iii] During lessons, Jacobs worked to resolve those deficiencies.

Jacobs wanted his students to allow their lips to buzz in coordination with their mentalizations. This approach, he found, was the most natural and efficient way to play a brass instrument. He wanted players to treat their lips as vocal chords so the pitch and intensity of each note was pre-determined by the time it reached the cup of the mouthpiece. "It's success or failure because everything on the other side of the mouthpiece is acoustics," he said. He described the approach of "singing while playing" a brass instrument as follows:

> Always motivate *Song and Wind*. *Song* is always vocal chords and buzz. *Singing* into the mouthpiece! That's what you must motivate. The fuel is the wind. It should motivate the musical message like a singer. If you order wind, you don't know what's going to come out. It's "pot luck." Maybe it will be good maybe it will be bad, but you are not in charge. You have to order song! Don't order wind. Order the sound directly as your main product. There is no buzzing without blowing. It doesn't exist. You can't buzz without blowing. You don't have to worry about blowing. You have to instead put your money where it pays off. Vibration pays off. There is no sound without lip vibration. Just because you blow air, it doesn't mean that you are going to have lip vibration. Blowing by itself creates silence so if you want sound, you have to order the song.
>
> Make sure the *singing* is the first thing you do—not the lips and not the blowing. Like a singer, there are habits you have to form that

have to do with taking charge of your music. In other words, you have to treat yourself like a vocalist. By that I don't mean in terms of breath applications or specifics of vocal techniques, but in terms of using a voice. The lips become the vocal chords. *Sing* with them! Put the notes into the cup of the mouthpiece. By the time it reaches the throat of the mouthpiece, it's success or failure because everything on the other side of the mouthpiece is acoustics. Don't depend on a three-valve instrument to give you three or four octaves of chromatics. You've got to *sing* perfect notes into the horn so it can resonate according to its acoustical laws—primarily based on sympathetic resonance.

Jacobs insisted in establishing the similarities between singers and brass players since—besides sharing the same performance approach—they share two of the three elements necessary in sound production. The first element is the motor force (the breath) and the second is its source of vibration (vocal chords or lips). The third element—the source of resonance—differs as brass players amplify their pitches using a brass instrument and singers use their oral cavity. The main reason Jacobs stressed these similarities was to establish that up to the moment of buzzing their lips, brass players are close to singers:

A cup-mouthpiece brass instrument is the closest to the human voice. The three basic elements of tone production must always be motor force, a source of vibration that involves pitch, and a source of resonance (amplification). Of those three, a singer has all. They are part of his anatomy. The brass player has two. Most other instruments have one. For example, the factory sends out a piano with pitch-vibration and resonance built in. The only element needed is the motor force. Brass players have within their own body two of the basic elements of tone production, but they don't have amplification. As a brass player, you don't have a built in sound board and this is why you need an instrument. However, the pitch-vibration and the motor force (a wind column) are up to you.

Most other instruments are not like that. For example, instruments like the oboe, clarinet, or violin have all sorts of perceptions regarding what the fingers are doing. The nervous system involved in playing them gives players certain knowledge of functions (like string vibration where you have to vibrate a string while it's resonated by the instrument, but you find the pitch based on what you are doing with your left hand). Therefore, the violin—as well as other instruments—involves more mechanics and awareness.

Brass players don't know what they are doing in terms of mechanics. If you would treat a brass instrument like if it were your voice, you would have tremendous success. You simply can never get into the analysis of anything you are doing. Deliberately recognize that your playing is very much like a voice when singing. Playing a brass instrument and singing are very close because instead of the laryngeal nerve going down to the larynx, you get the seventh cranial nerve going to the embouchure. It's the same identical treatment in message. If you don't sing with your voice, *sing* while you are playing! Most players who get in trouble try to use their lip as a woodwind reed. You can't play by treating your lip as a wooden reed. Instead, it has to be used like the vocal chords of a singer. Then you have success!

While some students found it easy to *sing* with their lips, others did not. Jacobs helped those troubled students maintain a mental focus on their *singing* by giving them mental tools—such as singing *solfège* or singing sequential numbers.[iv] These mental tools stabilized the students' mental focus on singing—resulting in an improvement in their tone production. Jacobs said:

One of the most stabilizing influences in playing is counting in the head aloud and in pitch. That sends a signal down from, you might say, the motor cortex. It has to be a voice up there in your head so as if you were going to sing with your vocal chords, but instead you *sing* with your lips (which are the vocal chords of a brass instrument). This has to be one of the things you must rely on in this profession.

Other times, Jacobs gave students "repeated singing syllables" [not specifically *solfège*] to stress the importance of controlling their music with their conceptual thought. That conceptual thought was a form of music mentalization that appeared as "LA, LA, LAS" or "TOH, TOH, TOHS" in the player's mind. Jacobs insisted that players need those mentalizations to activate and control their conditioned reflexes. This was the means of control Jacobs wanted his students to use while playing music. In the following excerpt, Jacobs called this control process a reflex response:

Can you hear a voice coming out of your instrument? The voice of a wonderful singer singing "TOHHHHH"? Changing your lip shouldn't direct the changes from note to note, but instead you change from note to note by *singing* each pitch in your head. If you try to play by changing your lips, you are very apt to miss. You have to play from your reflexes in your brain and you are almost guaranteed results.
  I have been working on this in recent years because I would like to put some papers out on this subject, but it looks very much to me like brass playing is really a reflex response. We are so used to handling our embouchures, but in this case if you let go and handle the brain instead, you get better and easier results.

> You have to start each tune with great quality. Prepare the qualities of tone in your head before you play and you'll be better off. Prepare the sound and not the mechanics. Your body will respond as a result. Then we go back to what my thesis is, brass playing is a reflex. If I am right, you'll see that many things in your playing will change for the better. All of this has to do with your ability to mentalize your music before you play it.
>
> I have taught mentalization my entire adult life, but I have never really looked for the text or the ways to prove it. However, I am doing that now. The more I do it, the more I am convinced I am right.

Although Jacobs did not complete his research on the applications of mentalization to brass playing and teaching, he taught mentalization to his students. He also used mentalization—or *singing while playing* as he also called it—as a tool for improving his own playing early in his music career. This happened when he was a student at the Curtis Institute of Music in Philadelphia. He narrated:

> The habit of *singing while playing* has been an interest of mine from before I started teaching. As a kid, I used to sing when I was a voice student. I intuitively used my voice and I was lucky because when Fritz Reiner [then teacher at the Curtis Institute of Music in Philadelphia] would ask for orchestral parts a certain way, he would usually sing them. I couldn't hear what he said, but I would pay close attention to his vocal interpretation. That was what I really copied. It was much more successful than trying to interpret words. When I interpreted words, I usually screwed up. I noticed that when I copied his voice, it was only once through, and he was satisfied.

The *singing while playing* approach can also be called the *singing approach*. The *singing approach* is analogous to mentalization and *singing while playing*—all of which remain important concepts for the rest of this book.

In sum, Jacobs based his teaching on the concept of *Song and Wind*. *Song* signifies the artistic and psychological aspects of playing while *Wind* signifies the motor force as well as the physical aspects of playing.

A brass player's ability to mentalize—or to imagine mental images of sound—is of utmost importance. These mentalizations direct a player's physical functions by way of conditioned reflexes developed by years of practice. However, it is important for players not to focus on the physical functions, but instead let them happen naturally (while maintaining a constant focus on their mentalizations). According to Jacobs, this is how a good singer performs and encouraged his students to imitate that artistic approach. Jacobs encouraged his students to *sing* syllables in their heads—in the form of *solfège*, singing sequential numbers, or repeated syllables. This was to Jacobs the most natural way to make music. However, to achieve this "natural way of making music" at higher artistic levels, players must first become fluent in the art form of music.

The Art Form of Music

Despite the fact that Jacobs integrated what he learned from his physiological and psychological studies to his teaching, it is important to recognize that Jacobs based his pedagogical approach on the art form of music. The art form of music encompasses the aesthetics considerations players strive to express in their artistic message—e.g., beauty of tone, articulation, and phrasing.

Often, Jacobs used scientific terminology to explain essential aspects of brass playing—e.g., sympathetic resonance to explain how acoustical laws work in relation to mouthpiece buzzing and sound production. However, he did not want his students to focus on a series of scientific procedures as a recipe for playing music. Instead, he wanted his students to send a predetermined artistic message into their instruments:

> The more you get into the art form of music, the more the instrument becomes a stupid piece of brass governed by acoustical laws. Some brass players tend to adapt themselves and play as if it was a piano by simply pressing keys. The acoustical principles between a brass instrument and the piano are so vastly different that the acoustical relationships are altered. A brass instrument is an acoustical amplifier with strange laws based on "sympathetic resonance." The piano's acoustical laws are based on *forced resonance*. The piano has one sound board that resonates all pitches. A brass instrument has a "sound board" that resonates specific partials with all sorts of gaps in between. That means that coming from the player must be the motor function and pitch vibration. All the horn can do is amplify. You have to play a brass instrument as you would play a megaphone by putting a message into it.

William Scarlett, former Assistant Principal Trumpet with the Chicago Symphony Orchestra, remembered his early lessons with Jacobs in the 1950s. Scarlett was impressed by the concept of thinking artistically and not mechanically (or physically) while playing. Nonetheless, he admits not to have understood what Jacobs meant by "the art form of music." Although Scarlett had studied with other famous brass teacher of the time, he had not been taught this concept before going to Jacobs. Scarlett said:

> I can remember him [Jacobs] telling me in my first lesson that this is an art form. I didn't even know what he meant by that. If somebody says that this is an art form, what does that mean? It means that one makes music by thinking artistically, not physically or mechanically, which I had not been taught before. However, as a kid it came naturally.

Jacobs's assertion that his students would improve their playing by thinking artistically was based on the concept of mind over matter—i.e., the belief that the mind is more powerful than the body. Theories of mind over matter abounded in the 1960s and 1970s—Jacobs's most active developmental years as a pedagogue—and were commonly expressed in reference to paranormal phenomena and psychokinesis.[v] However, Jacobs's influence on this subject began during his childhood in Willowbrook, California, followed in subsequent years by the reading of related literature.

Mind Over Matter

Jacobs's *singing approach* to music performance was rooted in the principle of mind over matter. He explained that "players must focus on the art form of music by mentalizing the pitch, tone color, attacks, and other aesthetics details of each note throughout an entire piece. This is the way they can improve their playing." Jacobs added that, "If Bud [Adolph] Herseth could put his brain into your skull—and you play with his brain—your lips would do a much better job." In other words, positive changes in the players' psychology leads to performance development. He expanded on this idea by narrating some of his early formative experiences growing up as a child in Willowbrook, California:

> Don't hesitate to use personal psychology on yourself because it's amazing what it does in terms of mind over matter. I was brought up in the Christian Science Church and my mother was a very good Christian scientist. During my younger years, much of my imagination was opened by the mind over matter concept.
> I say that because the way I think is so different in so many ways when compared to most people that I think somewhere along the way I might have been influenced by something. I wonder if Christian Science was the influence. Later on, I became an avid science fiction reader and I ran into other pieces of literature of that sort.
> I mention this because what has to improve is the player's concentration. It's not about the embouchure or about muscles—they are already developed. It's how you think when you play your

instrument that's going to help you improve. The more you think about the psychodynamics involved, the better you'll do in this art form.

The late Vincent Cichowicz, former trumpeter with the Chicago Symphony Orchestra and a Jacobs student, described the principle of mind over matter as found in Jacobs's teaching. He said that it was specifically through the study of medicine that Jacobs made the connections between the human mind and its effects on the human body. Cichowicz stressed that it was not solely the study of anatomy, but instead it was the study of physiology in tandem with the study of motivation and behavior that made Jacobs's teaching effective. Cichowicz explained:

> You know, he [Arnold Jacobs] had a deep interest in medicine so he obviously started to study, I assume, medical books and then as you go from that connection into behavior you have to go into psychology. I say that because the study of medical books doesn't explain muscle function by simply saying, "this muscle is attached here and does this, etc." That doesn't give you enough of the picture unless you understand how the brain makes the application.

Jacobs defined the relationship between mind and body by saying that players must communicate with their bodies using honest simple thoughts and not rationalizations or peripheral thinking—e.g., complex step-by-step directions. In music performance, the human body understands commands in the form of mental images of sound. These goal-like commands are easily understood by the subconscious levels of the brain that handle complex body movements. When performing anything that requires skill, this is the *language* the body understands. Jacobs reiterated, "Your body doesn't understand complex rationalizations because they lead to the loss of the natural—childlike—connection between thought and action." He elaborated:

> I cooperate with nature in the sense that I study long and hard how our bodies work in many ways—in sickness, in health, and in music—as well as in other areas. You'll soon find that you don't have senses in your muscles, but instead you have divisions in the brain where muscle sensitivity exists at subconscious levels. People think that muscle sensitivity starts in the lip, but it's not there. Muscle sensitivity works at various levels in your brain. If you learn to use your head by honest simple thoughts, you'll learn to communicate with your body.
>
> You have to communicate in a language your body will understand. In other words, if you want to touch your nose, you simply touch your nose. Your body understands that because it's a clear

goal you want to achieve. If you start rationalizations and peripheral thinking, you'll lose the mind-body communication right away.

To maintain the seamless communication between mind and body, brass players need to concentrate on the one thought that will produce the best results. This thought is the sound of the their instrument—or a human voice—loud and clear, resonating like a bell, inside their heads.

Having One Voice in the Head and One Out the Bell

Jacobs often told his students that they should have two voices. One voice in their heads and another voice coming out of their instruments:

> Can I get you to be more of a singer in your head? You have to play down your instrument quite a bit, but you must instead play up the song in your head. So again, you are dealing with reflexes in your embouchure that respond to the stimuli in your head. Can you increase the stimuli? You do this by creating each phrase by its individual notes. Remember, there should be two voices: one in your head and one coming out of the bell of your instrument. The voice coming out of the bell should be a mirror of the one in your head.

It was essential for Jacobs to teach brass players to have a "voice in their heads" as they played. He was convinced that their musical thoughts affected their physiology. If they sang each note in their heads as they played, they would be giving their embouchures clear directions on how to form and vibrate. Jacobs explained:

> The lip will continue to vibrate if you continue to *sing* in your head. Otherwise, your lip will just become a shape and we don't know if it's going to vibrate or not. If you would simply *sing* the notes loud and clear in your head (like another voice up there), your lip will work. Keep *singing* the notes in your head even if your lip is tired. If nothing comes out the bell, I don't care. However, if your horn goes blank and your head goes blank at the same time, then I do care. Make sure your lips *sing* every note.

By *singing* each note in their heads, players can focus on perfecting their artistic message. For the rest of his teaching career, Jacobs used this simple and effective concept for teaching players at all levels of development. His teaching concepts, however, evolved over time toward simplicity and effectiveness. These simple and effective concepts remained latent throughout his long teaching career and collectively form the text of the following chapters and appendices.

Summary

Throughout his teaching career, Jacobs based his pedagogical approach on the art form of music. Although Jacobs explained aspects of brass playing using scientific terminology, he did not want his students to focus on a series of scientific procedures as they played. Instead, he wanted his students to *sing* in their heads and put perfect notes into their instruments.

Jacobs established a clear relationship between the human mind and its effects on music performance. He stressed that players should communicate with their bodies by using honest and simple thoughts and not rationalizations or peripheral thinking. He wanted his students to have two instruments, one in their heads sounding as clearly as a bell, and one in their hands amplifying their thoughts.

Chapter Two

The Evolution of Arnold Jacobs's Teaching

Contents

Preview	15
Arnold Jacobs's Evolution	15
Teaching with Simplicity	19
Adolph Herseth's Influence	21
Summary	23

Preview

- *Jacobs sought the most effective and efficient methodologies for getting his message of Song and Wind understood. He also wanted his students to get immediate performance results.*
- *Jacobs realized during the last 10 or 15 years of his life that to get his message across he did not need the medical jargon. This period coincided with his retirement from active performance.*
- *The use of simple instructions was the most effective form of teaching. Toward the end of his life, Jacobs felt comfortable and confident with teaching using what he had found most effective — simplicity.*
- *Adolph "Bud" Herseth served as an example of the "simple approach." Jacobs observed Herseth play beautifully season after season and asked himself, "What is it that makes this player have such great success while other players struggle?"*
- *Today, Jacobs's teaching and performance concepts are regarded as efficient and effective tools by musicians from all over the world.*

Arnold Jacobs's Evolution

The emphasis Jacobs placed on the psychology of *Song* — the artistic aspects of music making — rather that on *Wind* — the physiological aspects of music making — was a feature that evolved over time in his teaching. William Scarlett described the evolution of Jacobs's teaching as follows:

> I saw his teaching change over the years. His teaching was medically oriented in 1956. He would throw those long medical phrases like popcorn popping. I don't think that most of us knew the meaning of the words, but we got the idea of what he was saying and we tried to put those ideas into practice the best way we could.
>   At that time, his medical terminology sometimes translated into physical awareness. Physical thoughts can get in a person's way of playing and that's precisely why he changed his teaching over the years. He got away from the physical and more into making music; as he called it, "the song in the head."

In those early days, he was known as an expert on breathing. It was not until the later years that he began to emphasize the artist in the head. He did talk about the artist in the early years, but the emphasis was on good breathing. Later on, he got into the artistic output; the artist in the head, like when he said, "You've got a trumpet in your head, and you've got a trumpet in your hand."

Over the years, his teaching became much simpler. He still knew the medical words, but he just didn't use them very much. In the end it came down to *Song and Wind*. It was a real revolution in his teaching method, not in the ideas he was teaching. What changed was the method of delivering the ideas and I totally agree with him going towards that direction. Few students know those medical words anyway.

Some people think that Jake [Arnold Jacobs] used those words to impress everybody or to be two steps ahead of what everybody else was teaching. That could be, I don't know. But in the end he could see that playing was an "art form," which he said from the beginning, and it's not a "medical term form" in which you have to be absorbed in all the medical knowledge. You don't.

Vincent Cichowicz described his lessons with Arnold Jacobs during the 1950s in a similar manner. However, he added that without the technical aspects, the students could not evolve to the artistic aspects since both aspects had to work in tandem. He said:

When I studied with him, there was a much larger concentration on *Wind* than on *Song*. Later he started to move with more emphasis towards the *Song*. And yet, without that *Wind* part it can't evolve into the *Song*. It just can't evolve without that. In the years I taught, I couldn't dismiss it either. The two had to be working together in order to achieve the results. You could not say, "Here is a good sound. Imitate!" Because if your breathing is corrupted, there is no way you can achieve your goal.

An example of Jacobs's emphasis on using scientific terminology to explain technical aspects of brass playing occurred during a 1957 lesson with John Cvejanovich. Cvejanovich narrated:

So here is what Jacobs told me. I am playing through J.S. Bach's *Cantata No. 51* in a musical way and he says to me, "Well, I see you have been a shallow breather for a long time and what happens is that in order for you to have any chance at all in getting these notes out I must tell you that, first of all, you are violating Boyle's Law. Because of the elevated tongue that you are using, I can hear it in your sound, you are interfering with the Bernoulli Principle. Furthermore, you are playing at the lower quadrant of the pulmonary function curve. As a result, that's making you go into isometric contractions and as you are trying to continue to play the phrase, you are triggering the Valsalva reflex." I thought, "My God what's all this." However, he was right on the money.

Jacobs explained his position on the evolution of his teaching by saying that, occasionally, he had to teach with a heavy dominance on the technical aspects of brass playing because some of his students expected to be taught that subject.[vii] He elaborated:

> I would say the individual is very much involved when I teach. In other words, you go by what the individual wants to know. There are people who think along different lines in relation to what I do and you have to steer the person into a heavy dominance of the musical thought. I frequently have to be technical in the sense that I am responding to some of the needs of the student. There are teachers who come to see me. They have inquiring minds that won't stay with me unless I can first answer some of the technical questions. In other words, I gauge the student who comes to see me based on our first words together and then I try to establish some way of a "two-way" communication.
>
> Many times, I have to over teach because whomever I am teaching at the moment seems to feel that that's what he needs. At that moment, I can pull rank and say, "No, you do it this way," or I can cooperate, especially if it's somebody I am going to see for an extended period, and say, "All right we can start with the subject of anatomy and physiology." Then I tell them, "You are not going to use this in your playing."
>
> If you want to help a person, you'll find simple answers to complex situations. The complex answers don't fit the picture. If you talk about machine systems and find the anatomy of a machine, you have to also find a fine mechanic to operate the machine when something goes wrong.
>
> For the human body we have physicians who can do wonderful things for us when something goes wrong. It's not necessary to know your own structure unless you are planning to repair it yourself. It's like a car that has simple control panels. I have studied people in various situations — like athletics, like the Australian aborigines and the untutored people in parts of South America — and I found that they all do tremendous physical feats. They dance, they play flutes, they play drums, they use their bodies for tremendously complex things, and they have no "Ph.D. degrees."
>
> I have studied and I have put many factors together. I have used myself as an example of a fairly trouble free player, I had people with problems, I have people in other fields with whom I consult, I have studied the human structures, I have studied a great deal about the brain,

and I have followed the research that's going on in various disciplines. As a culmination of many years of investigation, I want to stress that the answers are all in simplicity, not complexity. The study of what we are has become very complex. I would have to live various lifetimes to finish the study. I came to realize that whoever designed this machine of ours has put in us magnificent brains. I don't think any of us begins to use our brain with real efficiency.

What I am trying to indicate is that the answers are in the study of motivation, the study of what people are like, the study of how to use our brains efficiently and not in the study of mind control over our bodies. Why spend hours studying how to lower your blood pressure— like in the study of Yoga—by conscious thought when you have built in ways to lower you blood pressure (like when you are happy and you have wonderful thoughts). To use your brain efficiently, don't waste time trying to control something you can't control, like an embouchure. When you control the music, you control the embouchure. You don't control meat to control sound; you control sound to control meat. This can be checked out. It's not just my statement.

Jacobs also called the simplification of the complex activities involved in music making a *childlike approach*. He said:

The psychology of what you do is very important. You already have proven that you have the tissue development. You have the reflexes, but now you have to provide the stimulus. To do that, can you begin to simplify your activities so that there is more of a *childlike approach*? I need the adult mind for interpretation and for the qualities of musical styles, but I want the child for the brass playing applications. I don't want your knowledge of muscles and feel phenomena—although a little of it is all right, don't put a magnifying glass on your breath or your lip anymore. Instead, think sheer music!

In sum, Jacobs sought the most effective and efficient methodologies for getting his message of *Song and Wind* understood. He also wanted his students to get immediate performance results. However, this teaching approach evolved over time. Some former Jacobs students recall how—during their lessons in the 1950s— Jacobs would recite long monologues describing the technical intricacies of brass playing. Jacobs, of course, used accurate and appropriate medical jargon. A former Jacobs student expressed, "We didn't understand half the words he was saying, but he seemed to get his message across."

Jacobs realized during the last 10 or 15 years of his life that to get his message across he did not need the medical jargon. This period coincided with his retirement from active performance. He said in 1990, "I have less problems now that

I just teach. Since I don't have a playing career anymore, I have actually become a better teacher. I think it's because I spend more time thinking about my students' playing problems."

During this period, he still knew the medical jargon, but instead he had found "buzz words" or "key phrases" as appropriate replacements. *Song and Wind* is one among many of those key phrases. The collection of Jacobs's key phrases includes: *round sounds*, *singing in the head*, and *the art form of music*. Toward the end of his life, Jacobs was confident that he had developed—mainly through years of trial and error—the most effective and simplest form of teaching to get his message of *Song and Wind* across.

Teaching With Simplicity

By the 1980s, Jacobs had found simple ways to help players overcome playing problems. He achieved this by teaching his students simple mental cues to improve their performance. Manny Laureano commented on Jacobs's ability to help brass players by teaching them those mental cues:

> He (Jacobs) would take time to tell you about the complex things, but the point he would make was to make sure you had very simple mental cues to deal with the complexities involved in playing. Only then, we would be able to make the complexities happen. Not the other way around.

In other words, by using simple mental cues, the player found the most effective way to control his body. Jacobs reaffirmed that all players have a set of controls in their brains to manage the complexities of elaborate skills such as brass playing. He explained:

> If we play by ordering a product [brass sound], we'll find that our playing becomes effortless. The main reason for this phenomenon lies in the great set of controls that we have in our brain (if we simply order a product, the necessary actions will be executed by the lower levels of the brain—the *cerebellum*). This is why it's important to go by the study of the product and not by the study of the mechanics involved.
> However, for the "chain of commands" to work effortlessly we have to get out of the way. In other words, think of how you want to sound in your instrument and avoid thinking of how you are going to do it (this would be like an actor trying to act while simultaneously writing his script). You must put a great deal of thought on what you are trying to accomplish musically and not on how you are going to

accomplish it mechanically. The "thinking" part of your brain is simply not competent enough to order the actual "machine systems" in your body directly. The thinking part of your brain is indeed competent in ordering what it wants and letting the lower parts of the brain do the handling of the specific "machine systems" for it.

By "machine systems," Jacobs meant that—at a basic physical level—the anatomical parts used in producing a tone function like a machine. That is, a human flesh and blood machine. This machine is perhaps the most complex in the world. It has—as related to brass playing—systems of "pulls and balances" (embouchure muscles), "chain of reactions" as in the "Valsalva maneuver," and a "biocomputer" (human brain). However, players must use such complex systems by issuing simple commands. Jacobs said:

> We must keep simple things simple. The human body is, perhaps, the most complex "machine system" on earth. However, complex machines have simple controls (like a car). In the human body, the simple controls are in our brain so we can be free to cope with life outside ourselves—not inside ourselves. To deal with life inside ourselves, we can study Yoga so we can influence our internal body by using mental concentration and emotions.

It was during the last ten or fifteen years of his teaching career that Jacobs was able to use simple key phrases without resorting to lengthy scientific explanations. This was a simplifying process that evolved in his teaching. He explained:

> One of the things I have realized throughout the many years of teaching—and that I have only been able to use in my teaching for the last ten years or so—is the simplifying process. Twenty or thirty years ago I did teach using simplicity, but people didn't come to see me because I wasn't teaching how to use muscles and they thought that I wasn't teaching right. That was until it was proven that playing with simplicity is the most efficient way to play.
>
> It's hard to convince a person until they achieve success playing with simplicity. Your habits don't include some of the things I am teaching. At this point, you have to recognize that. Don't undo anything you have done before. You are a fine brass player with what you've got. However, you are not a great artist yet. You just have to add more tools to your arsenal of thoughts.
>
> All the things we are doing in the lesson are to simplify your thoughts—not to complicate your thoughts. I still want *Song and Wind*, but I also want you to recognize that you have the tendency to over change and over do. I want you to be more dependent on your concept

of how these notes have to sound and make sure you pay attention to what's going on in your brain rather than in your lips.

Brass players usually don't think this way. Adolph Herseth does. He is a storyteller of sound. I mentioned that to him years ago and he liked that. You have to bring in developmental challenges even if those challenges are not included in your instrument's repertoire. In other words, take some of the violin music and interpret it. Take charge of your music and not of your instrument!

Adolph Herseth's Influence

Incidentally, Adolph "Bud" Herseth[viii] served as an example of the "simple approach." Jacobs observed Herseth play beautifully season after season and asked himself, "What is it that makes this player have such great success while other players struggle?" John Cvejanovich added to this line of thought by saying:

> What originally got Jacobs so curious and inspired to research brass playing was what Bud Herseth was doing that resulted in a tremendous success in a brass instrument. Basically, it was Herseth's thought process that was not encumbered by all the mental junk (such as the stuff which goes through your head while you are sitting on the stage thinking, "What am I doing here?) In other words, the bigger the challenge, the better Bud Herseth would play. The psychology of it was such.

William Scarlett commented on the same subject by saying the following:

> Jake [Arnold Jacobs] said one of the last times I saw him in the studio, "Bud never knew it, but he was one of my best teachers." All Jacobs had to do was to sit in the orchestra and watch him. He saw how Herseth did what he did and then he [Jacobs] would go to the studio and try it out for himself. Then he would teach it to the students. He said, "Then I knew the way it should be." Bud was so efficient. Unbelievably efficient! He was simply our model to try to copy.

It is of interest that Herseth's earliest musical influences were his high school band director as well as opera singers. William Scarlett narrated:

> Bud Herseth told me the story of taking a lesson with his band director and Bud was struggling with something so the band teacher picked up his trumpet and said, "Just play it like this," and he played it nice and free and simply gave Herseth a lesson in good thinking. That was started in high school, but Bud carried that approach throughout his career.
> Herseth also gives credit to his mother who had opera recordings playing in the house all the time. I feel that I was very

fortunate to have played a number of seasons at the Lyric Opera of Chicago. I listened to great singers from all over the world. The emotion and the little nuances they did with their voices were so subtle that we can't even describe them in words. They add up to some very emotional music making. Bud said that he was very fortunate to have had those opera recordings in the house especially singers like Jussi Bjorling.

Manny Laureano made the following connection between brass playing and singing when asked what specific conception of brass playing he thought Jacobs was after:

For Arnold, the conception to brass playing was really singing. He would use the expression that what came out of the horn was a mirror of what was inside your head and he wanted you to constantly *sing*. Therefore the horn was a vehicle, it was a tool, to make your internal voice external. So I would say that his concept was almost operatic, storytelling, which is what he told us all the time. He wanted us to be storytellers. He also encouraged us to put words to the music we were playing. So if you think of brass playing as an operatic sort of an event all of that starts to make sense. In terms of quality of sound, I think that he was always looking for great clarity and lots of fundamental in the sound.

I say the latter because of the way he used to play and the way I heard those characteristics in his playing. I would also say that, as he held Herseth as an example, this is also what I heard in Bud's playing that I enjoyed so much. Like in those Fritz Reiner recordings. The great fundamentals with the singing quality on top.

I don't think I can describe his concept of sound in any other way than as an operatic voice with great clarity and with lots of body coming from the fundamentals of the instrument.

Jacobs found the playing of another trumpet player, Timofei Dockshizer[ix], to exemplify what he was teaching. Jacobs said:

I listened to Timofei Dockshizer, when I did this thing with the Summit Brass this last summer, and he was very musical trumpet player. He simply is an extremely musical trumpet player. I was hearing very much what I am teaching in his playing — buoyant and a singing quality all over the horn. That's the type of playing you should imitate.

Today, Jacobs's teaching and performance concepts are regarded as efficient and effective tools by musicians worldwide. However, in the 1950s and 1960s,

Jacobs's teaching was not universally well received. For example, the opinion of a renowned New York City brass teacher from that time was that Jacobs was giving too much information to his students. That teacher added, "You don't want them to become your competition." Fortunately, Jacobs did not pay much attention to those comments and continued teaching his way for 40 more years.

Summary

By the 1980s, Jacobs had found simple ways to help his students overcome performance problems. He taught his students to use simple mental cues based on the "set of controls" they have in their brains. A brass player's body works similarly to a "machine system," which functions best by following simple commands—such as the mentalizations of a resonant tone.

This simple approach to brass performance was exemplified by the playing of Adolph Herseth. The playing of Russian trumpeter, Timofei Dockshizer also exemplified what Jacobs taught; "a buoyant and singing quality all over the horn."

Chapter Three

Arnold Jacobs in the Twentieth Century

Contents

Preview	25
Brass Pedagogy in the Twentieth Century	25
Playing with Freedom	25
The Process	27
Jacobs's Continuous Development	28
The Difference Between Teaching and Performing	29
Summary	30

Preview

- *For most of the contributors consulted for this book, Renold Schilke represented the tight belly pedagogical approach used during the 1950s, 1960s, and 1970s.*
- *Jacobs was a different kind of musician. He described his thinking as "different in many ways from that of most people."*
- *Jacobs had a process for achieving change in his students.*
- *Jacobs continued to develop his teaching skills and knowledge until the end of his teaching career.*
- *Even though Jacobs was a highly knowledgeable and dedicated teacher, he said that he did not have all the answers and that students had to find some of the applications of his breakthroughs.*
- *Jacobs insisted that teaching was different from performing.*

Brass Pedagogy in the Twentieth Century

Jacobs was a different kind of musician. He described his thinking as "different in many ways from that of most people." These "different ways" reflected in his pedagogical approach. For example, while already a highly successful pedagogue, Jacobs continued to conduct experiments with his students during lessons. Those experiments often led to pedagogical breakthroughs that later appeared in his teaching. Because of his constant research and curious disposition, his development of teaching skills and acquisition of knowledge continued until the end of his career.

In studying other popular pedagogical approaches used by brass teachers during the first half of the Twentieth Century, the following four characteristics set Arnold Jacobs's pedagogical approach apart.

Playing with Freedom

The sense of freedom while playing a brass instrument was the first characteristic that set Jacobs's pedagogical approach apart. During most of the Twentieth Century, the *tight belly* school of playing was common practice. This school of playing proposed the tightening of the abdominal muscles—in an isometric fashion—as means of air support. Jacobs found that such practice limited the performing abilities of brass players since it led to pelvic pressures. He explained:

> The old teaching of air support was based on abdominal expansion for breathing and rigidity so even when players inhaled, they couldn't blow out again; besides, they would only take a little quantity of air to start. Once they got a little bit older, or had to play louder than they were used to—so they needed more air—everything just tensed up and they would start to worry. As a result, their embouchure would stop functioning properly.
> When you are younger, the same breathing motion gets you more air. Later in your career, especially when you start teaching some one else, is when you really get screwed up. When I was a young teacher, those screwed up players would come to my studio, but they would question what I had to say and they put a lot of resistance.

Vincent Cichowicz found Jacobs's pedagogical approach different from other approaches used during the 1950s. He found the teaching methodologies of those years to be extraordinarily analytical and ineffective. When asked to elaborate on this point, Cichowicz responded:

> I would say Arnold's teaching was definitely different. All you have to do is to go back to some of the trumpet method books of this period and you will find that many are extraordinarily analytical.
> I make the comparison with going to the doctor because you have a temperature; so it's obvious that you are sick. If all he does is to give you aspirin, or give you some ice to lower your temperature, then he is not a good doctor. A good doctor would say, "What's making your temperature rise." I have to that find out in order to deal with that. It's the same thing with the theories of the 1950s

For most of the contributors consulted for this book, Renold Schilke represented the *tight belly* pedagogical approach used during the 1950s, 1960s, and 1970s. William Scarlett described Schilke's approach as follows:

> Very tight, shallow breathing and a tight belly. That was the approach that Schilke would teach, but what was revealing was when Jacobs put me in the respirometer.... I had to be free to take a full breath.

Vincent Cichowicz told of a similar experience he had in a lesson with Schilke:

When I studied with Renold Schilke, for example, he said, "Make your stomach hard." I tried that and it was terrible. So I asked, "Why is he telling me to do this?" It occurred to me that if you play a high "C" *forte* you would find that your stomach area gets hard. However, you can't start out that way. It has to be a result of what you are doing rather than something that you begin with.

To sum, Jacobs helped his students regain performance efficiency by using a well thought out system for achieving performance freedom. He based this system on his knowledge of human physiology and psychology. He obtained some of the information concerning human physiology from medical books and journals. The information concerning human psychology he found in books such as Percy Buck's *Psychology for Musicians* and Maxwell Maltz's *Psycho-Cybernetics*.

The Process

The second characteristic that made Jacobs's approach different was the use of a process for achieving positive changes in his students. Vincent Cichowicz acknowledged the existence of this process when he said that at first, he was skeptical of Jacobs's ideas, but later he found that there was a method (a process) to those ideas:

> At the beginning, I was very skeptical of his ideas. I told him that and he said, "Well, yes but in order to prove or disprove you have to give it an honest trial." I agreed and I said, "Absolutely. It's the only way to make a decision." Often at the beginning of something that you don't fully comprehend there is no way you can make an intelligent judgment. After working with it over a considerable period, and keeping in mind certain perceptions, I was convinced. It answered many questions that in my previous ways of going about my work never seemed to be fully solved.
> As I began to understand the system and to find my way through the logic of what he was teaching then some of the questions I had about playing were much easier to deal with. Also, they were more successful than the path I was following before.
> It was a whole *process* and as I said, Jacobs was clearer than most people about the function, teaching, and the principles of brass playing. He had medical knowledge and had vocal experience so those two things combined enabled him to get away from the brass part. Then he was able to say, "Now, how does all this tie together?"
> Certainly in teaching, you must have the basis for what you are trying to do in order to present it to someone. It's important to have a clear understanding of principles. You can't just say, "OK, make a beautiful sound." The student might say, "I'd like to but I can't." Then

you have to go into the principles of what goes into making a good sound. If you don't have a conception of a good sound, you can't get to it through mechanical means alone. You must have a clear image in your head, and then you can apply the technical aspects to achieve your goal. If there is something that's not functioning correctly, you can take steps to correct your approach.

So those ideas are the kind of things that, as you begin to understand this, you begin to work at what Arnold used to call *the process*.

Jacobs's Continuous Development

A third distinctive characteristic found in Jacobs's pedagogical approach was the continuous development of his teaching skills and knowledge. This was apparent towards the end of his teaching tenure. Two months before his death, on October 7, 1998, Jacobs said to a student:

> There seem to be thresholds and I have noticed them in so many aspects of playing. You see, I am still learning as I am teaching you and I am learning more and more about these thresholds. For instance, very soft conceptual thought doesn't register in the brain. For it to intervene, it has to be at a certain level even in your thought process. Now, this varies from individual to individual. I don't have codes, scales, or anything I can go by so this is virgin territory.

John Cvejanovich mentioned a similar experience when Jacobs was testing his own pedagogical approach:

> There was another aspect in my studies with Jacobs. If he had a difficult day of teaching, because students didn't respond well, can you imagine that he would think his pedagogy was faulty? Then he would ask me to play some of his usual things (drills) to test his pedagogy and make sure it still worked.... So, when he would have one of those bad days I would know because he would ask me to do some of that stuff. I would say, "Yes, I know what's going on here because he wants to see if his stuff works," and he would say, "Bravo John" when I succeeded, but I knew that he was actually saying, "Bravo Jake."

Even though Jacobs was a highly knowledgeable and dedicated teacher, he said that he did not have all the answers and that the students had to find some of the applications of his breakthroughs:

Find out what works for you because I don't have all the answers. All I have are some breakthroughs. The physical applications may vary a little bit, but the main point is when there is buzzing in the lips, there is tone in your instrument. That's a principle! We are just making it come much faster by focusing on it.

The Difference Between Teaching and Performing

A fourth characteristic that set Jacobs's pedagogical approach apart was his insistence that teaching was different from performing. He believed that players should not use a "teacher's thinking" while performing and often talked of great players who jeopardized their performing careers by teaching too much and by going on stage wearing a "teacher's hat." To him, this overlap of "ways of thinking" led to performance deterioration. Therefore, Jacobs recommended wearing different hats, or ways of thinking—i.e., one hat for teaching and one hat for performing. He explained:

> Teaching is fatiguing to the brain. Even though teaching and performing are allied, the constant analyzing a teacher does is habit forming (if you teach many hours a day). The first bad effect of teaching is that you are always analyzing and that tires the brain. You have to learn to bring this under control because I have seen many fine players go down hill once they start teaching heavy schedules. Maybe you can decide to teach when it does the least amount of harm. That's so when you go play, you have a fresh brain.

On the same subject, Manny Laureano said the following:

You see, one of the things Jacobs made me do in 1988 was to completely change my teaching load. I was teaching, for his taste, too many students. So he said, "I want you to cut back way down on your teaching. You are doing too much thinking about technical things and I need you to do more playing. I need you to do more thinking about music."
    One thing that I took from his playbook was not to teach on the days when he had to perform. He said, "You know, I can teach more now because I wear two hats. When I go on stage, I wear the hat of the performer and when I am teaching, I wear the hat of the teacher. I have done this long enough and well enough to know when to put those hats on." It has only been in recent years that I started teaching on days in when I perform and now I understand what he meant. When you go on stage in orchestra hall, you forget all of that other stuff; you leave it at home. You leave it in the studio and just become the performer on the stage.

Jacobs's teaching attracted many brass students starting in the 1950s. Young brass players of that generation—for example, Vincent Cichowicz—appreciated Jacobs's gifts as a teacher, and studied with him. Cichowicz mentioned that the most common answer to playing problems at the time was, "Go home and practice! With Jacobs, it was different. He would tell you exactly what the problem was and how to go about fixing it."

Summary

The characteristics that set Jacobs's teaching apart include: 1) the pursuit of playing with freedom, 2) the development of a teaching process for achieving positive performance changes, 3) Jacobs's own continuous development as a teacher, and 4) the belief that teaching and performing were allied disciplines in the art form of music, but conflicting in actual practice. He understood the difference between teaching and performing and encouraged his students to wear "different hats"—one for performing and one for teaching.

Chapter Four

Skills and Drills
Contents

Preview		33
Aural Skills		34
	The Study of *Solfège* to Improve Pitch Recall	34
	Entry Notes	37
	The Mental Signal for Each Note: Sensory and Motor Nerves	38
Breath		
	Physiology	40
	The Shallow Breather	41
	Common Breathing Misapplications	43
	Breathing Exercises	46
	The Aging Process	48
	Refinements of Breath Control	50
	Breath Modifications	50
Buzz		
	Embouchure	52
	Embouchure Formation	54
	Rim Buzzing	54
	The Embouchure that Wants to Vibrate	56
	The Singing Brain	58
	Mouthpiece Buzzing	58
	Embouchure Development	60
	High Range Development	62
	Lipping Up and Down	63
	The Damaged Embouchure	64

Bell's Palsy	65
The Warm Up	65
Endurance Development	66
Brass Playing Acoustics	
Musical Amplifiers	69
Instrument Makers - Concept of Sound	70
Importance of Equipment	70
Mouthpieces	71
Vibrato	72
Dynamics	73
Tongue	76
Thick Wind	77
Air and Embouchure	77
The Study of Vowels	78
High Air Pressures	79
The Use of the Rim	79
Tongue and Articulation	81
Multiple Tonguing	82
High Register Tonguing	83
The Aging Process	84
Summary	85

Preview

- *Jacobs recognized that the top brass players in the music profession had achieved an advanced level of ear training. This enabled them to play in the center of the pitch where they got the most amplification for the least effort possible.*
- *Jacobs found that there were players who did not need remedial work in ear training. Those players usually had early life experiences singing, humming, or whistling in formal or informal environments.*
- *The study of solfège (or similar systems) and the development of accurate pitch recall are essential for outstanding brass playing. One of the biggest drawbacks a brass player will experience is the inability to recall pitch.*
- *Jacobs referred to the players who did not take enough air as "shallow breathers." These players will experience playing problems at the end of their breath. If they continue taking shallow breaths throughout their playing careers, they will increase their chances of suffering the repercussions of the aging process sooner when compared to players who function on full breaths.*
- *The aging process becomes an important issue for players reaching 45 years of age. It was common practice for brass players to retire in their middle 40s or early 50s. However, with the advancement of contemporary performance techniques, some professional players today play well into their 70s.*
- *You educate an embouchure by playing music and not by logic or peripheral thoughts of any kind.*
- *Jacobs wanted the lips to vibrate in the direction of the wind. This makes the difference between playing with a "singing like tone" or an "edgy tone."*
- *A great big tone requires a "big effort," but a "big effort" might not get you the big tone.*
- *Players who experienced lip damage have to go through a recovery period to regain correct physical functions. However, most of them also have to go through a retraining period to normalize their "thinking patterns" as related to brass playing.*
- *The development of endurance is an important concern to brass players. Most players are required to play for extended periods during solo recitals, chamber music concerts, jazz solos, and in orchestra concerts. Constant playing, followed by appropriate rest periods, develops endurance.*

Skills and Drills

This chapter explores the pedagogical concepts and techniques Arnold Jacobs used when teaching skills and drills. The exploration starts with the discussion of aural skills and ends with issues related to tonguing. As evident in the lessons, interviews, and lectures transcribed for the writing of this book, Jacobs used the following concepts and techniques to target specific technical problems, for improving underdeveloped skills, and for developing new skills.

The Study of *Solfège* to Improve Pitch Recall

For some students, developing the mental image of sound requires remedial work in an ear training program. Jacobs preferred the study of *solfège* and he often talked about its importance:

> I can't think of any other shortcut for improving brass playing than the study of *solfège*. Accept this study to be a long-term goal (for about ten years). It will take you a week to notice positive changes in your playing, but in two years your playing will sparkle because of this study. That's a promise!

To Jacobs, the purpose of learning *solfège* was to develop pitch recall skills. However, he wanted this to be a formalized study. He said:

> If you formalize the approach of pitch recall using *solfège*, you'll train your brain in one of the most efficient ways to recall pitch. You should talk with your instrument as when you talk with your voice. Don't ask questions, but instead make statements. You should teach the audience what's on the page displaying a lot of show business. During the next six months, you can formalize this study and make a habit of it.

Jacobs believed that the *solfège* syllables facilitated pitch recall:

> When doing ear training, you must have a word or a syllable associated with it so eventually the word becomes the stimuli for the pitch. That's the purpose of the study of *solfège*. You can give the note any name you want. At first, some players might not experience a rapid improvement with this study because there are variables in pitch recall and recognition among people, but they will gain confidence with repeated practice and success.

> When you hear your voice, you'll get the pitch right away. People who have trouble with pitch recognition set up the physical mechanism for producing tone and there is no way you can do that successfully. You have to actually imitate something and that something is the pitch *sung* in your head.

Jacobs recognized that the best brass players possess an advanced level of ear training. This enables them to play in the center of the pitch where they get the most amplification for the least amount of effort. Jacobs thought it was best to study *solfège* in short practice periods away from the instrument. He explained:

> Get Pasquale Bona's *Rhythmic Articulations*—or any other *solfège* book—and do fifteen minutes a day of *solfège*.[x] There is no short cut to excellence, but there are shortcuts to maximum efficiency. This is the closest thing I know for brass players as far as a short cut goes. The quickest pay off is the training of your brain in pitch and rhythm independently from your instrument. Don't be discouraged if it goes slow at first.
>
> The one thing that will slow your playing down is when you get into nervous situations—which you'll get into—and your playing will start to revert to old habits. The *solfège* study will start to resolve that. To do this, you must have pieces of music that you sing many times over a long period.
>
> *Solfège* is a type of specialized training in pitch and rhythm. This is not like ear training, but actual singing of music using *solfège* symbols. This is a wonderful training for any brass player. Adolph Herseth, Dale Clevenger, and Jay Friedman are *solfège* experts.

Jacobs also suggested alternating—back and forth—between playing the instrument and singing:

> Do a portion of your practice singing and playing. A lot of the singing will start to feed back to your playing all by itself. As it starts to grow, it will become a skill. Keep this training going for now and don't put it away because it might slip in and out for a while. Sing and play all the time! You always must have the voice in your head because that's the signal that goes down the seventh cranial nerve to your lip.

For Jacobs, the study of *solfège* was a lifelong study. In other words, players should continue it throughout their entire careers:

> The study of *solfège* is a long-term proposition. In other words, the pay off is very apparent right away, but it has to be constantly renewed and made into a way of life and that takes years. I am still working

at it even now. So many good things diminish when you are in your 70s. For that reason, I have to keep perking up my ear training just like when I was a kid. I have to do that! In other words, it's like being on a ladder and you keep going down so you have to do something to prevent yourself from going down too fast.

Jacobs found that there were players who did not need remedial work in ear training. Those players usually had early life experiences singing, humming, or whistling in formal or informal environments:

Children who whistle and sing a lot usually have an easier time working on ear training. Singing is what develops the music centers in the brain. Those centers continue to develop regardless of age. You could start to develop your ear training at the age of sixty, and you'll develop beautifully. However, you just need the patience to do it. The simple fact that you sing will create neural pathways in your brain. However, don't rest on your laurels once you attain some success. Instead, keep singing every day. This type of training pays dividends in a week, but you'll hear a great difference in six months. Ear training is something that I have worked on all my life; and I continue to work on it to this day.

Jacobs added that advanced work on a brass instrument would be unmanageable if the player's aural skills were underdeveloped. He explained:

At the early stages of development, I am more interested in testing the student in ear training that on brass playing because the problem is not in the instrument. Instead, you often find that the problem is really in their aural skills. Not every player has the same problems, but everybody's weak points can become strengths. On a brass instrument, the player depends very much on the ability to conceive music in the brain. In a three-valve instrument with over a three-octave range, you have to give the pitches to the horn by putting perfect notes into the mouthpiece. The horn simply provides the valves to adjust the lengths of its tubing to amplify the pitches the player is sending. Most advanced players' embouchures have undergone tremendous developments. However, some of their inconsistencies are not tissue problems, but mental problems. Eventually this is something players have to address by themselves.

There is no way or reason to do the advanced technical work on a brass instrument before doing the ear training work. You must always get the "double sound." By "double sound," I mean the sound of the voice in the head and the one out the bell. The one in the head is the teacher. The teacher is the source of stimuli for the conditioned reflexes that you have developed through years of practice. Your body is like a biocomputer that will read out music as you conceive it in your head and it will send it as a command to the muscles. Your goal is to constantly develop the mental aspects as a musician so you are not blowing a brass instrument at all, but instead you are *singing*.

Ear training is essential to a player's advancement at any stage of development. Players can attain ear training formally or informally. Jacobs suggested to school administrators in conservatories and universities to include a formalized program of ear training for brass players in their music curriculum.

Entry Notes

Jacobs believed that the aural conception of the "entry note" (first note of a phrase) was of utmost importance. This aural conception is necessary for avoiding missed entry notes and for producing the greatest sound spectrum. He said:

> Remember that the first note after the rest in the one in jeopardy. You must protect those entry notes by having a clear mental picture of how those notes sound. Take chances with this. Your solos will become yours. As a result of this type of playing, your playing will become easier and more efficient.
> This is important for brass instrumentalists because you have to send a perfect partial into the instrument (so you get the full spectrum of sound and dynamics out of your playing efforts). This study can be very frustrating partly because it requires high levels of mental efforts. This mental effort is important because brass instruments are stupid pieces of brass. They can't give you the pitches like a piano would, so we must put "perfect notes" into them.

An early performance experience at the Curtis Institute of Music taught Jacobs the importance of clearly hearing the entry note of a melody in his head before playing it. Jacobs narrated:

> I used the idea of hearing the pitch in my head before I played long before I taught it to anybody else. This was one of my techniques from when I was a kid. Once I knew you had to hear the notes before you play them, I started to play with authority. My first year at the Curtis Institute of Music in Philadelphia[xi] was a disaster in a way. They put me in an opera orchestra playing an opera by Leopold Auer[xii] titled *The Spanish Hour*. I remember that I had to come in a middle "E-flat" and I couldn't hear the pitch. I had no idea where I was. I was a kid, just sixteen years old, so I took a chance, and fortunately, I made it. That's

a terrible feeling to sit there and not know where anything is. You can put the valve down and anything can come out. I learned that when I was sixteen years old and I thought, "This is no way to live your life!" I started to study these things, and the result is my career and the way I teach today.

It's not hard to play when you can hear a note just by looking at it on the page. It can get very hard to play if you don't know the note and you have to guess what pitch it is. That way you are half dead before you start playing.

After the entry note, Jacobs wanted players to continue *singing* each note—one at a time—in their heads as they played. This marked the difference between being a performer and being an audience member. To Jacobs, the performer played note by note while the audience member listened to entire musical phrases. He elaborated:

> Don't play by the phrase, but instead play note by note. As an artist, you must play note by note so audiences can hear the phrase. You must narrow down your mental focus to the note you are playing now, so there is a stimulus for a reflex.
>
> If you are playing by the phrase, your mind is playing the whole phrase the same way the audience hears a phrase. Don't do that! Instead, create the phrase by the individual notes. Each note as it comes. You put each individual note into a series, but your brain has to put in the stimuli for each individual note—one note at a time. You can't do it by listening to yourself play, but instead you have to do it by conceiving of each note individually.

The Brain Signal for Each Note: Sensory and Motor Nerves

The *singing* of each note provides the necessary brain signal to trigger motor activity in the player's "effectors"—i.e., lips, torso, arms, and fingers. Jacobs affirmed that a player's ability to perform was tied to that player's sense of "sending a message" to his audience. He explained:

> As human beings we move about and influence the external environment through motor activity that is fired—or activated—by brain signals. Those signals go down to a very special type of motor system that we can call the "effector." The "effector" might be a finger, an embouchure, or the arm holding a violin bow ready to play.
>
> These messages are motor messages and not sensory messages. The young person has a tremendous gift of learning through the sensory nervous system. In other words, the ability to gather knowledge in a young person is enormous. Biologically, this is a very active period in

our lives where acquiring knowledge is given every possible chance that can get and it's favorable to the person at all times while she is growing up. I think that at my age I can still learn, but it would be at a slower pace than when I was young.

The two types of nerves mentioned above are like "one way" streets. Where you have a motor nerve, it's a "one way" path from the brain to the lips (the effector). If you are a ball player, you want to hit the ball with the bat. That's motor activity. Anything that influences the external environment in any way is "motor." When I talk to you, I am using motor systems for me to communicate messages to you, but you are hearing those messages through sensory nerves that travel through from the ear to the brain.

Jacobs went further in explaining the importance of the seventh cranial nerve by saying:

The seventh cranial nerve (the facial motor nerve) is similar to a wire hooked up from the brain to the lip. It has branches out into the trigeminal nerve (facial sensory nerve) for various functions. For example, if you touch your lip, you can feel it because that is a message going inward. That's felt through the fifth cranial nerve (trigeminal) that has nothing to do with actual performance. The ability to perform is tied into your sense of sending a message (as when you use your lips as vocal chords). That's the job of the seventh cranial nerve.

Manny Laureano talked about the importance of separating the functions of the seventh and the fifth cranial nerves:

When I made people aware of the seventh and the fifth cranial nerves, it made sense to them instantly. Just the whole concept that one has a whole set of messages that are going from the brain down to the lip only to meet the resistance of incoming information the fifth cranial nerve transmits. I said, "You have a mission here and it's to override all of that no matter what you are feeling." To use Arnold's phrase, "You have to flood your mind with all of these thoughts about music and you have to do it really well."

The seventh cranial nerve has to be completely convinced of what you are doing no matter what doubt the fifth cranial nerve sends back. You have to completely erase that. You have to cover up the pictures of doubt with the pictures of success. So that's the concept I find myself using all the time. You have to have that in order for the mental image to be able to drive everything you are doing. The mental image of music has to dictate everything you do. It's where the sound, the *vibrato*, and the tone color is.

Making people aware of what the seventh cranial nerve does is my borrowing from Arnold to help convince people that everything has to be about *sound, sound, sound, sound, sound,* and nothing else. It's like I say, they have to create their own wall to keep doubt away. People have their own walls that they create that prevent them from playing with doubt.

To sum, the study of *solfège* (or similar system) and the development of accurate pitch recall are important to all brass players. One of the biggest drawbacks a brass player will experience is the inability to recall pitch. When asked, "What was the most difficult problem you encountered in a lesson?" Jacobs responded, "A student who couldn't recall pitch." Pitch recall is also essential in directing the brain signals—and the resulting motor activity—necessary for great playing.

Breath - Physiology

Jacobs often described the breathing aspects of brass playing in accurate and picturesque detail. Although human anatomy and physiology was his hobby since the 1940s, Jacobs said that he could not use most of what he knew about those subjects in his lessons. He added that when he played music, he did not think of the details of human physiology, but instead he thought of the details of music. He wanted his students to do the same as they learned about the physiology of breathing. Jacobs described the breathing system as follows:

> We have about 659 muscles in our body and 654 of those are set in antagonistic pairs. In other words, they have a great potential for shortening to exert great power (the same muscles also have the potential for stiffness). However, you can't teach a person about breathing by telling him what to do. Instead, you have to provide the correct stimuli and the brain will activate the correct muscle groups. A good example is blowing out matches. Here, the blowing out muscles activate while the inhaling muscles deactivate.
> The abdominal muscles are expiratory in nature. When they "push in," the diaphragm will raise to a certain level and when they relax, the diaphragm is free to come down. The main function of the diaphragm is inspiratory in nature (when it comes down it lowers the air pressure in the lungs and it will also increase the abdominal pressure).
> Like a bellows, the abdominal muscles go up and push the air out (the intercostal muscles are also involved in blowing out). However, the abdominal muscles are involved in three other actions. Those actions—or blueprints—in the human body are: 1) pelvic pressures (childbirth, defecation, etc.), 2) combat (tensing up the abdominal wall to protect the vital organs in case of an attack), and 3) blowing (brass instruments, birthday cakes, etc.). The latter are listed in order of importance from the standpoint of survival on this planet.

These separate "blueprints" (pelvic pressures, combat, and blowing-bellows activity) are part of life and they are quite necessary. However, when we try to blow large quantities of air while being in "pelvic pressure" or "combat" modes, blowing becomes very difficult. This misapplication of activity is what the "old school" of brass playing (*circa* 1920's-1970's) advocated.

There is tremendous potential for stiffness (instead of efficient function) in the respiratory system so players have to make sure to order the right product. In other words, the player could trigger the wrong blueprints with his thoughts. Consequently, players have to make sure to order the performance product (in the case of inhalation it is suction at the tip of the lip and for exhalation it is blowing outward).

The Shallow Breather

Jacobs referred to players who did not take enough air as "shallow breathers." He thought that shallow breathers encounter playing problems at the end of their breaths. If they continue to take shallow breaths into their 40s or 50s, they will probably suffer the repercussions of the aging process sooner when compared to players who function on full breaths. Jacobs talked about shallow breathers as follows:

> Shallow breathers will have trouble playing the end of their phrases. If they take a poor second breath, they will really be in trouble because their reflexes are going to be activated and they will start to tense up (or start to close) their throat. Their chest will also become tense and everything will go in a downward spiral from that point on.
>
> Shallow breathers will also have playing problems with age, as they will experience a decrease of breathing abilities. In other words, they will use the same muscular activity with less results. Consequently, shallow breathers find it difficult to continue their profession by age 45-55.
>
> However, if you have formed your breathing habits correctly, you can get around that problem by simply taking large breaths. You develop correct breathing habits in the practice room and not in performance. If you follow through with the study of taking large breaths in an orderly fashion, you'll age gracefully as a player.

Jacobs found that there were useful strategies for teaching how to take more air. These teaching strategies required the sense of touch, vision, and sight. Jacobs believed in enhancing a student's learning by multiplying their sensory experience:

> There are various options for helping a student take more air. You can use tools such as visualization and other musical challenges. The question is, which one will fit the student's psychology? To find out you have to talk to the student and investigate.

By using the tactile sense, you have the student touch his abdominal region, feel the movement in the region, and establish a range of motion. If the student feels stiffness in this region, provide them with resistance at the tip of the lip. This way his muscles, instead of fighting each other, will start to work together against the resistance at the tip of the lip (This works because you can control the resistance at the tip of the lip, but it's more difficult to control it at the back of your mouth or any point farther below). You are always striving to work toward the use of minimal motors.

You can use the tactile sense to teach the student about the wind outside her body. If you just talk to the student about an efficient breath, you might not reach the student but if you have the student feel the breath, the student will learn much faster. Have the student do a full bellows movement. Have her put her hands in her belly and tell her to push in as she plays. This way she will start a program of proper air support.

William Scarlett talked about his experience of learning that he was a shallow breather:

> At that point in the lesson, he [Jacobs] found out that I had more air than somebody my size should have. Actually, I found out later that I had 6.8 liters. I don't have that now.
>
> That was very revealing because normally I would take a shallow breath and it would be the same quantity as my neighbor in the trumpet section. I was always very inefficient in my breathing. I was always breathing down low in my lung capacity, but it was an equal amount to what my neighbors in the section were using. I was being very inefficient when I was breathing in a shallow way.
>
> I didn't fill up to where I could get into the positive air pressures where your body wants to blow air out. That's when you have extra air inside and it's a lot easier to get quantities of air out. It's much easier to do that when you are full than when you are almost empty.
>
> I found out that I was gifted with a great air capacity, but I was using it very inefficiently and that was a problem for me — which I didn't know until I went to see Jacobs. It was the beginning of an understanding for playing better and Jacobs found this out in the first lesson.

Shallow breathing is one of the simplest breathing misapplications Jacobs encountered in his teaching. Shallow breathing is easy for the student to understand and it is swiftly remedied. However, other types of breathing misapplications are more complex, more difficult to diagnose, and take longer to comprehend.

Common Breathing Misapplications

Jacobs recognized that many brass players played with breathing misapplications. Some of these misapplications result from the involuntary activation of isometric muscular activity. This muscular activity is difficult to notice since—to the "untrained eye"—it shows subtle physical changes in the player's physique. However, it often reflects in the player's decreased sound quality.

There are three reflexes—or blueprints—that evolved in humans to create pelvic pressures, to assist in combat situations, and to exchange gasses. Breathing misapplications stem out of two reflexes associated with isometric contractions. However, it is a third breathing reflex—used for blowing air as wind—that great brass players use. The effects of playing with the wrong reflex immediately shows in the player's sound. Hence, players must go in the direction of blowing air as wind and not as pressure. Jacobs explained:

> Every human being responds to certain kinds of stimuli to affect built in reflexes. You have three sets that involve the respiratory musculatures. We have to get you into the bellows set and away from those that involve the pressure syndromes because they react completely differently when you start getting into the supportive aspect of pressure. That is: childbirth, defecation, pelvic pressures, and combat. You can easily move in either direction. Either the direction of the bellows aspect (blowing) or the pelvic pressures. We have to have it in the direction of the "big wind." When you go into the power of pressure, you think big wind and never pressure. With big wind there is pressure. There is no such thing as wind without pressure, but there is such thing as pressure without wind.

Jacobs found the following problems with breathing applications related to brass playing. The first breathing problem is regional breathing:

> Regional breathing happens when you inhale using a small part of your lung structure (e.g., if you bend down, you'll be collapsing the lower part of your lungs and as a result you'll 'regional breathe' with the upper part of your lungs). Incidentally, some overweight people will have their diaphragm go up (because of the extra pounds below) making their lungs shorter. In other words, the extra pounds will cost them about .75 litter of air capacity. (Mr. Jacobs, after his heart attack and hospitalization, lost about 40 pounds and gained one liter of air capacity).

With reference to the last quote, Jacobs recommended for brass players to keep their weight under control:

> I think I have more air than I had last year simply by losing weight. You have to keep your weight within reasonable bounds—then weight is not a big deal. If you start getting a "big pot" on you, then that's going to cut down on your total air capacity. I have picked up almost a half a liter already since I lost weight. As I lose another 20 pounds, I'll probably gain another half a liter. Now I am about 3350 ml (milliliters) and I am more comfortable playing in the orchestra.

Jacobs described the second misapplication as "expanding instead of breathing," leaving the player with small air quantities:

> The way you order your body to breathe is very important because sometimes a player will order expansion instead of air. You must always tell the truth to your body. Always order wind, not expansion. In other words, when you take a breath, you must order suction of air from the tip of your mouth. The psychology of wind is at the tip of your mouth.

The third misapplication is "tensing the abdominal wall before playing the first note." Jacobs explained:

> When you take a breath, the air will go into the lungs (via the bronchial trees) following a trajectory based on what part of your anatomy has expanded. At that moment, it's not like water that fills up from bottom to top. This is why it's so important to sit tall as you breathe. However, if your abdominal wall gets hard, the ribs will be too stiff to move up to create a vacuum (the vacuum is necessary to lower the air pressure in the lungs so the air in the atmosphere—outside the lung—can rush into them) and not much air will be able to get into the lungs. To alleviate this problem, you can exercise your breathing with the "breath builder."

Jacobs described a fourth misapplication as "pressurization":

> If there is pressurization of the breath before the release of the first note, you might play with a hard attack or miss the note. To avoid pressurization, you should take as much air as you can and start counting out loud, "1, 2, 3, 4." You'll notice that there is no internal pressure as you count. This is what we call zero pressure. You'll also notice that your body regulates itself beautifully—in between the numbers—as you count.
>
> Very powerful air comes from zero pressure. As you learn to control your breath, you learn to control the breathing apparatus—not the other way around. Zero pressure—up to the moment of sound—

happens when great players play. To inhale, you must have less pressure internally (in your lungs) than externally (in the atmosphere). Point zero is where the inside and outside pressures are balanced. At this time, all the airways are opened.

If you use antagonistic movements in your breathing apparatus (e.g., lungs and abdomen), you'll feel that you are always playing with more effort. However, when you experience zero pressure, you'll still have the necessary muscle activity to perform.

That is to say, the use of pressurization leads to playing with static pressure. Most players do not understand the complications related to static pressure. For example, air is a gas and as such, it is compressible. When playing with static pressure, the player is compressing his air supply and as a result, he will reduce it. Other playing problems follow once the air is compressed:

Static pressures in a cylinder go up and down (they also go up and down in the in the walls of the cylinder). Some players have static pressure behind the tongue that can easily move to the throat and as a result, the sensors in the lungs adjust to the signal of pressure at the tongue and at the throat. The majority of players will accept that fact. Pressure in the lungs is supportive to a downward contracting diaphragm (it gives an additional two or three pounds of downward pressure) and it will always involve closures in the throat region.

When playing the instrument, you must pretend that you are blowing something outside yourself. Blow the air out as if you were blowing a candle and avoid blowing pressurized air. Order motion rather than air pressure! You must practice a few minutes a day blowing out candles, papers, etc. You must always remember that when talking about air, 15% is about air but 85% is about music.

Jacobs recommended the use of the "breathing bag" (also known as a test lung) to alleviate some of the problems related to static breathing. A breathing bag can be purchased as a five liter or six liter size bag and it is helpful in exercising the breathing system. While using the breathing bag, the player inserts a tube into its opening and fills it up with air. The player then inhales the air inside the bag and exhales it once more back into the bag. The player can repeat this exercise 15 to 20 times before fatigue sets in. Jacobs described the benefits of using the breathing bag:

The use of the breathing bag allows for a visual illusion that helps players take larger amounts of air. (One of the ways to use the breathing bag is to fill it up with your own breath, cover its end spout so the air stays inside the bag, empty your lungs, and inhale the air inside the bag. You can repeat this inhalation-exhalation process many times without suffering from hyperventilation). If the player takes a full breath with the breathing bag and he plays his instrument immediately afterward, the player's sound (and general technique) will improve. The improvement in sound and technique is due to the availability of blowing more wind at a lower pressure (helping ease some of the tensions the player might have).

Jacobs also recommended the use of the "breath builder":

> To use the "breath builder" try to keep the "ping pong" ball up as you blow in and out. You'll notice that the tension in your abdominal wall will stop, but you'll still be able to move large volumes of air in and out of your lungs. (This is what the expression 'use of minimal motors' means. In other words, it's when you achieve an action using only the necessary muscles).

Jacobs thought that the danger in using these "breathing gadgets" begins when players replace their musical thoughts with mechanical thoughts. In other words, some players become experts at using the "gadgets," but in becoming so preoccupied with using them, they forget about making music. To remedy this problem, players should take plenty of air, but at the instant of playing, refocus their minds back to music.

Breathing Exercises

Jacobs recommended various breathing exercises—practiced away from the instrument—to establish positive breathing functions. Brass playing requires an extraordinary amount of air intake when compared to normal breathing functions. Some untrained players might find this type of breathing odd at first. What follows is a specialized set of breathing exercises Jacobs prescribed to his students:

> When doing breathing exercises, you should be in front of a mirror (naked from the waist up). You should observe (without self analyzing) your body movements as the air moves in and out. Create a mental picture of yourself. Achieve maximum changes—from small to big—going from empty to full (tip to frog) following no rules (e.g., allow your shoulders to raise).
> By observing yourself breathe, you'll learn faster because you are multiplying the senses. (Incidentally, by using the sense of sight, while doing the breathing exercises, you will also cancel out your sense of feel).
> When doing breathing exercises, you should also aim for contrast going from black to white. You do this to move the awareness of your body movements far apart. In actual performance, you can

compare your breathing movements to subtle changes between shades of gray. However, in your breathing practice you should strive to go from black to white (full to empty).

Another way to help you achieve ease of breathing is by using a piece of tubing (about the length of a trumpet mouthpiece and the circumference of a trumpet mouthpiece rim). You use this small piece of tubing by wrapping your lips around it (slightly passing beyond your teeth) and breathing in and out. This exercise will introduce strangeness to your training (this is specially useful when trying to throw off a negative or old breathing habit). When breathing with the tube, you will also be able to feel a "cold spot" in the back of your mouth—that's the point where the air hits meaning it bypassed your tongue. When taking a breath while playing your instrument you can also try to feel the same "cold spot" as you breathe in.

Air quantity intake depends on the clear communication between your brain and your body. You have to tell your body how much air you want and then tell it how fast you want it. Always be specific about it. Most players will order a cup (or a pint) when they should be ordering a full gallon. If you simply order your body to breathe, that's non-specific (this way you get into the negative curves of pressure fast; by not taking enough air in).

Practice the following exercises at home to get used to taking large air quantities. Remember to practice them away from music and use a black and white approach (from very big to very small). Only then, you'll have two opposite patterns so you can learn faster. In other words, put your instrument down before practicing them and concentrate on breathing.

Exercise 1: Breathe in keeping your mental focus at the tip of your mouth because this is where you have the most nerve sensors (you also have nerve sensors in the chest, but they are subtle). Make guesses on how much air you have just taken in. Then fill up a "test lung" [breathing bag] and see how much you actually took. Repeat this exercise several times.

Exercise 2: Take a full breath "from tip to frog" (empty to full) and watch your body movements (You can use the test lung or, if you don't have a test lung, repeat only three times to avoid hyperventilation). Then divide your breath into thirds. Each third has to have a sufficient pause for you to self examine. Now, make a guess as to how much air you have in your lungs.

The next step requires to put your hand on your mouth and, as you exhale one third of your breath, move the hand forward one third of the way. Then you let out the second third and you move your hand forward one more third. Repeat this exercise and let out two-thirds and take one third back in (all while moving your hand back and forth accordingly). This way you will learn specific quantities when inhaling air.

Exercise 3: In 5/4 time, start with full lungs and exhale while counting to four and inhale on the fifth beat. (Counting in 5/4 adds the time factor. You can also try this exercise in 8/8 time (exhale to beat seven and inhale on beat eight). While inhaling, make sure you keep an "OH" vowel to avoid throat closure. It's important to know that if the opening of your mouth is larger than the diameter of your throat, you will — because of an innate reflex — close your throat (to avoid foreign objects from flying into your 'naked lungs').

Exercise 4: Breathe in counting to five while raising your hands to your side. Then hold your breath for about two or three seconds and let go of the breath. Watch yourself in the mirror as you do this and watch your ribs go up while your diaphragm goes down. This is called the "bucket handle" effect (With the bucket handle effect, you have the greatest distance from rib to rib. The opposite is when you are out of breath your ribs are closer together). For the "bucket handle" effect to happen, you have to sit straight up. Only then, the sternum will go up — as the diaphragm goes down — to create a huge chamber in your intercostal area for the air to rush in.

The Aging Process

The aging process becomes an important issue for players reaching 45 years of age. Throughout most of the Twentieth Century, it was common practice for brass players to retire in their middle 40s or early 50s. However, with the advancement of performance techniques, some professional players today play well into their 70s. William Scarlett commented on one aspect of the aging process — the loss of breath capacity:

> As you get older, you lose breath capacity. I don't have 6.8 liters any more. I have trouble getting to 4.5. I lost a big third. That's not shocking, it's just normal. Bud Herseth, when in his prime, had 4.5 liters. A couple of years ago [*circa* 2001] I asked him if he wanted to measure his breathing capacity with a spirometer I had and he said no. He just didn't want to know the news but he did say that he suspected that his capacity was somewhere in the three-liter range or less.
>
> Yes, you have to breathe more often to get the same quantity of air you had when you were young which is what Bud did at the end of his career. He was taking more frequent breaths than he had never taken before. He simply had to. I know that and I perfectly understand. Recently I got a call from a first trumpet in the east coast who was asking, "What can I do about my playing? Things are not as easy as they used to be." The person was taking a breath "feeling" the same quantity as he did ten or fifteen years ago. It feels like the same quantity but it isn't. A musical phrase that was easy fifteen years ago is more difficult now and as a result playing, in general, becomes more difficult. I told him, "You have to take what feels like a bigger breath

now than you did fifteen years ago in order to get something close to the quantity that you took then." You also must keep the same artistic goals as before. The quantity of air your body can take in diminishes as you age because you are not as elastic as you once were. More frequent breaths are also needed.

It was common practice, I have found just by observation, that the players who played inefficiently retired earlier. The ones who played efficiently had longer careers. Right now, I am retired but I can go down to orchestra hall and play a concert and know that I could fit right in. I still practice a couple of times a day. I have to breathe more often, but playing is still easy and fun for me. I still try to put the same artistry into my playing value and I still enjoy playing.

Jacobs added the following:

Shallow breathers will have playing problems with age, as they will experience a decrease of breathing abilities. In other words, they will use the same muscular activity with less results. Consequently, shallow breathers find it difficult to continue their profession by age 45-55.

However, if you have formed your breathing habits correctly, you'll get around that problem by simply taking large breaths. You develop correct breathing habits in the practice room and not in the job. If you follow through with the study of taking large breaths in an orderly fashion, you'll age gracefully as a player.

The aging process includes a psychological factor that is rooted on feelings of insecurity and on the constant questioning of the player's performance abilities. Jacobs explained:

The aging process not only includes a physical deterioration and the lessening of some of our potentials—which a person in their 50s are still very viable functional people—but there is an attitude change where enthusiasm tends to lessen. There is a change in perspective.

When you are young, you can't wait to demonstrate what you can do with difficult music. There is no worry about anything that could go wrong. As you grow older, you become more cautious and you begin to ask, What if? What if I miss this note? Gee, I missed that note ten years ago and I hope I don't miss it today.

The first thing is that you start to think negative thoughts instead of positive thoughts. This is what I am talking about. In other words, if you fail to provide the stimulus in the brain, you won't have the physical response. If you play perfectly all your life, the filing cabinets in your brain will have automatic responses that are good. If you want to take charge, you have to sing to your audience. The deterioration that we are talking about is an attitude change that comes with the aging process. Of course, there is physical deterioration as well.

Refinements of Breath Control

For Jacobs, a refinement of breathing functions occurred when players played lyrically. Jacobs compared this refinement to the efficient use of fuel in a fine tuned engine. He said:

> To me, the love song is one of the basic factors in tone production. I prefer to hear tone production based on lyricism where we have the finest qualities. This is like tuning up an engine in a car. You get your finest performance based on motor activity and the response of minimal use of gas with a finely tuned engine. You can untune the engine and the car will move slower, but you won't save gas. In other words, you have lost efficiency.
>
> The love song—or the lyric aspect of brass playing—acts just like the tune up in a car. You get your finest tone production and you maneuver it into other emotional states. You maneuver it into the fanfares, but with quality. You maneuver it into a variety of interpretations of styles. Then you'll have tools as an artist.
>
> If you want stridency, or you have an emotional state where the music calls for someone to have his throat cut, you don't want a wonderful love song. At that time, you'll deliver stridency based of conceptual thought. However, the basic emotional state should be lyrical. Always sounding good.

However, Jacobs warned against developing a player solely on lyrical materials as they will not develop the rapid air speed changes necessary to successfully perform the brass repertoire. He explained:

> When you develop a player based on the singing line, that player never develops a flexibility of breath to quickly change dynamics or to suddenly speed up and slow down his tempo. These musical changes are done by parts of your body of which you can't be aware. However, you have to be aware of the musical changes you are introducing to your playing. The physical changes will be subconscious, but your choice of practice materials has to be conscious.

Breath Modifications

The breathing requirements of high brass players differ from those of low brass players. Therefore, high brass players have to modify what Vincent Cichowicz called "tuba breathing." Cichowicz explained:

SKILLS AND DRILLS   51

>   There were some students who were doing what I call "tuba breathing" and I said, "No, you can't use that for the trumpet. There is a modification there that needs to happen." Other than that, there were no conflicts between Jacobs's teaching and mine.

Along with the breathing modification, Cichowicz introduced the use of the *wind patterns*[xiii] as a way to further simplify the use of breath as applied to trumpet pedagogy and performance:

>   Another interesting thing for me was the *wind patterns*. That came about by watching flute players. I observed that of all of the wind instruments, the one that seemed to have the best breathing was the flute. I thought, "What is it? Are they smarter than we are? I don't think so. Maybe it's being taught in a better way." So, I thought, "How could I apply this to trumpet playing so the player could experience this kind of thing of taking the breath and blowing freely without having to worry about notes or about embouchure." So I came up with the wind patterns.
>   The idea that once the body experiences that, once you put the mouthpiece in front of the embouchure there is resistance of course, but you will have the impression of what the release must be like. As soon as you hold back a little on the breath, there are compromises in what you are doing. Whereas if you take a breath and blow, without the trumpet, there are no inhibitions and everything is very direct. Now you say, "Take the instrument and get as close to that as you can." The general idea is if you are making a sound you are going to think in a linear way.

John Cvejanovich talked about another modification—called *wedge breathing*—to what he referred to as "going pure Jacobs." This modification is used by some contemporary lead players:

>   I remember Roger Rocco (tuba teacher) saying that if you "go pure Jacobs," you might not be able to play certain things. I remember Howell talking about *wedge breathing* like Bobby Shew talks about. Sometimes I thought that if Jacobs heard some of the things these people talked about he would faint. In *wedge breathing*, the player inhales once and protrudes the abdomen wall to the take 90% of the air in the upper chest. I tried it and the high notes seemed to be floating out easily.

To sum, breathing serves as fuel in brass playing. Jacobs recommended playing with thick wind in order to obtain an open and resonant sound. Playing with thick wind requires the player to play with an efficient breathing system free of isometric pressures. Some players refer to thick air as warm air. Breathing misapplications affect various aspects of brass performance. For example, the resulting lack of thick air to serve as a reliable source of energy in buzzing.

Buzz: Embouchure

Before discussing the function of lip buzzing, a physiological description of the embouchure is necessary. Much has been written about the embouchure formations of brass players.[xiv] Nonetheless, Jacobs preferred to describe the anatomical function of the embouchure based on its physiology in music performance. He said:

> The embouchure starts where the lips vibrates. It always starts at the center of the lip and it moves outward to the peripheries.[xv] Other parts of your embouchure, such as the chin, are not as important in the beginning stages of development (Incidentally, the *mentalis* is involved in brass playing by pulling the lip down or pushing it up. However, avoid putting too much emphasis on this right away at the cost of leaving music out of the picture).
> Remember to always form the embouchure based on how you think it's going to vibrate so it's not at the rim of the mouthpiece. That's simply a holding device. Intuitively, you might be moving towards the rim. In the psychology of it, the embouchure shouldn't radiate in from the rim just as my bass fiddle playing shouldn't radiate from the shoulder to the fingers. It should radiate from the finger back to the shoulder. We want the vibrating part of the embouchure to be your endeavor. Not the rim aspect in, but the buzzing aspect out. Set the lip to where it's going to vibrate.

Jacobs also gave a detailed anatomical description of the embouchure to illustrate its anatomical formation:

> The lips are quite complex in structure. The lower lip starts back in the upper part of the cheek area. The top lip starts in the lower part of the cheek area. Interwoven in between the large muscle groups you have feeding up—like a basket weave—all sorts of muscle groups (quite small) that have to do with the protraction and retraction of the lip. You have to have a fresh cadaver to study those small muscles because after the cadaver dries out, the small muscles will be very difficult to define. The small muscles are outclassed by the mass of muscle fiber of the *obicularis oris*. To put them into function, you have to use a rim as isolation pressure (Hence, there must be mouthpiece pressure). (According to Jacobs, the trick of playing a trumpet hanging from a string is non-sense because you end up developing a muscle mass

out of the *obicularis oris* that will overpower the protractors and the retractors. If you give those able players something to play that 'moves around,' they won't be able to do it).

However, brass players develop their embouchures based on the music they play and not based on their knowledge of muscular structures. Jacobs said:

> You educate an embouchure by playing music and not by logic or peripheral thoughts of any kind. You have to actually play the notes. Bad sounds can be made into good sounds, but silence can't. You develop an embouchure by playing music.

Jacobs wanted his students to play with slightly larger embouchures. A larger embouchure will help the player produce a warmer tone and gain agility in up and down maneuvering. Jacobs explained:

> If you can thicken up your air column, it will be easier for you to play. When you feel your sound thinning out a bit, stop and get organized. Strive to get that thick air column and the round sound again. The round sound will indicate a slightly longer embouchure. When the embouchure gets too small, you begin to lose control and it will be hard to find your pitches. When your embouchure is longer, there are more fibers for shaping the lips than when the embouchure is short. Actually, you'll feel a little more comfortable when you play with a longer embouchure. You lose the ease of the sustained high *tessitura* as the embouchure gets a little longer, but the up and down maneuvering gets a little easier because there are more protractors and retractors involved. You'll find that your general playing is always better with a little longer embouchure.

Brass players develop their embouchures based on the type of music and the musical concepts with which they play. In general, the embouchure is one of the healthiest parts of the human body. There are few maladies that affect a brass player's embouchure. Most cuts or bruises in the embouchure area will heal promptly if the player gives them a chance to heal. The accelerated healing process is due in part to the embouchure's healthy blood circulation.

Embouchure formation—as related to brass playing—is based on a system of *pulls and balances*. Jacobs referred to those *pulls and balances* as protractors and retractors. These separate sets of muscles help brass players maneuver the embouchure changes involved in performance—e.g., a two-octave major scale.

The protractors and retractors strengthen based on the music a player performs. The protractors and retractors also—when developed and balanced properly—serve as support for the center of the embouchure to vibrate.

Embouchure Formation

Jacobs wanted players to form their embouchure's aperture in the shape of an oboe reed—with a small oval shape—rather than a squeezed closed circuit. This oval-shaped aperture applied to all registers, but it became smaller for the high notes and bigger for the lower notes. Jacobs wanted a brass player's embouchure to vibrate in the direction of the wind based on the player's *singing approach*. He explained:

> In the middle and lower middle range, if you can get your lips a little farther apart so the vibration—psychologically speaking—will be in the direction of the column of air rather than having your lips pressed and squeezed. This is especially important in the upper end of the horn where you have to let a little contact while trying not to squeeze your lips. Make sure your embouchure is tiny up there by a little more retraction as your embouchure will need to be reduced in length but increased in tension. Now, in the lower end of the horn you'll have more length and less tension. I also want you to look for that while buzzing the mouthpiece.
>
> Your lip is actually being used like a closed circuit and the wind has to work harder than it should because it has to force the lips apart. Your lip is vibrating inward instead of outward toward the direction of the wind. Your lip has to be in an "oboe reed" shape so you can blow in between its aperture. In the high register, the lips will be closer together, but not in the lower register. Because of your habit of having the wind press your lips apart, your pressure line is too high. The shaping process in your lip is like having a dozen oboe reeds. The lip will change according to the pitch and it will do it subconsciously. In other words, your lips become a tiny little reed up high, and it gets bigger in the low register.

Rim Buzzing

Jacobs also recommended buzzing the lips with a rim [sometimes called a visualizer or buzzing ring] to gain a kinetic feel of lip buzzing. However, Jacobs advised against buzzing the lips without a rim—as it could lead to playing with high air pressures. He advised:

> Don't buzz without a rim. It's so close to being right that it's dangerous. You see, the lip forms like a little oboe reed so there is a space between them. The vibration will be around the oval space opened up in between the aperture. When you buzz without the rim, you can't achieve the proper function of the buzzing unit because the breath becomes elevated in order to move the lips apart (This in turn will activate all sorts of pseudo-functions in the respiratory system). The act of buzzing brings focus to the function of buzz while the rim brings the shape of the lip.
>
> Use sensible mouthpiece contact, but isolate the small muscle fibers. You can't isolate them by buzzing without a rim. You have to work too hard to keep the lips apart and you'll run into the danger of transferring that "hardness of blowing" back to your playing (Also, you'll have a tremendous resisting power in the embouchure). Remember that the lips have more power to close compared to the wind's power to open them up. It's an unfair contest between the two.
>
> There is length, thickness, and tension in vibrating surfaces and you must have all three variables at work. You had eliminated some of the thickness in the lip by having them constantly closed. You gain a lot of range that way, but you run into problems because you'll work harder than you need to in the lower and middle registers. Now, this is quite proper for the notes above the high "C," but it's in the middle range that you have to keep your lips apart. Remember that the embouchure changes not only for pitch, but also for quality of tone. When you keep the best quality of tone, you make the embouchure's work easier.
>
> When your lips are closed, your air will work as pressure instead than as wind. Now, the way you buzz is very important. The lip can't shape unless it's isolated by the mouthpiece rim. You won't have the ability to shape the lip to where it shapes like an oboe reed if you don't have a rim pressed against it. You see, the rim will isolate the vibrating area. That's the danger of buzzing without the rim. Buzzing without a rim develops the ability of your lips to stay too close.

Rim buzzing carried more benefits than hazards. However, Jacobs warned about the hazards associated with buzzing the rim in the high register:

> There are benefits and hazards in buzzing the rim. However, with mouthpiece buzzing there is benefit with no hazard. You can go to a vacation and take the mouthpiece so you can play anything you want. If you know what the danger is in rim buzzing, you can avoid the danger.
>
> I don't recommend too much high range playing on the rim. Lower register playing is fine. Only advanced players can benefit from high range rim playing. The rim is not an acoustical device. The pressure relationships are different when compared to the way you play on the mouthpiece. There is a little more effort on the rim than on the mouthpiece. The danger of playing on the rim is that you might transfer the increased pushing of the breath and the decreased ability of your

embouchure to vibrate back to your instrument. This way, you might harm your playing. In the instrument, you must reduce the back pressure but if you are not familiar with buzzing on the rim, you might transfer the high pressure back to the horn.

You must have your lips always vibrating. They are like vocal chords. Psychologically, they have to want to vibrate.

The Embouchure that Wants to Vibrate

Jacobs stressed the difference between an embouchure that was forced to vibrate and one that wanted to vibrate. The embouchure that is forced to vibrate is static and it tends to produce an edgy tone. On the other hand, an embouchure that wants to vibrate tends to buzz in the direction of the wind and produces a rounder more *singing like* tone. The player will "help" his embouchure "want to vibrate" if he pretends to *sing* as he plays. Jacobs explained:

> You must always go by the tone production properties of your instrument. You want an embouchure that wants to vibrate, not one that is forced to vibrate. You also want to isolate that vibrating area. When you play a brass instrument, you must think *buzz, buzz, buzz* and not *blow, blow, blow*. In a car, the engine moves the wheels (It's not the gasoline moving the wheels). Your buzz is like the engine of a car.
>
> Embouchure is important because we function based on motor skills. The seventh cranial nerve (the facial motor nerve) is similar to a wire hooked up from the brain to the lip. It has branches out into the trigeminal nerve (facial sensory nerve) for various functions. If you touch your lip, you can feel it because that's a message going inward. That's felt through the fifth cranial nerve (trigeminal) that has nothing to do with actual performance. The ability to perform is tied into your sense of sending a message (As when you use your lips as vocal chords). That's the job of the seventh cranial nerve.

An embouchure that wants to vibrate depends on the artistic thoughts a player mentalizes when performing. In other words, up to the moment of buzzing, brass players function like singers. It is good practice for brass players to first sing their music before playing it on their instruments. Players will notice that their playing will sparkle as a result of this practice. For Jacobs, the meaning of *singing* as applied to brass playing was as follows:

> Now, don't confuse using *vibrato* with *singing* because the meaning of *singing* to me is simply that there should be two voices: one in the head and one coming out the bell. The one in the head always directs what's coming out the bell. In other words, we want the stimuli in the head to

always direct what's coming out the bell. We want the stimuli in the head to be pure song!

A cup-mouthpiece brass instrument is the closest instrument to the human voice. The three basic elements of tone production must always be motor force, a source of vibration that involves pitch, and a source of resonance (amplification). Of those three, a singer has all. They are part of his anatomy. The brass player has two. Most other instruments have one. For example, the factory sends out a piano with pitch-vibration and resonance built in. The only element needed is the motor force. Brass players have within their own body two of the basic elements of tone production, but they don't have amplification. As a brass player, you don't have a sound board built in and this is why you need an instrument. However, the pitch-vibration and the motor force (a wind column) are up to you.

Most other instruments are not like that. For example, instruments like the oboe, clarinet, or violin have all sorts of perceptions regarding what the fingers are doing. The nervous system involved in playing those instruments gives us certain knowledge of functions (Such as string vibration when you have to vibrate a string while it's resonated by the instrument. In this case, you find the pitch based on what you are doing with your left hand). Therefore, the violin—as well as other instruments—involves more mechanics and awareness.

Brass players don't know what they are doing in terms of mechanics. If you would treat a brass instrument like if it were your voice, you would have tremendous success. You simply can never get into the analysis of anything you are doing. Deliberately, recognize that your playing is very much like a voice when singing. Playing a brass instrument and singing are very close because instead of the laryngeal nerve going down to the larynx, you get the seventh cranial nerve going to the embouchure. It's the same identical treatment in message. If you don't sing with your voice, sing while you are playing! Most players who get in trouble try to use their lip as a woodwind reed. You can't play by treating your lip as a wooden reed. Instead, it has to be used like the vocal chords of a singer. Then you have success!

The seventh cranial nerve is similar to an electric cable used by the brain to send down message carrying neurons to activate the lip muscles—the message is the artistic statement the artist wants to communicate. The seventh cranial nerve splits into branches. These branches are the pathways musical messages take when traveling to the nerve ends in the correlative facial muscles. Singers send their artistic messages down the seventh cranial nerve as do brass players. For this reason Jacobs said that, in terms of sound production, brass players were the closest instrumentalists to singers. Brass players should *sing* at all times to make their playing free, buoyant, and resonant throughout their entire register.

The Singing Brain

Jacobs wanted players to discipline their brains to keep *singing* at all times so their artistic message—going down the seventh cranial nerve—continued to motivate their buzzing lips even in moments of discomfort:

> Can you discipline the brain to continue *singing* even when discomfort comes? The human brain won't want to do that. It won't want to cooperate because it likes to always be alert to know what the dangers are so they can be corrected. It's a survival instinct. In our art form, however, we must overcome that. I want for your survival in this profession to get the results. I want you to *sing*! At the very instant you think you should be feeling, I want that voice in your head to flood out any other thoughts. Can you sense the direction I want you to go? This approach will produce a sort of purity in tone production where enough airs gets through so you are not pushing your lips apart. In other words, you don't want your lips holding together so tightly that to make them vibrate, you have to pull them apart with your wind. Instead, they must move in the direction of the flow of the air very much like the hairs of the violin bow pulls the string in its direction or a singer's vocal chords move upward in the same direction of the wind. However, without singing in your head, your lip doesn't know what you want.

Mouthpiece Buzzing

Jacobs recommended mouthpiece buzzing as a training tool for achieving efficiency in brass playing. He suggested to some developing players to buzz up to an hour a day—practiced in ten-minute increments—for training purposes. Mouthpiece buzzing focuses the mind and the lips. It also accelerates the musical connection between the player's thoughts and his lip tissue. Jacobs suggested the following:

> While playing the mouthpiece, you must search out for music without thinking of technical rules (Just use the rules of sound and music). When playing the mouthpiece, think that you forgot the instrument at home, but you still have to entertain your audience.
>
> You'll see that as you play the mouthpiece, the storytelling aspect of your playing will increase. (This has some to do with the introduction of strangeness inherent in mouthpiece playing). When you add the mouthpiece to the instrument, your sound will sparkle. This mouthpiece training will connect your artistic thoughts to the tissue so I recommend to some players to do one hour of mouthpiece playing a day—in ten minute segments—to start the training aspects of storytelling in music.

Conceive the vibration of your lip the same way you feel its vibration when buzzing in the visualizer (This way the buzzing of the lips will become the challenge). Keep buzzing at all dynamic levels. Also, keep using air as a fuel and buzz your lip like a little engine!

When you play softer, there will be less vibration but the quality of your tone must continue into the *pianissimo* level. We call this way of playing veil *pianissimo* (It's a thinner piano that sounds beautiful—it's created by a small surface that vibrates minimally). To achieve this kind of playing, you can start with a note at full volume and *decrescendo* while keeping the same quality of sound (just like turning the volume down in your stereo).

Veil *pianissimo* is like putting a small reed into your instrument. You can carry the veil *pianissimo* to all registers. Both, veil *pianissimo* and regular *pianissimo* are good and useful under different musical circumstances.

Remember that you *sing* with your lip (That's where the vibration appears) and the instrument serves as an amplifier of whatever comes out of your mouthpiece. From the buzz of the mouthpiece, there is a 20 dB increase by the instrument (If the pitch of the mouthpiece is in tune). You always have to provide the motor activity and the vibration.

You've got to be in control of the notes all the time because the seventh cranial nerve transmits that right down to the lip for the reflex response to work. There will be no reflex responses without stimuli. Players take that for granted and instead of thinking of music, they pay attention to how their embouchure feels. This is what the so-called "naturals" avoid all the time. While the naturals are sending clear musical messages down the seventh cranial nerve, the other players are trying to learn fingering and embouchure and don't play as well.

Jacobs stressed the importance of motivating lip buzzing by musical means—i.e., concentrating on the quality of sound—instead of physical means:

> Woodwind players have reeds and they work with them. Brass players have to know how to work their "flesh and blood reeds." Lips can fight back the breath. When you have a strident sound, that's a symptom of an embouchure that's starting to fight back against the pushing power of the breath.
>
> There is no way you can blow and pull your lips apart with your wind because it's an unequal struggle. We can't encourage this at all. We have to encourage increasing the vibration of our lip instead. Take a mid-range note and give it a great tone and a beautiful singing line. Maybe play it with *vibrato*. Then you can approach fairly large dynamics with beauty of tone. The *vibrato* will throw the instrument into resonance (pitch average) without forcing it. Increase your sound, not your effort.

If you have a larger quality of sound, you'll also have a larger volume of sound. The tendency of putting larger physical effort for producing a larger sound is like lying to your own tissue. You must order the sound. The other approach has to do more with the methodology of how to produce that sound.

Mouthpiece buzzing is a good substitute on occasions when players cannot play their instruments. Other benefits associated with mouthpiece buzzing are the greater mental focus on pitch and the emphasis on healthy tone production habits—i.e., the reliance on lip buzzing as a means of sound production and on connecting the air and the lip without the interference of the tongue.

It is recommended to buzz in 10 to 15 minutes at a time since extended mouthpiece buzzing sessions of 20 minutes of longer tend to temporarily disorganize the muscle fibers in the embouchure. This occurs because the mouthpiece is not a full acoustical device—as the instrument is—so players will usually over stress their embouchure to create the pitch. Jacobs explained:

> If you play the mouthpiece for too long, that can affect the sound in your instrument because you might get too fatigued. In other words, you can buzz independently from your instrument, but at some point you'll disassociate yourself from it and the buzzing will start tearing you down instead of building you up. Instead, I would back and forth between your instrument and mouthpiece. You can play five or ten minutes on the mouthpiece, and then I would start alternating. I have seen this all the time. I don't do as much isolated mouthpiece buzzing, except when I was very young and I was sick, and even now I associate very quickly back to the horn. You can make music that you get sheer pleasure from just to make you feel better. I do this many times when I feel depressed. Since I've been ill, I have had moments of depression and buzzing tunes on the mouthpiece makes me feel better.

Embouchure Development

Embouchure development needs periods of work followed by periods of rests. However, players have to find the balance between work and rests periods by themselves. That is to say that brass players differ in terms of their physiological and psychological characteristics and therefore need to develop their own practice habits and practice schedules. Jacobs suggested the following:

> Don't try to follow a strict formula for resting. Fatigued muscles accumulate lactic acid and the neural transmissions are impaired as

soon as that happens. If your muscles are not accumulating lactic acid, then it doesn't matter. You are playing safe by resting as much as you play, but you can generally go by how the lip feels. What I am saying is that you can guide yourself very much by how your lip feels and by how you sound.

Don't become dependent on the "resting as much as you play" routine because you might get into situations where you can't rest and you'll still need to play. In your practice, gradually reduce the rest periods and see how the lip feels. If there is real fatigue, then you stop and see how you do. In the professional sense, you don't always have the opportunity to rest. It's like other types of physical exercise in which your muscles pick up strength as they are challenged. The principle in building strong muscles is to have certain amounts of contractions followed by rest periods. You can contract your muscles from repeating drills or from heavy stress while playing solos or excerpts.

In weight lifting, after some of the heavy lifts, it takes 72 hours or so for the muscles to recover. If you continue to train on a daily basis, you'll show a lack of strength. However, if you have the periods of rests, you'll have increasing strength.

What I am suggesting is to use your head. If the lip feels great when you are playing, then don't stop. If the lip doesn't feel great, then you stop. Eventually you'll learn a little bit more about yourself as a player. When you formalize your practice by resting as much as you play, you are following a pattern that's habit forming in itself. Your lip can even get used to that and you can start to become dependent. However, if you feel that your lip is deteriorating, then stop. I'd rather you become dependent on resting than on abusing your lip.

When practicing or performing, brass players might experience pseudo-fatigue. Pseudo-fatigue occurs when the supporting muscles around the embouchure tighten up—or get disorganized—due to the lack of mental focus or lack of muscular development. Jacobs described pseudo-fatigue as follows:

> Sometimes it's not only lip fatigue as it's mental fatigue. It's also a disorganization that gradually sets in. It's all based on the fact that your playing requires stimuli from the brain to innervate the muscles. As the stimuli start to lessen in the brain, there will be less stimuli for the lips. In other words, your lips don't have to work just because you blow. They are like vocal chords and it's the sense of having a constant renewing message in your brain—just like if you were a speaker reproducing from a stereo. You just can't do these things by the mechanics of brass playing alone. Instead, you have stay focused on the art form. Other types of embouchure development include the physical requirements necessary for playing the extremes. That is: 1) very high and low, 2) very loud and soft, and 3) very fast and slow.

High Range Development

Playing high notes on a brass instrument requires the formation of a small embouchure. This small embouchure depends on supporting musculatures so its center is free to buzz at high vibration rates. Brass players can begin to develop their high range by holding long tones in their upper register. Jacobs explained:

> You depend on long tones for developing your high register abilities. For instance, you can use J.B. Arban's exercise number one on page one an octave or a perfect fifth higher. It's four beats to each note. To develop a note, it always takes sustaining that note for more than four beats.
> There will be hypertrophy in various the muscle groups—which shape and gradually strengthen to give you the shaping processes—you need for particular pitches. You must handle your high register with kid's gloves. In other words, don't bully it.
> You have to consider yourself elementary when you begin to study your high range. Don't worry if you are successful or not. However, in your brain you have to be successful. Your high range comes from playing up there. Just make sure it doesn't deteriorate your normal playing. When you finish playing the piccolo, make sure you open up your airways as you come back to the larger instrument.

Jacobs reminded his students about the inherent dangers in practicing their high range. One danger is the tendency of playing with small airways—which implies the gradual closures of the player's intraoral cavity and consequently raised intraoral air pressures—after playing in the high range. He explained:

> Allow plenty of rest in between your high excerpts. Recognize that as you play high excerpts you are apt to end up with very small airways that are compatible with very small embouchures—but incompatible with the middle range embouchures. You've got to go back to the big oral cavities and the thick air when you play in the middle or low registers. Don't go into the point of real fatigue when you are practicing J.S. Bach's *Brandenburg Concerto No. 2* or pieces like that.
> Don't make the mistake—like so many of the players who have come to see me for the past 40 years or so—that after extensive high playing their lip becomes a little less responsive so they blow harder and soon they find there is no sound at all. In other words, keep sensitizing the embouchure for vibration so that it can respond to comfortable breaths—not pushed breaths. The embouchure's duty is not to provide resistance, but instead it's duty is to provide buzz. Also, it's not the breath's duty to force a reluctant lip into vibration. Protect your high playing by going back to mouthpiece buzzing and middle range playing.

After the practice of high range passages, Jacobs recommended playing a few *vocalises* in the middle or low register to regain control of the "normal register." Jacobs referred to the middle and low registers as *the norms*. While players play in *the norms*, they regain suppleness and response in this register. In sum, high brass playing tends to close the player's airways. It also makes the musculatures involved in sound production tight and fatigued. Going back to *the norms* will re-open the airways and it will relax the musculatures involved in tone production.

Lipping Up and Down

Another aspect of embouchure formation is the ability to *lip* up or down the notes that are out of tune. However, whenever a player *lips* up or down, there is a technical compromise—usually in the form of a raised tongue or a tight embouchure. Jacobs recommended the following:

> After you have the quality and the style established, then you should start to worry about the intonation. The problem with *lipping* your notes is that when you *lip* up or down—or you false finger—you have lifted your tongue. You have also reduced the aperture size, compressed the air further, and sent it through a smaller space. In other words, you have created a different set of conditions than you would have in your normal playing. That's going to interfere like hell with your embouchure. Instead, give me an "AH" or "OH" vowel. The point is that I have had a lot of experience on this with many players. I could tell you in advanced what happens. If you finger "E" 1 and 2, there will be a little less perfection in the sound (The sound gets better with less tubing and not with more tubing). Now, you'll also have changed the intonation. Even if you *false finger*, you must find the quality and match it using 1 and 2.

Jacobs talked about other technical problems associated with *lipping* up or down:

> If you *lip* your instrument sharp, that will cause a diminution of your dynamic range coming out the bell. That means that you are going to have to put more energy into the mouthpiece because the horn is losing the ability to resonate as you lip up sharp. Sometimes, you *lip* up sharp because you are trying to achieve a "C" trumpet sound on a "B-flat" trumpet. Now, there are many fine players who do that and have great playing careers.
>
> Bud Herseth is almost unique because he finds the center of the partial. Most players don't. Many successful careers are based on

lipping the pitch up. It's simply that the ability of the horn to resonate a signal diminishes as you *lip* flat or sharp. Only at one point in each partial, you get maximum resonance. I once experimented with crude equipment and it turns out that the horn amplifies the center of the partial at 20 dB (becibels). With refined equipment, I don't know what it would be, but I think that it wouldn't be to far off.

As you *lip* up, you would be cutting down your resonance potentials to 18 or 17 dBs. The point is that as you round up your tone, you increase the output—meaning that you can back off on your energy input. This is why in playing constant high notes, there will be a tendency to start to increase energy levels.

There will also be a danger that you'll start *lipping* up or *lipping* down out of the "channel of resonance," and still be satisfied. In lyrical playing, find the beauty of the "big bore" type of playing and get back to *the norms*.

The Damaged Embouchure

Players who experience lip damage have to go through a recovery period to regain correct physical functions. In addition, some of them must also go through a retraining period to normalize their "disoriented" minds. They become disoriented because their kinetic factors have changed. In other words, their playing does not feel the same as before. Jacobs said that, "If they would simply concentrate on the art form of music, coming back to good playing would be much easier." He explained:

> I keep getting people with damaged embouchures. Most people don't know what the hell I am talking about even though the statements are clear. People with lip damage get their brains all tangled. It's not that the lip doesn't recover. I have one with me now who is coming out of it very nicely. He had an operation and a lot of tissue was removed. The lips are not that sensitive. It's amazing how resilient the lips can be if you don't try to feel like how it felt before an operation or accident. If you simply try to sound like you always sounded, that's the way to go. As soon as you try to keep the feel of playing like it always was, then you lose the ability to have collateral activity take over for some of the damage parts.
>
> Every so often I get these people in my studio and I have never found one whose lip was damaged enough to keep them out of the profession. They have enough lip to go on. I had this guy come to me and play the music satisfactorily on the mouthpiece, but he couldn't play the same music on his instrument. The trumpet was not off, but his brain was off. I had to have him run around the room doing deep knee bends while playing so he couldn't think of what he was doing on the trumpet. Then we found out what his lip could do. People with lip

damage have to be willing to recognize that it's not going to feel how it did before the lip damage. They have to accept that they can sound like they did before. I have helped many of them.

Bell's Palsy

Bell's palsy (idiopathic facial paralysis) leads to another form of embouchure ailment. Players suffering from Bell's palsy are unable to control their facial muscles in the affected region. Although serious and debilitating, the prognosis for this ailment is good—i.e., taking anywhere from three weeks to six months. Jacobs successfully helped players suffering from Bell's palsy by shifting their embouchure position, playing simple music, and buzzing. He elaborated:

> Even with Bell's palsy, you can usually play some things with the instrument. This is a self-limiting ailment in that eventually stops. There will be residual damage from it and it might require considerable embouchure shift depending on the neurological tests and the electromyographical studies. There again, you get the students playing in different parts of their embouchure with the mouthpiece. They don't have to stop playing. If they try to pick up where they left off, then they usually quit playing. If you are willing to make a lot of music that is quite different and more elementary, then you do well. After Bud's accident, he started playing many simple songs. His lip felt horrible, but he started sounding good. If you approach it as a musician, you always win.

The Warm Up

Warming up is important to all brass players. Advanced and professional players who play many hours a day never cool off. However, they still need to ensure muscle flexibility at the beginning of their practice session. Jacobs said the following about warming up:

> If you play every day, you never cool off. Warming up has a connotation of increasing blood supplies. In other words, warm up means that something was cool and the temperature is changing. In athletics, the warm up leads to an increase of the blood supply to the tissues so that they have more elasticity. Warming up is also getting a good tone. If you change the terminology and couple yourself to the instrument at the start of the day for wonderful tone production, that's just another way of saying "warm up." You have to do this every day. Every time you put your instrument up, you always search out quality. You must establish quality early in your playing and then you transfer that quality to everything you play throughout the day.

At some point, you have to make sure your tongue is also being trained not to destroy your tone production by staying in the way of the air column. That means that your articulation has to be established to the point where you keep your quality of tone. If you are in the high *tessitura* all the time, your air pressure will increase. That also means that as the bodily activity of compressing air increases, the need for air decreases and the need for pressure increases. You also have to make sure that is brought under control at this stage. You have to make sure you are not playing all tightened up.

Someone like Bud Herseth warms up every day on a beautiful "C" trumpet. Even if he is playing the J.S. Bach's *Brandenburg Concerto No. 2,* he warms up on the "C" trumpet.

Jacobs added that during the warm up, the player should also strive to find the most lyrical and purest tone production possible to increase performance efficiency:

The warm up is where you find the finest qualities of tone. That's the most efficient tone production. That's when you find the efficiency you are looking for. It shouldn't be done by looking for ease of playing, but instead you should be looking for the quality of tone. The fact that you are looking for the beautiful tone is what counts.

When you look for a beautiful tone based on lyricism, you are automatically cutting down on the overwork. Overwork won't be lyrical because it will sound forced and strained. The lovely love song is where you'll find the ability of producing sound for the least effort. The goal is to go for the product and not the method. The intelligence of a human being is always directed toward the product; while other areas of the brain go for the methodology.

Endurance Development

Endurance development is essential to brass players. Most players are required to play for extended periods during solo recitals, chamber music concerts, jazz solos, and in orchestra concerts. Constant playing followed by appropriate rest periods develops endurance. Jacobs explained:

The endurance that's built over the years of playing in an orchestra is tremendous. You figure that we have rehearsals in the morning (maybe two or three hours), then a concert that same night, and maybe an afternoon show. In other words, we are with our horns all day long. If you do that, you would also have that type of endurance.

Playing that much you'll feel stiff, but you don't let that bother you. You have to loosen up by doing flexibility studies, but don't stop playing. You have to also gauge if your lip is swelling at all. If it's swelling, then you back off. If you study weight lifting in terms of physiology, you'll find that power contractions damage the muscles. The damage is not much, but you have to have a 48 to 72 hour wait to do more training. In other words, developing players need time off to help their muscles recover. If you train heavily every day, you'll get weaker, but if you do it every second or third day, you'll get stronger. The same applies to your embouchure. At the stage you are in now, if you start to do heavy orchestral blowing, you don't want to do it every day. I would wait one or two days in between because this is the "weightlifting" of the small fibers. If you treat it like that, your strength will come in gradually and your tone will get as big as a house. You should develop your dynamics way up and way down to minimal levels. Both have to be studied musically so you don't blast. It's all based on music with excellent qualities.

Some professional players develop what Jacobs called *leather lips*:

When you play every day—some of the professional players play matinees in the afternoon and then again in the evening—for eight hours or so, you develop tremendous endurance. You indeed need to develop tremendous endurance to work professionally. We used to call those players *leather lips*. By playing certain types of materials, you'll improve your endurance for now.

However, there are many factors that contribute to the decrease of muscular endurance. One of those factors is mental fatigue:

It's never lip fatigue alone. It's brain fatigue and nerve fatigue among others. It's not only in certain fiber groups. Put it this way, if you were to play the duets in the back of the J.B. Arban's method book for a long practice period, you don't need to rest as much. On the other hand, if you go for music that needs intense concentration, you'll need to rest the brain. If you go into high and loud playing, you'll need to rest the muscular tissue. You'll judge for your own playing, but it's important to have rest periods and high standards. I had a fellow—who played trumpet for one of the television orchestras—who wanted to work for endurance. He left me because I wouldn't let him work on endurance. I told him that endurance would come based on the music he played, but you don't work on endurance for endurance's sake. Instead, work for the excellence in music so you gain endurance as a secondary factor.

As you continue to work as an artist, you'll develop the endurance. Don't start pounding high notes for the sake of endurance. In other words, don't take something bad and lock it in. Endurance is hypertrophy of tissue that comes from playing. There is now way you can work like a weightlifter to develop your embouchure. Even weightlifters go by certain forms. In music, hypertrophy comes from the music you play.

Unfortunately, there are complications with endurance. For example, blood pressure. How much blood pressure is there in the arteries? In other words, how much mouthpiece pressure does it takes on the lip to completely stop circulation? The point is that it's different with different people. The general muscle tone of the individual also comes as a factor in this. Many things come in when you talk about endurance. The simple way is to play a lot and you'll have the endurance.

At some point in a player's career, she will have play when her lip is tired. To deal with this problem, Jacobs recommended playing softer—as most audience members will not notice the difference—and more musical. He said:

When your lip is a little bit insecure, make sure your mentalization of music is louder in the head so you increase your source of stimuli. You'll suddenly find that it's compensating in the lip end. Try not to force. If your lip is tired, let it rest. I tell you, Walter Smith's *Top Tones* and the Theo Charlier's etudes are marvelous to keep your endurance and strength. The Wassily Brandt is also good.

Jacobs established the difference between *pseudo fatigue* and true fatigue— true fatigue, in his opinion, comes as a result of accumulated lactic acid. He explained:

Many endurance problems are due to lack of practice. One hour a day is not enough to compete with people like Bud Herseth. Two hours will be better. You need at least three hours to compete with Bud. You have to create the endurance not by practicing the virtuoso studies, but more by the ballad type of playing and the sustained type of playing. The tonal studies are the ones that bring the endurance to you. Virtuoso studies—like Walter Smith's *Top Tones* No. 9 or No. 15—will tend to disorganize the embouchure to where you'll experience *pseudo fatigue*.
True fatigue will be the accumulation of lactic acid in the embouchure so your embouchure will tend to swell up a little bit. When you get tired and you take your mouthpiece off and buzz, you suddenly find that you are not fatigued. At that moment, you know that your embouchure fibers are simply disorganized. This will give you the same sensation as if you were fatigued, but you'll discover that you are not. *Sing* more in your brain so there is more artistry and you'll see that you get less fatigued. You have to keep your standards very high.

Some amateur musicians complain of endurance problems. Jacobs suggested that the minimum amount of practice required for competing with professional players, such as Adolph Herseth, was three hours. However, with one or two hours of practice, an amateur player can accomplish a high stage of development. Jacobs said:

For you to develop the type of strength some of these jobbing musicians have—those who go to the job and play all night long—you can't do that on two hours of daily practice. Instead, it has to be a considerable number of hours of actual playing. If you practice an hour a day, you shouldn't expect the type of endurance that you get from practicing three hours a day.

Three hours of personal practice is about the minimum if you were to replace a guy like Herseth. He doesn't have to practice three hours a day at home, but I said if you were to replace him, you would have to build yourself to it. He has already got it so to maintain it is far different. His practice is involved in the orchestra and at home. He does a tremendous amount of playing and he has tremendous endurance.

At this stage, if you can't put in six or seven hours of playing don't make endurance a big issue. In other words, endurance is going to come about by itself. If you know your music well, then you are going to be able to extend yourself further through the studies. Even on an hour a day, you'll be able to play an etude from beginning to end. I just don't want you to do that at the beginning stages of learning the piece.

Brass Playing Acoustics: Musical Amplifiers

Jacobs talked about brass instruments as amplifiers of the player's musical thoughts. Musical instruments were important to Jacobs, but more important was the player's ability to buzz perfect pitches into his instrument. Putting perfect notes into the instrument is necessary because there are acoustical laws—primarily based on sympathetic resonance—which each brass player must follow in order to play with efficiency. Jacobs talked about the acoustical nature of brass instruments:

> Don't depend on a three-valve instrument to give you three or four octaves of chromatics. You've got to *sing* perfect notes into the horn so it can resonate according to its acoustical laws—primarily based on sympathetic resonance.

According to Jacobs, the instrument's potential to amplify a particular pitch depends on how in tune that pitch is buzzed into the instrument. If the note is buzzed flat, the instrument will amplify it at *circa* 17 dB (decibels). However, if that note is buzzed in pitch, the instrument will amplify it at *circa* 20 dB.

The importance of daily mouthpiece buzzing for improving intonation and sound production could not be stressed enough. The player should not depend on his instrument to give him the pitch. Instead, the player must put perfect pitches into the cup of the mouthpiece. In turn, the mouthpiece buzz will be amplified by the instrument.

Instrument Makers - Concept of Sound

Jacobs believed that many instrument makers design their instruments based on their concept of sound. To him, this was especially apparent in the instruments made by Renold Schilke. Other instrument makers, however, seek the opinion of great players to find the ideal sound for their instruments' design. According to Jacobs, this was the case with the instruments Vincent Bach designed. Jacobs said:

> There are men who are artists at building instruments. You get a fine player and a fine maker and you come up with something excellent. Vincent Bach was a good example. The gorgeous Bach trumpet is the product of great players stopping by the factory and trying them out. You can never make a good instrument just by using pure mathematics. You can standardize the measurements of the instruments, but you have to have great craftsmen making those instruments. Machine instruments are fine if you have a good "first design." However, if you have to change anything in the design, you have to go through the whole factory changing things.

Brass instruments made by computerized machines need to have a good "first design" to produce good instruments. The advantage of this type of assembly production is quality control and the disadvantage is the homogenous sound produced by the instruments rolling out the production line. In addition, players might not find that one "gem" of an instrument that stands apart from the rest.

Importance of Equipment

Jacobs also talked about the importance of brass instruments as acoustical devices—i.e., choosing the right equipment for the right job. He said:

> If you use the right equipment for the right job, you'll avoid frustration. Otherwise, you'll be ordering more volume potential out of a small mouthpiece. The overtone characteristics will also be altered by using different equipment. Big instrument equals big fundamentals, which equals small overtones. Small instrument equals big overtones, which equals small fundamental.
>
> You have three variables in you playing: 1) player, 2) instrument, and 3) mouthpiece. You can initiate change by changing the embouchure, the instrument, or the mouthpiece. All of these changes affect the relationship of overtones to their fundamental.
>
> With small instruments, you'll have more high overtones, but you can bring them to a balance by getting a bigger mouthpiece.

However, you can never change the amplitude the instrument can give. An instrument can't make up for its size.

Mouthpieces

Jacobs said that, occasionally, he would carry a bag of mouthpieces with him to rehearsals to experiment with changing tone colors and instrument response. He humorously said that, while sitting in the back of the orchestra, the bag of mouthpieces also kept him from getting bored during long rest periods. He advised against experimenting during a week the player has exposed solos. He added the following general comments about mouthpieces:

> The thinner the wall of the mouthpiece, the more dissipation occurs in the energy of its sound waves. Much less sound comes out, but it's a good quality sound. It reduces the entire dynamic range. I had a Renold Schilke *thin mouthpiece* that I used to play in the brass choral section of Gustav Mahler's *Symphony No. 2*.
>
> This adjustable cup mouthpiece was made by Schilke *circa* 1951. I used it for the first time in the Chicago Symphony Brass Quintet. It's like a small trumpet cup. It's good for brass quintet, but not for orchestral playing because it's got the overtone range of a trombone and therefore it would get crowded out.
>
> There is nothing wrong with experimenting with mouthpieces — different thickness and lengths. By experimenting you'll have greater control over your spectrum of sound. Switch around depending on your musical requirements. However, all your mouthpieces should have similar rims — either all flat rims or over-rounded rims. This has to do with the development of the protractors and the retractors in your lip. I used to change mouthpieces to keep things interesting in the orchestra in terms of variety of sounds.
>
> When you change mouthpieces, you don't get as dependent on the feeling of the familiarity of the mouthpiece. If you play based on feel, you'll limit yourself because you would always have to have the same equipment and acoustics.
>
> From time to time, you should change mouthpieces because it brings strangeness. Think of Maynard Ferguson changing from trumpet, to trombone, or to the slide trumpet. Keep in mind that there are limitations in doubling so if you are a player in a major symphony orchestra, you might want to do your work on your main instrument

Mouthpieces also have acoustical laws that govern them:

> The mouthpiece alone is a bugle. The wavelength is so short that your mouthpiece acts like a bugle — so you can only get certain notes.

There are players who can play all the notes on the mouthpiece, especially up high, but usually they are forcing the lip into a shape. You could plug-up the end of your mouthpiece (except for a tiny hole) with your finger and get more notes. If you leave the end of your mouthpiece open while buzzing, you'll get partials. It's just like a bugle.

It's simply that you've got enough length in a regular shank mouthpiece—when compared to a small shank mouthpiece—so your notes will come down much lower in terms of partials. When you get around high "C," you'll see that you get into partials—so your next note will be up a fourth or a fifth. If you want to fool around with your mouthpiece, just take a "spare mouthpiece" and cut most of the shank off so it's a shorter length.

Once you get around your high "C," you'll get blank spots because the mouthpiece has become an instrument. That's because the shortness of the wavelengths and the length of the tube you are blowing through have already created a partial. If you want to play the high notes on the mouthpiece, you have to cut the most of the length off its shank. You see, the wavelengths in the high register are so short—when compared to the tubing it has to go through—that you are getting the effect of blowing through a tube with partials. For example, in the lower register, you could take a garden hose and it would act like a bugle. In the lower register your tones a wider apart and they get closer together as you go up. This follows the same laws that pertain to the vibrations of any pipe.

Jacobs advised players to keep the same rim size when changing mouthpieces, but to feel free to change the depth of their cups or their backbore. Keeping the same rim size prevents players from playing with undeveloped muscular tissue around the mouthpiece rim.

Vibrato

Jacobs thought *vibrato* was a specialized embellishment used in performance—especially useful when giving character to the interpretation of music. Some types of music, like some of Gustav Mahler's symphonies, required what Jacobs called "ethnic *vibrato*." Certainly, some ethnic music—such as the music found in the *Mariachi* repertoire—requires the use of *vibrato*. Jacobs liked to use *vibrato* as an expressive tool as well as a therapeutical tool. He explained:

> I like a lot of *vibrato*. I'd rather hear you play with too much *vibrato* than with too little *vibrato*, but I would like you to play the same music with it and without it (so you always keep it under control). *Vibrato* should be associated with the interpretation of your music. In other

words, *vibrato* shouldn't be a thing that just happens, but instead it should be used as a tool. Now we have a tradition already set up with *vibrato* with Bud Herseth—and with other players of wide ranging ability—where they legitimize the *vibrato* in various ways. The whole point is that you should have versatility and flexibility in the use of *vibrato*. You don't use it only one way. You can use it in different ways.

If you play music that's traditionally played without *vibrato*, then you should play that music without it. If you are playing the chorale music from Anton Bruckner's *Symphony No. 4* or some work of Johaness Brahms, then you don't want *vibrato* there. That's why I am saying that you don't want *vibrato* so ingrained that you can't turn it off. I keep a "scope," even though it's a converted TV set, and we use it as an oscilloscope to watch the *vibrato* there. I teach *vibrato* based on vision as well.

Jacobs also used an exaggerated form of *vibrato* as therapy. This type of *vibrato* was played by oscillating the instrument with one hand to create sound fluctuations. Jacobs said that with this form of therapeutical *vibrato,* a player could "fool" the instrument into getting more resonance. He explained:

> I often teach *vibrato* as a remedial tool and because of its pitch averaging, you get more resonance—that's more output for less input. *Vibrato* can be a therapeutic tool because the fluctuations of pitch and dynamic always ensure the player will find where the instrument resonates most efficiently. *Vibrato* introduces a pitch averaging that has a psychological connotation of mellowness. Then there are fluctuations in dynamic and pitch, which could be measured with the various pieces of equipment. Those fluctuations oscillate above and below where your horn gives its maximum resonance. By using *vibrato*, you'll suddenly find a round sound and playing gets easier because the horn is amplifying at its maximum potential.

Dynamics

Jacobs taught dynamics as part of the study of phrasing and of the extremes. He wanted his students to have a scale of dynamics the same way they have a scale of pitches. This scale of dynamics became useful to achieve subtleties of phrasing once the student reached an advanced performance level. Jacobs said:

> You should have wonderful *pianissimos*. When I was in school at the Curtis Institute of Music in Philadelphia, Marcel Tabuteau taught me phrasing. He considered himself an expert, and I guess he was. He challenged my mind with phrasing when I was sixteen or seventeen years old that, while I didn't have much required phasing on the tuba, I

had a great deal of knowledge of phrasing by listening to my colleagues and by singing with emotion.

One of the things he used to stress was the scaling dynamics the same way you scale pitches. Your entire dynamic range has to be under control. You establish the norm somewhere in the middle dynamics and then you move it back to the *pianissimo*. You have to establish the quality first. At any dynamic, your tone has to be a wonderful product.

Jacobs encouraged brass players to practice at various dynamic levels to retain their entire dynamic spectrum. He explained:

You should practice at various dynamic levels. Otherwise, you'll specialize in playing at one set of dynamics. If you just practice a few soft etudes and an easy concerto, that won't take you into the massive big pieces. There are tremendous differences in physiology between playing *pianissimo* and great *fortissimo* and you have to stay comfortable in both.

As you play softer, it will become easier to play softly. When you first learn to play softly, it's better to find *the norms* of great tone production in the mid-dynamics. You also get your musicianship, artistry, and phrasing. Whatever you do, don't fight the dynamics. Get the music digested the way you want it, then you can begin to go for the extremes. The main thing is to form a concept where it's soft in the brain, then you'll see it's easier to play softly. After all, brass playing is all a reflex response to a stimulus.

Similarly, the maintenance of the extreme loud dynamics was of importance for the advanced and the professional player:

At large dynamics such as 113 dB (decibels)—like the ones we reach in the Chicago Symphony Orchestra—still keep physical but tonal. The big danger in the big *fortissimos* is that there is so much physical awareness of the effort involved, that you'll begin to use the effort to get the big tone rather than just going for the big tone (which will include the big effort). You give the priority to the tone and not to the effort. When practicing the large dynamics, you should pair them with *pianissimo* playing. You should scale your dynamics as you scale pitch.

There are players who have a horrible sound by the time they reach 108 dB. They have a very small embouchure—like a small reed— and when trying to play loud, they force it. They show signs of physical stress, but on the decibel meter they are not getting any louder. There is just more resistance and more push. It has to be a tonal phenomena. Loud playing always has to be related to what you are playing. That is, what are the relationships to the acoustics of the hall, to the orchestra, and what the conductor is asking for?

> Pitch should be constant when you are playing loud. When you go sharp, you are also cutting down on the ability of the horn to resonate. That's why I ask for the *vibrato*—because of the pitch averaging. The whole point is that, if you were going to play deliberately loud in an ensemble, you would be getting in everybody's way. If you, on the other hand, were sensing the situation that they need more from your instrument, then don't hesitate to use it. There are many factors involved. You go by what you sense the ensemble is doing.

Jacobs also found that there were technical complications when playing at loud dynamic levels—mainly the use of unnecessary physical efforts:

> Loud playing doesn't connote big physical efforts. There is a whole number of parts that have to cooperate to play loud and an embouchure has to learn to make use of increasing amounts of air to give amplitude of vibration. As you get used to playing extremely loud, anything less than that gets easier.
>
> Forced loud playing is brittle and hard. Many times when I put the decibel meter on, I see that when a person tries to play louder, they are actually playing softer, but it sounds more strained. They get more edge, but less tone. At home, get used to playing extremely loud as well as extremely soft every day. There is a great deal of physical effort involved. You have to lie to the audience and make it sound as musical as hell.
>
> I have professional students who before getting loud, already have a strident tone. They are so chocked up that even at a low dynamic level it's as if they are grabbing themselves by the throat. Do about 20% of your practice in the extremes. No more! Don't be afraid of playing wrong and ugly. This is music and music making is like acting. You should make people laugh and cry, you can be a villain or you can be a hero. There are varieties of interpretation and sound is part of it. I wouldn't be afraid of playing with the wrong sound.
>
> By playing musically, your embouchure is learning to cooperate. In other words, the big increase in effort is for a big sound. Some players simply blow as a big physical effort, but they don't get the big sound. Instead, they get big resistance and airy tones. They play with a great deal of physical efforts and their tones get rough and hard. That's not right.
>
> It's the same concept of the ball riding on top of a water fountain. When playing loud, you simply use a bigger fountain. In fact, when I get very loud I don't get very physical, but I get very musical. If you get physical without getting musical, you might push against resistance. As a result, you increase the resistance and then you have to increase the push and pretty soon, they'll cancel each other out. I have players who have completely lost their performance function because their embouchures are fighting against their breath. The contest between air and lip is so unequal that the lip always wins over the breath and you lose your ability to function. When I play loud, I think of a big voice. I go strictly by the orchestra. A great big tone requires a big effort, but a big effort might not get you the big tone.

Tongue

Jacobs believed that the incorrect use of the tongue in brass playing was a common problem. He added that the unwanted interruption the tongue exerted on the air column was one of the biggest problems he encountered as a teacher:

> One of my biggest problems as a teacher is the relationship between the tongue and the air. The brain—very frequently—tends to make the tongue the dominating part for controlling the breath rather than the lips. The needs of the embouchure are what predicate the use of breath. The tongue is a villain in many ways and you have to make sure of its downward stroke—the vowel rather than the consonant. Always use a good vowel—AH, OH, or OOH—when you play.

The tongue could be a player's best friend or his worst enemy. For the tongue to be a player's best friend, the player must get his tongue out of the air column's way. Jacobs explained:

> You must play down the nuisance value of the tongue. The problem is that the brain will start to accept your tongue as the regulator of the breath and it will send signals based on what your tongue needs and not on what your embouchure needs.
>
> Neurologically, you must handle the tongue by specific stimuli to fire up your conditioned reflexes. As you learn these concepts, use your voice often in your practice of different vowels like "TOH" or "TOO." You have to get into the spirit of tonguing based on the vowel and not based on the consonant. If the tongue stays in total closure while pronouncing the consonant, there is no way you can get air through it. The tongue has to swiftly pronounce the consonant and learn to get out of the way of the wind by moving to its vowel form right away.
>
> When tonguing, the vowel has to be dominant over the consonant. The vowel is always open, and the consonant is always closed. In other words, if you analyze the consonant "T," you notice that it will have, for a moment, no air getting through. The consonant "T" simply acts as a barrier between the breath coming from the lungs and your lip. The culprits are the lower branches of the Genio-hyo-glossus group that protrudes your tongue. Biologically, when you put your tongue forward, that forward movement is initiated down in that muscle region. What frequently happens is that those muscles, instead of being innervated off and on, remain innervated and the tongue gets clumsy. You can't feel these things. It's like a tug of war between muscle groups. You can't even be aware they exist because you won't get any feedback or sensations of their motor activity.
>
> As soon as your tongue starts to move forward, the brain will innervate the intrinsic and extrinsic musculatures—those muscles that

help the tongue move around — but often the tongue becomes stiff. When the tongue moves forward, it has more power. I mean, it becomes more isometric within itself. If you start this combination in fast tonguing and you start to stutter, you know that's a problem down in the genioglossus group and not a problem with the tip of your tongue. That's why you can't stop practicing single tonguing. When you practice your double and triple tongue, don't neglect the single tongue. Either that or walk around singing "TA-TA-TA-TA" as Herbert L. Clarke used to do.

Thick Wind

Jacobs wanted his students to reshape their tongues, as when pronouncing the vowel "AH," to create an open oral cavity. An open oral cavity enables the wind column to freely reach the embouchure — where it is used to propel the lips into vibration. Jacobs called the quality of this unobstructed wind column "thick wind." John Cvejanovich explained how Jacobs conceptualized the concept of thick wind:

> Jacobs compared the use of thick air to the bowing of a violin player. Jacobs would say, "Imagine a violin player who plays with a violin bow. Imagine now the same violin player playing with a viola bow. He would then get a much bigger sound. Now imagine the same player playing with a cello bow and then with a bass bow. Imagine the kind of sound you would pull out of those strings." Now, that would be ridiculous to see a violin player put a bass bow to a violin, but some of these things have to be put into clear analogies to be understood.

Air and Embouchure

Jacobs wanted to have a direct connection between air and embouchure — not air and tongue. The combination of air and tongue produces thin air — or cold air as it is sometimes called — and the combination of air and embouchure produces thick air — or warm air as it is sometimes called. Jacobs explained:

> What you want is to have the release of the air toward the lip and not toward to the tongue — this is what gives you thick wind. Otherwise, at that moment when the air hits the tongue, the brain will form a pattern of response based on the control of the tongue rather than of the needs of the lip. When you buzz on the rim, you bypass that problem by getting a strong sense of buzz — immediately setting the correct air-lip relationship. You have to pretend you feel your lip buzzing when you play your instrument. The other way of playing — with the air hitting the tongue — will get you in trouble after a few measures.

The Study of Vowels

Jacobs devised effective and efficient training exercises to get more air to the embouchure. One of those exercises was the study of vowel forms for teaching his students to get their tongues out of the way of their air stream. He gave the following instructions to begin the study of vowels:

> First, you have to make sure that your tongue is not too long. Say, "DOH" and "AH-LAH" and you'll find that the tongue gets shorter. Now say "KEEH" and "OH." "OH" is the smaller tongue (either 'OH' or 'AH'). The study of the vowels I just mentioned should become an airway study.
> There is a continuity of procedures and we must start with the tongue. First of all, start with taking a deep breath because the shallow breath will have the brain assign a priority of closures in the mouth area (the tongue included) and it will close no matter what you do simply because you don't have enough air coming up your trachea. So take lots of air in and then play with a small tongue (lowering your jaw).

Jacobs's study of vowels is a form of specialized training that he developed through years trial and error. He also used this training to help his students develop a kinetic awareness of their tongue placement. He said:

> Go to "KEEH, EEH, and TEEH," so it's the back, middle, and front of your tongue, and inhale and exhale while you practice those vowels. You'll feel your tongue staying at the top of your mouth and you'll also feel tremendous pressure. Now, go to the other extreme. Try "AH, OH, OOH" and inhale and exhale. Now, go back to your instrument and try to feel that open oral cavern. Remember to take huge breaths when you are working out your tongue position this way.

The study of vowels is based on the study of the extremes. In other words, the study of a black and white contrast instead of the study of shades of grey:

> The study of vowels is an exaggeration, but I want the exaggeration for your own recognition. Later you can find the tongue level and the tone production you want. I want you to be able to function with a closed or open oral cavity. It doesn't have to feel good, it just has to sound great.

Ultimately, a player will play anywhere in between the "AH" and the "EEH" tongue positions. During performance, the player is advised not to think about vowels or feel the tongue's position, but to instead concentrate on sounding great. The study of vowel forms is a type of specialized training that belongs in the practice room and not in the concert hall.

High Air Pressures

Jacobs warned about high air pressures that could build up behind the tongue—pressures which often activate reflexes such as the Valsalva maneuver:

> You don't want to build up the air pressure behind the tongue. It's air and lip that plays music. Use the "rim" to put the focus back on the relationship between air and lip. Of course, it will feel differently when you play your instrument, but you pretend it feels the same. Air and lip and not air and tongue. The psychology of it is that the air should be at the outer part of your lip, and not inside of your mouth.
>
> You want to play down as much of the interference of the tongue as you can. Your job is to connect the air with the lip. There will be manipulation caused by various movements of the tongue, but keep that to a minimum. The tongue will want to take over. To avoid that, take the tongued passage and play it slurred. Notice the ease of playing and blowing. Now, take some of that ease to the tongued passage. Always look for the lack of back pressure.

The use of the rim—or the mouthpiece—serves as a remedial tool for connecting air and lip without the interruption of the tongue. Jacobs advised players to buzz a few low pitches on the rim and to try to remember the feel of buzz once they played their instrument. According to Jacobs, it is impossible to feel the lip buzzing while playing the instrument, but he wanted players to pretend to feel it. Air and lip (buzz) is what makes music, not air and tongue.

The Use of the Rim

Jacobs used the rim (sometimes known an a visualizer) as another tool for connecting the air and the lip while bypassing the interference of the tongue. He explained:

> Can you play down your tongue a little bit so the buzz of the lip creates the *staccato*? You know how the buzz would be like on the rim [visualizer]. Right now, your brain wants to involve the movements of the breath, the tongue, and the lips to buzz. That's wrong. I want the connection to be breath and lips only. Then you simply use the tongue as when you use it in speech—so you use it for timing and diction

purposes. Music is always a combination of air and the embouchure buzzing.

Even a short note is a short buzz. You have to use the tongue, but basic tone production is air and buzz. You are giving the tongue too much emphasis to the point where the brain is beginning to accept the tongue as a control factor in tone production. For that reason, your brain is accepting the tongue as part of the musical equation with more importance than it deserves. The tongue does belong in the music making equation, but it's on a very small basis. In a graph, the use of the tongue would show as a small line when compared to the importance of air and buzz.

When you buzz the rim, you'll feel the lips as well as your tongue. Can you forget about the feel of the tongue and instead put a magnifying glass on the feel of the lips? When you go back to your instrument you won't be able to feel the lips, but you have to pretend you do. Simply, remember the feel of the lips vibrating. Somewhere along the line, this has to become a learned function with you because it's very basic to your playing. You can't unlearn something that has been already learned and has reached a "habit form." You simply have to add and develop this new tool [using the rim for a few minutes twice a day] and frequently touching your lips where they vibrate so you are sensitizing the feel of buzz.

You want to play down much of the tongue's interference. Your job is to connect the air with the lip. There will be manipulation of the air column caused by various movements of the tongue, but keep that to a minimum. The tongue will want to take over. To avoid that, play your tongued passage slurred. Notice the ease of playing and blowing. Take some of that ease to the tongued passage. Always look for the lack of back pressure.

Nothing has to be perfect when you start. At home, you can play simple tunes on the mouthpiece or the rim. Feel through the skin where the vibration is actually happening. It doesn't have to be exact, but it's simply that the brain is now concentrating on providing the motor activity while feeling the same motor activity. Can you make a study of connecting the vibration of the lip and the air so the tongue is almost like an accessory that works going up and down like a valve in a car? The tongue is important, but it's not the whole engine.

Jacobs went further in stressing the connection between the air stream and the lip by saying the following:

Always find the rhythm of your music in the buzz and not in the tongue. If you connect your buzz and your mind, your authority will increase right away. Years ago I had a gauge—which had a tube connected to the player's mouth—mounted on the music stand. This gauge produced a read out of the player's attacks. Often—in troubled players—the gauge indicated air pressure first followed by the player's tone. The brain will be satisfied that the first note was in rhythm because the tongue was on time—even though the tone was late.

Can we make sure that we play by wind and buzz rather than by wind and tongue? Buzz! Your lips are always supposed to vibrate. Open a little space in between the lips so the air goes in between them instead of pushing them apart. The air has to go in between the lips just as it does in an oboe reed. Blow more wind so you blow "out here" in front of you. Your breath is not used to working quite the way it should because it's gotten used to feeding the tongue and not the embouchure. Using your imagination, you have to pretend you can feel and see the lips vibrating for each note you play. Do this from time to time to activate your lips.

Tongue and Articulation

When tonguing, Jacobs wanted the downward motion of the tongue and not its back and forth or upward motion. He described the tongue's role in articulation as follows:

> The attack is always built upon the downward stroke of the tongue and not the upward stroke of the tongue. You have to blow your attacks and not release them. Don't let the attacks have an uncontrolled air column that has been manipulated by the tongue. You always blow air for the need of the embouchure. Remember that air is like a violin bow. Don't let your air column be like a pressure device. Use zero pressure when you play.
> The closer you get to speech, the better the tongue will be. Say, "It's ten 'till two." Where is your tongue when you say that? Do this daily and you'll notice a sense of freedom coming to your embouchure.

According to Manny Laureano, his lessons with Jacobs helped him clarify the tongue's importance in brass playing. Laureano narrated:

> The most significant thing he [Jacobs] did for me was to make me realize that when I was exhaling I was holding my stomach in a very still and stiff position. He said, "No, you don't do that. You have to pull in as you are playing concurrent with your tongue (articulation)."
> The second thing Jacobs made me realize was that the tongue was very important in the production of sound. He wanted me to accentuate the use of the vowel, which is the real sound, and to diminish the beginning consonant of the note. So he drew a little picture with a small "t" and then a big "O" and then a big "H." He said, instead of a large "T" (large attack- small vowel) he wanted a small attack and large vowel. That was it, within twenty minutes all the problems I had had

finally went away, and my playing entered a whole new era. Now I don't have that problem, but I would have never gotten there had it not been for the way Arnold showed me to play. Playing with maximum efficiency and using less tongue.

You know what's funny, in the four years I studied with [William] Vacchiano he would say over and over, "The tongue is the greatest enemy of the trumpet player" and he was right. I didn't know it then, but now I know what he meant. The tongue is what really starts the tone for many people. They use it like a weapon and as a result, they are not going to get the correct use of the vowel. That's partly due to of all of that internal pressurization the tongue can lead to.

Multiple Tonguing

When playing multiple tonguing, Jacobs wanted his students to maintain a high quality of tone. This, in his opinion, was achieved by few players who came to his studio. The learning of multiple tonguing has to start at a slow tempo. This way a player can concentrate on achieving a good tone. Jacobs explained:

> It's easy to slow down your playing to raise your standards of tone. Otherwise, if you face the immediate challenges of double-tonguing head on and at a fast speed, you might not achieve success. I hear so many players with deteriorated tone production as soon as they multiple tongue. In fact, very few players sound as good in multiple tonguing as they do in single tongue or slurs. Work your tonguing based on the concept of a "loaf of bread" and all its excellent ingredients. Now, you simply cut off slices from that loaf—those slices have the same ingredients as the big loaf. You have to work the same way with your long tones. That's the basic principle behind it. Then if you want to change for other purposes, then that's valid and it's part of the art form.

The application of multiple tonguing must be lighter in approach. Jacobs described this lighter approach as follows:

> Don't make a big issue out of triple tonguing in the sense that usually its application is too severe. In other words, triple tongue is a light movement of the tongue. Say "TA-TA-KA-TA" and say "LAH-LAH-LAH-LAH." Can you have your "TA-TA-KA-TA" to sound more like your "LAH-LAH-LAH-LAH"? Make sure you "AH" vowel stays equal throughout. Can you get the tone "AH" to be equal in quality? Match the tonal quality. You need a tonal triple tongue. Say "LAH-TAH" and match the tone of the vowel. I don't care what type "AH" vowel you use as long as they match. Any single little tonal changes are shape differences in the tongue. As you triple tongue, because it goes so fast, you usually change the vowel and your tone quality changes.

It's maybe getting a little harder, a little less, or a little more. In other words, there are tonal differences of which you are not in charge.

There are also dangers in the practicing of multiple tonguing:

> Whenever you go very rapidly, your tongue will want to remain much more in closure. In other words, it will tend to—I suppose for conservation of energy—reduce the distance between vowel and consonant. The first thing you've got is a closed sounding "TEE." We need an exaggeration of whatever vowel gives you space, not closure. We must find the neurological pattern that will have the brain motivate the vowel so you simply use the consonant for articulation, but you don't over motivate it. You motivate the vowel as tone production.
> If you don't have much space in your mouth, there will be almost no room left for the air to get to the lips. You'll also have all kinds of pressures and almost nothing coming out the tip of your lip. If you say "KEE," you'll see how your mouth will close up in the back. Now say "KEE-HO." When you say "HO," your tongue will come down and it will become shorter in length. Say "OH" and then say "TEEH." When you say "TEEH," right away you can visualize the air traveling through a very small space to get to the tongue. If it gets too small, you are going to get a hell of a resistance. If you are also holding down in your abdominal region plus tonguing continuously, you are going to have a difficult time producing a good tone.

Jacobs suggested limiting the practice of multiple tonguing to give room to the maintenance of an agile single tongue. He also wanted his students to memorize the sound they produced while tonguing, not its feel. Jacobs elaborated:

> I would only do 10 or 15% of your practice time on multiple and single tongue. There is a tendency of losing the single tonguing if you just practice your multiple tongue. You want to have a flexible tongue. You want to memorize the sound and not the feel of your tonguing. If you memorize the feel, you'll be apt to soon forget and you'll upset everything else. It's like forgetting a couple of items out of a formula and before you know, you have the wrong formula.

High Register Tonguing

The continuous practice of high register tonguing often leads to intraoral closures and to embouchure starvation (from the air it needs). Jacobs explained:

> Tonguing in the high register can deteriorate your playing if you just keep practicing it. The whole point is that when you introduce the tongue—even in normal use—it will cut down a small percentage of

the flow of air at the lip. In other words, the use of the consonant will tend to reduce your airflow. If we use a decibel meter and have you tongue a B-flat, you'll see the gauge dropping in volume. It should have been at the same volume. You can sense that, even though you are blowing the same, what's getting to the embouchure is actually far less than what it was in the slurs. Try to keep the gauge the same.

The tongue's interruptions will be exaggerated when you play in the high range. The starvation of the lip will be greater. It's simply that as you use the tongue, you create a hazard for the embouchure in the high range. That's why I teach the high range slurred first. If you practice your high range as a tone study, you'll be all right.

One of the problems is that as you get into high pressure, you apply more pressure and as a result, there will be a reduction phenomena. Boyle's law! When you are playing and you are up in the high register, you don't have very much air in the lungs. Instead, you'll have intense pressure, but there can't be much quantitative air usage because there is not much room left. In other words, your tongue is in the way and what you are getting to the lip is a *hiss* of very high pressure. If you can thicken that air up by getting your tongue out of the way, you'll go far in solving this problem. If you can keep this "thick air" approach, you'll be fine.

The Aging Process

Jacobs experienced a change in his tonguing abilities as he aged. He also noticed a similar change in other aging players—specifically some of his colleagues in the Chicago Symphony Orchestra. Jacobs advised older players to take surplus quantities of air and learn how to use that air as airflow, not as air pressure. He suggested the following:

> Practice your single tongue and double tongue to the point where you have an overlap; so you can go either way. There is a funny thing that comes with age. I noticed it with myself and I think I notice it with Bud Herseth. I also know what it is. There are changes in the airways that come in with aging that are unfavorable to single tonguing. Particularly as the air slows up, if you don't have enough air in the lungs, you'll find that the tongue goes on duty closing the airway down (So that the pressures remain and when that happens your tongue slows up even further). We simply have to make sure we have enough air in the lungs.
>
> Bud Herseth is doing more double-tonguing and less single tonguing now that he is aging. It's just that as you get older there is less air that comes up the trachea and there will be more distress in your single tonguing. You have to try to take more air in and let it come out faster, but your habits were not formed that way. You can also re-develop your tonguing abilities.

Summary

The discussion of tonguing includes the study of its physiology in the articulation of music. It also includes the study of vowel forms for shaping the tongue inside the player's oral cavity. The shaping of the tongue, as a result, will shape the brass player's tone. Players should allow their tongues to be allies and not enemies in their tone production. The tongue becomes an ally when its shape—inside the player's mouth—allows a thick air column to flow without interruption to the lip. The tongue becomes an enemy when it arches upward to the point of becoming a barrier between a thick air column and the lip. This barrier thins out the air column and starves the embouchure of air.

All players benefit from the study of vowel forms as a tool for learning both extremes of tongue placement. That is, the vowels "AH" (or its variations 'OOH' or 'OH') and "EEH" (or its variations 'KEEH' or 'TEEH'). Jacobs said that as performing musicians, brass players have to play music anywhere in between those two extremes.

Chapter Five

Artistic Concepts

Contents

Preview	87
Artistic Concepts	87
The Use of Imitation	88
Imitate a Better Player	89
The Use of Imagination	89
The Voice Singing in the Head	90
Round Sounds	91
Show Business	93
Playing with Authority	94
The Art of Phrasing	95
Storytelling in Music	97
Summary	97
Notes	98

Artistic Concepts

Preview

- *Great brass players focus on the mental image of their end product (sound) as a means of controlling the elements involved in sound production.*
- *Jacobs went further in saying that there should be no separation between the player and his instrument. In other words, the instrument becomes an extension of the player if the player concentrates on singing.*
- *Jacobs described his approach toward music performance as extroverted. He said that as a kid he was a "ham" and had a strong desire to entertain an audience. This is indeed a positive attitude to have in the art form of music.*
- *Jacobs wanted his students to play with the same sense of authority he saw in players such as Adolph Herseth. He also wanted his students to be sure of what they wanted to play in terms of sound, phrasing, and all the other elements involved in the art form of music.*
- *For Jacobs, playing music was like telling a story. The storytelling aspects of playing were the ultimate goal of any musician. Musicians are in show business to entertain an audience.*

Artistic Concepts

Great brass players focus on their mental image of sound as a means of controlling the elements involved in their sound production. The quality of that mentalization—in terms of clarity of conception and exactitude of its various musical elements—determines the quality of the end product. The end product is the *Song*, as found in *Song and Wind*, and it is created based on the player's artistic concepts.

Jacobs recognized this type of artistic playing in the so-called "natural players." These natural players play with a direct connection between mind and lip without the interruption of peripheral thoughts. Some of the peripheral thinking includes thoughts about physical procedures or about the physical feedback involved in playing.

Playing artistically requires a high degree of extroversion from the player. For this reason, Jacobs wanted his students to communicate as entertainers by delivering a pre-determined artistic message to their audience. Jacobs said:

The big thing about music—or any other art form—is that you can enjoy what you are doing, but others must also enjoy what you are doing. Its orientation should be like when you draw a beautiful picture on canvas for others to enjoy. When you are playing a solo, you are not playing for you, but for the people who are listening.

Jacobs used the following concepts to improve his students' artistic playing. Those concepts were: the use of imitation, the use of imagination, the concept of round sounds, and having a show business attitude toward performance.

The Use of Imitation

Jacobs stressed the importance of having a clear mental image of sound as a modeling source during the brass playing learning process. He believed that the use of imitation is the most natural method for the attainment of the mental image of sound:

> Imitation is a powerful tool for learning. In learning through imitation, you can use your sense of sight, touch, or hearing to imitate something or someone else. (This way you will tell your brain how to proceed to play music). This is indeed an attitude that has the dominance in the art form of music and not on the physical function of making music. For example, you could use your breath (as applied to brass playing) to perfection and be a horrible player (musically speaking). The use of breath is nothing more than the use of fuel (like gasoline to a car); it's not music, it's just part of music.
> Imitation is especially important to a young person learning a musical instrument. That young person should be aware of the musicality expected from them. They should also have a great sound to imitate because if there is a great sound in their brain and a horrible sound coming out of the horn, it won't be long before that sound becomes better. That happens naturally by a process of trial and error and by the agitation of muscle tissue that leads to hypertrophy. In other words, eventually what comes out of the horn will match what is in the brain.

The use of imitation for improving brass performance implies the use of the method of trial and error. During the learning process, players should allow themselves a quota of mistakes. In other words, some of the attempts at achieving the ideal sound might not be successful. Nonetheless, after several more attempts players might come closer to their ideal concept of sound. This learning process comes naturally to most children as they learn to talk. However, adults have to often be reminded that imitation is one of the most powerful learning tools they possess.

Imitate Great Players

Jacobs encouraged his students to imitate great players—i.e., a brass playing role model that seemed appropriate for that particular student. For example, Jacobs told a trumpet student:

> Be an actor and pretend to be someone else for a moment. Use imitation (or create your own model) and hear the different players in your head. Put great examples in your head and demonstrate how a great player sounds. Imitate Maynard Ferguson, Adolph Herseth, or Doc Severinsen. Remember that you are always selling a musical product. Always start with the sound in your head and not with mechanical preparations.

On another occasion, Jacobs told Ron Hasselman the following:

> Now you are going to be away from Herseth, but you've got a really fine trumpet player (Bernie Adelstein) up there in the Minneapolis Symphony Orchestra and you'll be working with him. When he plays a phrase, you go home, you practice that phrase, and you play it just like him. You play just like Bernie because he is a beautiful player.

A brass student may choose a favorite player to imitate. However, Jacobs said that it is best if that "role model" is a better player than the student. The student may also choose to imitate specific performance aspects of a particular player. For example, the student might imitate the clear articulation of Maurice André or the trumpet tone of Adolph Herseth.

Most advanced players have learned the stylistic and technical aspects of brass playing from commercially recorded albums. Jacobs, however, advised his students to listen to great players in live concerts—whenever possible—to gain a "realistic picture" of their tone and articulation. (Commercially recorded albums often give an "unrealistic picture" of a player's tone and articulation).

The Use of Imagination

Jacobs stressed the importance of having a clear mental image of sound before playing by encouraging the use of imagination. He said:

> The use of imagination is a strong tool for getting the body to react to whatever you are trying to accomplish. When playing, always imagine

a great sound (even if you are sounding rotten at the moment). Imitate a player better than yourself.

The use of your imagination is also important in rehearsals because you have to be able to transfer into musical sounds whatever the conductor is asking you to do (you must transfer the spoken word into images of sound). In other words, you have to transfer the critique of something wrong in your playing into musical thoughts and not into mechanical thoughts.

Jacobs found that the lack of musical imagination was a common problem among some of his students. He said:

The lack of musical imagination in the musical endeavors is the number one problem in most cases. You find that those students who crowd their brains with how to play their instrument from a technical standpoint, are not able to play music from a musical standpoint. One should learn first how to play music and by doing so, learn to play the instrument.

The Voice *Singing* in the Head

Jacobs wanted his students to "hear" the mental image of sound in the form of a human voice *singing* in their heads. That voice *sang* each note as a student played his instrument:

The notes have to be more in the brain and less in your lip. You are missing notes in the same place where there is not enough singing going on in your head. There should be two voices, one that comes out of the bell of your instrument (which is not too important), but the other you conceive in your head is the most important. Can you let that grow more inside your brain? I won't be able to hear it, but you'll be able to hear it.

This way of playing will keep slipping in and out and you won't know it. The unfortunate part is that you'll suddenly feel that you can't control the notes. When you feel that way, don't blame your embouchure or try to correct your lips or your breath. Instead, correct the song in your head and "she" [your playing] will correct itself quickly.

You have good conditioning behind you now. You'll start growing as soon as you start to mentalize your music. You've got to train yourself so that all the ink spots on the page of music are converted into sounds in your head.

Jacobs went further in saying that there should be no separation between the player and his instrument. In other words, the instrument should become an extension of the player if the player concentrates on *singing*:

You are taking to blowing your instrument like if it were a separate from you. Your instrument should be like an extension of you—as if it belongs to your body. You should *sing* and blow air out here so you forget about your instrument. I want you to think less about playing a brass instrument and more about singing with your vocal chords [lips]. This way you are very close to a singer. For you, this should translate to being much more vocally oriented and much less mechanically oriented.

Round Sounds

Jacobs encouraged his students to play with a round sound throughout the entire register of their instruments. That is, the low, middle, and the high registers. For playing the extreme high register, Jacobs wanted his students to pretend that the sound was round. However, he knew that playing round sounds in the extreme high register was difficult under most circumstances. He said:

> Always protect the high notes by giving them a roundness of tone. Once the range gets into the upper high range, the round tone changes. You must even out the roundness of tone over your entire register. You don't have to do the manipulation physically, but you do the manipulation mentally. Controlling the embouchure is an illusion because you can't control the embouchure by using direct commands. Nobody can! You can only control your sound. I know of some teachers who teach controlling the embouchure, but I know that that's wrong.
>
> Can you round out your tone in your brain? In listening to Herseth play the little trumpets (Eb trumpet and piccolo), you hear that the psychology of his playing is based on the round and thick tone of the large trumpets.
>
> So many players with a round tone can't get up to the high register. Herseth had the round tone anywhere he wanted. I had it anywhere I wanted it simply by allowing my embouchure to readjust so that the embouchure is not important, but that the music is important. Get used to coming up from the low register with a round sound rather than coming down from the high register with a thinner sound.

Jacobs used the concept of round sounds toward the end of his teaching tenure. By round sounds Jacobs meant that the shape of the sound could be visualized as having a round shape and a solid core as it came out of the instrument. The sound produced by players who *sang* as they played usually has a resonant and round quality. The concept of round sounds also implies the lack of unwanted distortions in terms of sound production.

William Scarlett talked about the concept of "round sounds" by stressing its importance as an artistic thought :

> The concept of round sounds is a wonderful idea. It's an artistic idea. If I were teaching you and I want you to play a high "C" with the most brilliant penetrating sound and I tell you, "Play it right now," you would have many muscles engaging. Now, if I ask you play to play with a nice warm round sound, what happens? You don't have the same muscle activity. For Jake [Arnold Jacobs] to say that you should play with a round sound worked as a muscle relaxing idea.

For Manny Laureano the concept of the "round sounds" correlated with the shape of the player's embouchure when pronouncing the syllable "TOH." He explained:

> I think that it has to do very much with the shape of the mouth when we go "TOH"; it's a round shape and when we go "TEEH" it's not round. Not only is the sound not round, but also what we are doing physically is not round. "TAH" is a little bit rounder, but it's still somewhat elliptical or oval. "TOH" is round and when we get the round vowel, we get the round sound. Every once in a while if you want a certain musical effect you may go to "EEH," but you don't use that for your normal way of playing.
>
> I find myself using Arnold's concepts to get people away from the "EEH" type of sound and more towards "TOH" because I teach "TOH" all the way up to the highest note you can play. I do that fully accepting that the tongue does change. To have people do those changes consciously is to exaggerate what's already a natural process. In other words, I have students doing "TOH, TOH, TOH" (singing upward arpeggio) because I don't want them to go "TEEH, TEEH, TEEH."
>
> The conscious adaptation of vowels will make the sound round as you go into the upper register and as you descend into the lower register. I think that you have to keep the round sound from the bottom to the top. We all know that when we get to the top the sound is not going round but your mental concept of roundness has to be there. You have to pretend that that's what you are doing. So that you are always articulating the same way and you are doing whatever it is you want to do in a purposeful way. There is nothing arbitrary or accidental about what you are doing. Why? Because we are supposed to be creating these sounds from a mental image. Therefore, every sound we make is supposed to be the sound that we expect. The sound that we are anticipating. There shouldn't be any accidents.

In contrast, Vincent Cichowicz related the concept of "round sounds" to other similar concepts—such as that of singing sounds or dark sounds:

It's hard to put the characteristic of a sound into words and I think most people have individuality in their sound, but all the good players have similar qualities. You can call them round sounds, full sounds or dark sounds. Singing sound and sometimes those words strike a chord with some people. Most of the time if you refer to a free sound or natural sound it also works.

Show Business

Jacobs taught the concept of "performing with a show business attitude" as a way of encouraging artistic extroversion. He said that as a kid he was a "ham" and had a strong desire to entertain audiences. This is indeed a positive attitude to have in the art form of music. He elaborated:

> Developing musicianship, interpretation, and aesthetics sometimes takes the experience of being on stage while reading many types of "stories" to an audience. You always have to "ham up" your stories so you become entertaining when you read. That is, dramatic when you need to be dramatic, funny when you need to be funny, and sad when you need to be sad. If I could just get you in one walk of life to be like that, so you could then transfer that sense of storytelling to music. Just take a chapter of a book at home and make it come to life. As the creative part of your mind awakens, you'll find that it will make brass playing easier.
>
> I was always a ham. I was in the movies when I was a little boy. I don't know anything about those movies, but I remember that I was paid five dollars and was given an ice cream cone. As you see, I was brought up in show business. My mother was always playing the piano in movie theaters and I used to see the movies for nothing. (She played for the silent movies in Hollywood). There was a lot of show business in my family so I came to realize that a lot of what we do in performance is based on extroversion.
>
> I need you to imitate artistry. To do that, you have to pretend to be a great artist. For example, if you have to pretend that you are dying, you can't do it by really dying. However, you have seen enough films of people dying so you can imitate the actors you are watching. Those actors have studied how to pretend to die with doctors guiding them through the dying process. If you want great joy, you don't have to jump fences or eat an ice cream cone to attain it. All you need is to respond to a feeling of joy. This approach will pay off in our art form.
>
> You have to realize that you don't play by listening to yourself play. That's playing by asking questions. We receive information by asking questions, but we impart information by issuing statements. You have to play by issuing statements. Then you would be entering into show business the way you should. We need to issue the statements with enthusiasm and as a product of our imagination. Be a storyteller of sound.

Don't play as if you are putting your toe in the water. That would be like listening to yourself as you play. Instead, you should go into show business and play like an artist. Imitate great artists. Pick great role models and use the power of imitation. Don't prepare yourself to play your instrument. Instead, prepare the sound in your head. Play four "G's" in a row and pick the best one. Then start your phrase with it.

Asking questions is not undesirable. I do it too because that's the way we learn many things. However, when you play your instrument I have to get you into show business and be a storyteller of sound so you avoid self-teaching.

Cheat a little! Sound great even if you feel rotten. Be like a "used car salesman." It's simply that in order to use your nervous system properly (to influence the external environment using your motor systems), you have to issue statements.

Playing With Authority

Jacobs wanted his students to play with the same sense of authority he saw in players such as Adolph Herseth. He also wanted his students to securely establish their artistic interpretations in terms of sound, phrasing, and all the other elements involved in the art form of music before they performed them. Jacobs explained:

> I want to introduce the psychology of playing with authority into the student's interpretations. Some students have had too much grounding over the years in insecure playing. Everything a human being repeats is habit forming—even insecurity. Then the brain will accept insecurity as a norm.
>
> You need to have more preparation in the *Song* aspects of brass playing. The teacher can play a pitch on the keyboard and the student can play back the pitch on the mouthpiece. With this exercise, you make sure the student goes more by the pitch than by the lip. Make each pitch authoritative in your brain. If the student is not confident with the pitch, it will show in the student's over all recital, concert, or audition preparation.
>
> Increase the strength of your mentalizations. Make sure you don't get distracted. The messages to the lip must come from the brain. Always protect that. Make sure you are less aware of the feel of the embouchure and more aware of your mentalizations. Then all you have to do is to take enough air so you have a surplus and sing.
>
> Sometimes, the application of that mentalization is insecure in terms of tone quality (it has a lack resonance). Put yourself on the stage of Orchestra Hall (Chicago) and imagine that you have to play solo right after Adolph Herseth. He has just played your solo beautifully and the audience in clapping. Can you hear him playing? Now you go play and compete with him!

Artistic Concepts

> When you play a lyrical passage softly, you have to play it with a positive pitch sense. You have to play almost like if you were an actor and you were going to cry, but at that moment don't let it go too far into mush. If you do this, there will be a change in the qualities of the music, but you must always suit the style of the composition you are playing. On the other hand, you must keep more of the brass playing aspect when playing fanfares so you get more into the brass family. Whatever you play, you have to be in the character of the piece you are playing. A musician has to expect to be excited. There is no way you can be a fine musician and just be placid and dull. Life involves many exciting experiences and you express all aspects of live in music just like an actor would.

While playing on the mouthpiece, Jacobs wanted players to demonstrate their authority as excellent interpreters of pitch. He said:

> When buzzing the mouthpiece, be careful with your pitch interpretation. Decide what you want to play and with great authority go for it. You should always carry a pitch source (pitch pipe) with you to challenge yourself. Don't rely on your mental recall. You'll find that your relative pitch will get better and your absolute pitch will relax. Absolute pitch is not important. As long as you have a pitch source, your recall will improve. When I am testing you for pitch recall, I always do it away from your instrument. I want my student's pitch recall to be superior.
>
> Even when you are wrong, I need very much to ask for more authority in your interpretation. In addition, you should pay more attention to your attitude. A positive attitude is very important for a musician in terms of confidence even when you know it's not deserved. However, you've got to play music with authority. If you miss, you miss, but you'll find that you'll miss much less if you play with authority.

The Art of Phrasing

Jacobs taught phrasing based on his vast artistic knowledge, his experience as teacher and performer, and his experiences as a student at the Curtis Institute in Philadelphia. He often talked about the concepts he had learned from oboist Marcel Tabuteau [one of his instructors at Curtis]. Jacobs also encouraged his student to imitate great artists as a way of learning the art of phrasing. He narrated:

> In phrasing, there could be a consistent use of small *crescendos* and *diminuendos*, which lead from one note to the next. You can put a little lift in some of the notes or you can smooth out some of the others. Put some *vibrato* in one section or take it away for another section. There are many tools you can start using when learning to phrase. You can experiment with phrasing when you are learning a piece of music.

I went to a class at the Curtis Institute of Music in Philadelphia that gave us many suggestions on how to phrase. They really didn't teach us rules of phrasing. We studied the *crescendos*, *diminuendos*, and the changing of pulse between down pulses and up-pulses to give us ideas on phrasing. Real phrasing has to come from the performer. If it helps, you can pretend you are singing the lyrics of a song. I studied voice for many years so my phrasing is more from the vocal school. I studied phrasing instrumentally as well. The idea is that you can have various versions of the same phrase. You take a set of notes and you do them in many styles. You could do them in the style of Mozart or Brahms.

In the orchestra, I phrase depending on the part I am playing. For example, in Gustav Mahler's *Symphony No. 6* there is a tuba part that, whenever I played it, Georg Solti used to smile. A number of other conductors used to come and congratulate me on my phrasing after the concert. I just did it for myself since I thought nobody would notice the tuba part. These little details on how to phrase some of the major orchestral works are very important. For instance, in the symphonies of Gustav Mahler, there are ethnic flavors in some of the parts—little *crescendos* and *diminuendos*—so maybe in one beat you might have to go up and down in dynamics. Those details keep you mentally focused and very close to the character of the music. You must keep up the study of phrasing along with the other things you are doing in your playing.

Whether you are playing solo or *soli*, like when I used to play with Bud [Adolph Herseth] two octaves apart, I would adjust my phrasing to his. Whatever he would do, I would try to adjust to it two octaves lower. If it was my own part, I would phrase it according to my own concept, but I would usually create a phrase. I would try not to play a straight line.

If you hear a singer, you usually hear wonderful story telling and phrasing because she has a story to tell with her music—she has lyrics. For example, you can hear the subtleties when a singer sings a love song. When you have a story associated with the music, it's much easier to phrase. The idea is that words have meaning. You can put lyrics to your solos and excerpts as you sing them. You can emphasize some words more than others depending on their meaning. The idea is for you to experiment, record yourself, and then listen to the play back. For example, you can play *America the Beautiful* as a march or as a choral piece and see what you think once you listen to the playback. It might be a bit embarrassing at first and you might not know what you are doing, but after you listen to the playbacks a few times, you'll start making decisions about your phrasing.

As a brass player and musician, if you hear another brass player's phrasing you might be able to analyze it and you might be aware of what he is doing differently from the norm. There are few people who are able to analyze phrasing, but you could find many who simply enjoy phrasing. By imitating others, you are getting the materials so you can work on your own artistic ideas. Take one portion of your practice, perhaps 15 or 20 minutes, and work on phrasing. You have to find, however, the appropriate music materials to study phrasing. You can play love songs or some music that has some sadness or sorrow. You can make music that makes people laugh as well.

Storytelling in Music

For Jacobs, interpreting music was like telling a story. The storytelling aspect of performance is the ultimate goal of any musician. According to Jacobs, musicians were in show business to entertain an audience. He reminded one of his students—who was a full time teacher—about the dangers of interpreting music in an introverted fashion:

> You are beginning to play music too much like reading a book at home, "Once upon a time in a far off land there lived a little boy, and his name was Joe." In front of an audience that becomes, "ONCE UPON A TIME IN A FAR OFF LAND THERE LIVED A LITTLE BOY AND HIS NAME WAS JOE." There is a big difference between words being interpreted for you and words being interpreted for an audience. With a lot of teaching, there is chance that you are playing for yourself. We must be in an art form where we work for audiences.

Summary

Jacobs found that great brass players focus on the mental image of sound they want to produce as a way of controlling the various elements involved in their sound production. Jacobs believed that the so-called "natural players" approach music making this way. Jacobs also recommended the use of imitation as a powerful tool for learning to play a brass instrument. Players must embrace the method of trial and error, as mistakes are part of their learning process. Players can also imagine their ideal sound. This becomes especially important during rehearsals—when the player translates the conductor's instructions or suggestions into mental images of sound.

Jacobs encouraged his students to maintain a round sound throughout their entire register—except in their extreme high register. He also wanted his students to play with a "show business attitude" and a sense of authority (or lack of insecurity). Finally, Jacobs wanted his students to be storytellers of sound—following consistent phrasing—and work within the art form of music to entertain their audience.

This concludes the exploration of Arnold Jacobs's pedagogical approach. It is the author's hope that the readers will find the information in this book helpful in their pursuit of conveying their artistic expressions, through the medium of a brass instrument, for many years to come.

Notes

i. The concept of mentalization is used by Hungarian psychologist Peter Fonagy. In his book *Affect Regulation*, about mentalization and the development of the self, Fonagy and his co-writers present a theory that describes the ability of individuals to mentalize and regulate affect in relation to their successful development. (Fonagy et al. 2002)

ii. The concept of "singing with the lips" is considered synonymous with the concept of *Song* and with the "singing approach" term used in this book.

iii. Some of the deficiencies included the underdevelopment of aural skills, the misapplication of breathing functions, the lack of examples of great brass playing (lack of musical exposure), and misguided performance dispositions.

iv. Jacobs prescribed the singing of numbers as a simple and flexible exercise—e.g., counting 1-2-3-4 for groups of four notes or 1-2 for groups of two notes.

v. Paranormal refers to activity that is not scientifically explainable (Merrian-Webster). Psychokinesis (abbreviated as PK) means motion created by the mind and it refers to the direct influence of mind over a physical system.

vi. The psychology of *Song* refers to the ability to *sing* with the lips—instead of singing with the vocal chords.

vii. Jacobs was responding to a question asked by a student at the *Second Brass Congress* held at Indiana University at Bloomington in 1984. The question was the following: I had my first lesson with you 22 years ago and I think there has not been a year since in which I have not had a lesson or two. In the early years, you were extremely informative about the physical aspects of playing. In more recent years, it's almost entirely musical. Is this a general change in your teaching or is it specific to me?

viii. Former principal trumpet with the Chicago Symphony Orchestra.

ix. Timofei Dockshizer was student of Mihail Tabakov (1877-1956) and soloist with the Bolshoi Theater orchestra since 1945. Dockshizer also served as successor of Tabakov at the Gnesin Music Academy. (Tarr, p. 184-185). Dockshizer passed away in 2005.

x. Pasquale Bona's *Rhythmical Articulations* published by G. Schirmer, Inc. and distributed by Hal Leonard.

xi. The Curtis Institute of Music in Philadelphia, PA.

xii. Leopold Auer (1845-1930) Hungarian violist and teacher.

xiii. A player does a *wind pattern* [air pattern] by blowing air from the tip of his lip in the same manner as when blowing his instrument. Some players call this action "air trumpet."

xiv. As evident in the literature published during the 1950s through 1970s. Most notably Philip Farkas's *The Art of Brass Playing* published by Wind Music, Inc.

xv. The center of the lip is where the *singing command* needs to start. The *singing command* should not start at the peripheries and radiate inward.

ANNOTATIONS

Reference List

Arban, J.B. (1982). *Complete conservatory method for trumpet*. New York, NY: Carl Fischer, Inc.

Bona. P. (1900). *A complete method for rhythmical articulation*. New York, NY: Carl Fischer, Inc.

Brandt, W. (1956). *34 studies*. New York, NY: International Music Company.

Buck, P. (1944). *Psychology for musicians*. London, England: Oxford University Press.

Charlier, T. (1946). *Trente-six études transcendantes pour trompette*. Paris, France: Alphonse Leduc.

Clarke, H. L. (1934). *Technical studies*. New York, NY: Carl Fischer Inc.

Csikszentmihaly, M. (1993). *The evolving self*. New York, NY: Harper Collins.

Farkas, P. (1962). *The art of brass playing*. Rochester, NY: Wind Music, Inc.

Fonagy, P. (2002). *Affect regulation, mentalization, and the development of the self*. London, England: H. Karmac, Ltd.

Gregory, R. (1987). *The Oxford companion to the mind*. New York, London: Oxford University Press.

Herseth, A. (Speaker). (2003). *A portrait of Bud*. WFMT Radio (Producer). Chicago, IL: WFMT Radio.

Jacobs, A. (Speaker). (1991). Master Class. Northwestern University School of Music (Producer). Evanston, IL: Northwestern University Deering Library.

James, W. (1911). *Talks to teachers*. New York, NY: W.W. Norton and Company.

Random House. (2001). *Webster's Unabridged Dictionary*. Boston, MA: Random House Reference.

Rochut, J. (1928). *Melodious etudes for trombone*. New York, NY: Carl Fischer Inc.

Schlossberg, M. (1965). *Daily drills and technical studies for trumpet*. New York, NY: M. Baron Co.

Smith, W. (1936). *Top tones for the trumpeter*. New York, NY: Carl Fischer, Inc.

Tarr, Edward. (1988). *The trumpet*. London, England: B.T. Batsford, Ltd

Thiecke, W. (1928). *Thiecke's daily studies for cornet and trumpet*. Milwaukee, WI: H. Bechler.

Webster, N. & Merriam. C. (1985). *Merriam-Webster's dictionary of English usage*. Springfield, MA: Merriam-Webster, Inc

APPENDIX A

EDITED LECTURES

Preview

- *The use of imagination is a strong tool for getting your body to react to whatever you are trying to accomplish.*
- *One should first learn how to play music and by doing so, learn to play the instrument.*
- *You don't want mediocrity because everything is habit forming.*
- *When you stabilize the product, you'll also stabilize the tissue.*
- *You must give a great deal of thought to what you are trying to accomplish musically and not on how you are going to accomplish it mechanically.*
- *We must have a sense of communication as we play. You just don't make noise with the instrument; you always put something extra into it. In other words, we don't do push-ups and sit-ups in music.*
- *When you listen to music, you always hear phrases, but the person playing those phrases builds them one note at a time.*
- *The lips can resist the air. You can blow against your lips and they don't have to vibrate. You have to make them vibrate by thinking of each note as you play—note by note, one note at a time.*
- *Rules are meant to be broken, but in music they have to be broken with wisdom.*
- *A young player should have a great sound to imitate because if there is a great sound in his brain and a horrible sound coming out of the horn, it won't be long before that sound improves.*
- *If I pick the three most damaging phenomena that I know for a brass player, the first is isometrics, the second is the inadequate ventilation of the lungs, and the third is the inability to have a thick air column that moves to the lip.*
- *Your horn should reflect your best artistic thoughts.*

Song and Wind

I am noted today as someone who favors *Song and Wind*. That's the way I use to express my approach to music making. Today, we are increasingly recognizing *Song and Wind* as an important thought process for several reasons. One of the reasons is the simplification about it. *Song and Wind* immediately begins to cut through the clutter of individual thoughts that come about on how to create *Song* and how to control the *Wind*. I found that this was very important because as you study a human being in structure and function—which was actually a hobby of mine since about the year 1944—you get into utter complexity. In other words, the study itself is a lifelong study, and probably more, and the answers to some of the problems are not in yet. However, this study is a terribly complex subject and you can see that we deal with it in a very simple manner. It doesn't take a genius to play a little on a brass instrument or to dance; or even just to simply walk. Nonetheless, what we are is a very complex structure with enormously complex controls and that way you can talk about *Song and Wind* and not be frowned upon by the powers of today.

The Use of Imitation (Vicarious Learning)

Imitation is a powerful tool for learning. In learning through imitation you can use your sense of sight, touch or hearing to imitate something or someone else. (This way you'll tell your brain how to proceed to play music). This is indeed the dominating attitude in the art form of music. For example, you could use your breath (as applied to brass playing) to perfection and be a horrible player (musically speaking). The use of breath is nothing more than the use of fuel (like gasoline to a car); it's not music, it's just part of music. You must make sure music is the dominating factor.

Imitation is especially important to a young person learning a musical instrument. That young person should be aware of the musicality expected from them. He should also have a great sound to imitate because if there is a great sound in his brain and a horrible sound coming out of his horn, it won't be long before that sound improves. That happens naturally by a method of trial and error and by the agitation of muscle tissue that leads to hypertrophy. In other words, eventually what comes out of the horn will match what's in the brain. Your major should not be listening (or paying attention) to what comes out of the horn, but rather your major should be the conception of sound in your brain.

The use of imagination is a strong tool for getting your body to react to whatever you are trying to accomplish. When playing, always imagine a great sound (even if you are sounding rotten at the moment). Imitate a player better than yourself. The use of your imagination is also important in rehearsals because you have to transfer into musical sounds whatever the conductor is asking you to do (you must transfer the spoken word into mental images of sound). In other words, you have to convert the critique of something wrong in your playing into musical thoughts and not into the mechanics of playing.

The Controls in the Brain

If you play by ordering products (brass sounds), we will find that your playing becomes effortless. The main reason for this phenomenon lies in the great set of controls that you have in your brain (if we simply order a product, the necessary actions will be executed by the lower levels of the brain—the *cerebellum*). This is why it's important to go by the study of the product (brass sounds) and not by the study of the mechanics involved in playing.

However, for the "chain of commands" to work effortlessly, we have to get out of the way. In other words, think of how you want to sound and avoid thinking of how you are going to do it (this would be like an actor trying to act while simultaneously writing his script). You must give a great deal of thought to what you are trying to accomplish musically and not to how you are going to accomplish it mechanically. The "thinking" part of your brain is simply not competent enough to order the actual "machine systems" in your body directly. The thinking part of your brain is indeed competent in ordering what it wants while letting the lower parts of the brain do the handling of specific "machine systems."

The Biocomputer

We have what I call a biocomputer. This is a so-called living computer simply because it acts like that. It follows certain rules that modern computers have to follow. In other words, when you think of the ability to stand, or to walk, or to play a trombone, you reach for the fifth position and you don't get the sixth. Whatever it is you are trying to accomplish, when you are going to do something, you plan it and then you do it.

What I want to say is that part of the brain will accept your order as you go thorough a period of conditioning—which we will call practice and conditioning studies, scales, intervals, and so on. During this practice time, we are creating a programming that goes into the brain where the things you have practiced can be absorbed to become conditioned reflexes. In other words, a reflex is something we are not born with, but it becomes a reflex simply by the fact that we have done a number of repetitions. From that point on, once you have a reflex, all you need to bring it into function is the proper stimulus. It's a thought process in the brain that says, "I want to touch my nose," and you reach and touch your nose. It's not a big deal. Somebody throws a ball and usually if you have eyes, you catch it. Maybe you can throw it back at them.

You don't perform any of these actions by thinking of musculatures or planning what to do with the various parts of the physical structure. They are responses to the stimulus of catching the ball, or touching your nose. Now, in playing music there are physical factors involved, as we all know so well. Some of them are quite complicated and actually very serious and we have to do them well.

The Process of Development

What we are dealing with here is the art of playing. It's a series of developments that come through taking a musical instrument and going through the course of training with the teacher and the student relationship in which the teacher says, "Do this and do that," or "I want this, I want that." The student listens and the teacher advises and guides. You'll base these actions on a repetitive type of maneuvering. Now, if you play a C Major scale and then repeat the C Major scale a second time, then a third time and maybe one day you repeat it five times, you'll be getting many repetitions. Your brain is indeed absorbing all those repetitions.

Human biology requires repetitive maneuvers before it becomes a permanent neural-pathway in the brain. Now, the reason I am saying this is simply that right from the time we start to play, we are actually developing these reflexes whether we realize it or not. This is a very beneficial approach in the study of music. If Phil Smith (Principal Trumpet of the New York Philharmonic) takes his trumpet and plays a beautiful scale for a young student and says, "Now listen to this," that doesn't mean that the student can imitate it right away. However, the student has the example and she will try to imitate it. By trying to do it, she is developing in her brain a recall and a recognition of what she wants her audience to hear.

The Young Mind

This is what we are up against when we teach. We take a young mind. We take somebody who is just learning something new, but we are showing him excellence in terms of results and not in terms of muscular activity. You tell him, "Here is your trumpet, here is your mouthpiece, and it can sound just beautiful. Imitate, go by trial and error, and be willing to make mistakes." It's not a big deal if there is something wrong. However, you should have a definite concept of what you want the audience to hear. It's a very important type of thought to have in the music making business.

What I want to get across is simply the fact that we are developing based on the *Song*. Now, that doesn't necessarily mean a tune. It can be a scale or it could be telling a story of music. It could be anything we want, but it is the message that comes from the player to the audience that matters.

Motor Nerves

Now, here is the important part. As human beings we move about to influence the external environment through motor activity that is fired—or activated—by brain signals. Those signals go down a very special type of nerve we can call the "effector." The "effector-end" might be a finger, an embouchure, or the arm holding a violin bow ready to play.

These messages are motor messages and not sensory messages. The young person has a tremendous gift of learning through the sensory nervous system. In other words, the ability to gather knowledge in a young person is enormous. Biologically, this is a very active period in our lives where acquiring knowledge is given every possible chance that can get and it's favorable to the person at all times while he is growing up. I think that at my age, I can still learn, but it would be at a slower pace than when I was young.

The two types of nerves I just mentioned are like "one way" streets. Where you have a motor nerve, it's a "one way" path from the brain to the lips or to the effector-end. If you are a ball player, you want to hit the ball with the bat. That's motor activity. Anything that influences the external environment in any way is "motor." When I talk to you, I am using motor systems for me to communicate messages to you, but you are hearing those messages through sensory nerves that travel from the ear to the brain.

Sensory Nerves

You process the visual aspects of what I am doing on stage similarly, but you process them through your eyes instead. In other words, the sensory system always picks up information and drives it to the brain through your senses.

When you play a musical instrument, you are sending information outward instead of receiving information inward. However, young students go to school every day and they are growing up with this tremendous ability to learn through their sensory systems. Frequently, that way of learning tends to transfer to how they learn to play their instruments.

If they would try to learn to play music with their instrument just by making statements—so the psychology of it would immediately move to the art form of music—they would learn to play their instrument correctly. They could play for their fathers or mothers, or their schools.

If you are an actor, this is what you do as well. You don't express your own life, but you might have to imitate somebody else's life. Whatever it is, it has to go into the brain so it can come out of the brain to affect the nervous musculatures.

The programming is in the brain, but the effectors are receiving information on what to do based on what you are trying to accomplish. All this becomes very complex when you study the biology and the anatomy of what we are doing, but if you instead study the art form, it becomes very simple.

When I say *Song and Wind*, I do it for a specific reason. *Song* to me involves about 85% concentration of your intellectual input into playing your instrument based on what you want your audience to hear. If there is no audience, what do you want somebody walking around the corner to hear?

What you want to compete with is your colleagues and other professional players. What you consider a great sound or great music might vary from your colleagues' concepts, but whatever you do, try for the results of a great sound, great music, and great phrasing.

The Study of Emotions

In music, we have the study of emotions. Emotions are involved in the style characteristics of our art form. This is indeed an important study. You can make people laugh, you can make people cry, and you can make people want to come down and enlist in the services. You can help them by the moods associated with music and you have all sorts of abilities to communicate these moods through sound. If you want to enter this profession, you have to do it as a musician who plays with emotions.

I don't like the terms trombone player, tuba player, or trumpet player. I know we play these instruments, but we are artists, we are musicians. We use music as a medium to express ourselves with those particular instruments, but they are stupid pieces of brass. They don't have any brains. What you do with them is what really counts, *Song and Wind*.

You can't get anywhere without wind because if you think of an automobile, you have its body, four wheels, but you also have an engine. Now, those wheels won't turn without that engine turning it (unless you are being towed). That engine could be running on electricity, gasoline, or methane—it could have different types of fuel.

Our musical engine is the vibration of the lips. It's important that you always make your music with the lips vibrating. Like the automobile, the lips can't vibrate unless there is an energy source being fed to it. In this case, it would be our breath. If we could substitute the breath with electricity to vibrate the lip, we wouldn't need any breath.

The Study of Motivation

You must learn how to think like a child when it comes to communicating with your body. Think like an adult to order a musical product, but get out of the way to let the lower parts of the brain do their job when it comes to performing. When you stabilize the product, you'll also stabilize the tissue.

We all are a product of the life we have lived. For example, I [Arnold Jacobs] was a singer, a tubist, a trombonist, a Dixieland bass player, and a trumpet player. I had a varied approach to the production of sound. However, I also found similarities in all of the instruments I played and I also found that to produce a musical sound you need: 1) motor function, 2) a source of vibration, and 3) a resonance chamber.

The Lack of Musical Imagination

The lack of musical imagination in the musical endeavors is the number one problem in most cases. You find that—with those students who crowd their brains with how to play their instrument—they are not able to play music from a musical standpoint. One should learn first how to play music and by doing so, learn to play the instrument.

With this subject in mind, I should mention that there are people who warm up for one hour before they play any musical tunes. By the time their hour is up, their brains are already tired. It would be wiser to take a few moments to get used to the instrument and then take a few musical challenges (easy cornet solos or folk tunes). For example, take a soprano solo and put all of the emotions into it from the very start.

The Music We Play

We are the product of the music we play. Don't learn to play your instrument in order to play music. You should instead establish musical challenges that will bring in the required muscle development. For example, you can practice your high register in the form of a Joannes Rochut etude played an octave higher (avoid playing long phrases because you'll be more likely to play with a mediocre sound towards the end of the phrase).

Anything that's good music, is good for practice. Your goal is to be comfortable through the entire range of the instrument. Play with an extrovert attitude, having each note in your head, and blowing "out there." In brass playing, we are close to how singers conceptualize music if we play by singing in our heads first (what comes out of the bell is a mirror of your thoughts).

The Study of *Solfège*

If you formalize the approach of pitch recall using *solfège*, you'll train your brain in one of the most efficient ways to recall pitch. You should talk with your instrument as when you talk with your voice. Don't ask questions, but instead make statements. You should teach the audience what's on the page displaying lots of show business. During the next six months, you can formalize this study and make a habit of it.

We must have a sense of communication as we play. You just don't make noise with the instrument—you must always put something extra into it. In other words, we don't do push-ups and sit-ups in music. Yes, we have to do drills, but we put them in a musical context (e.g., the scales could be part of a cadenza). This has to do with your response when you see the "ink spots" in a piece of music. You have to visualize—or mentalize—what your music sounds like.

Playing One Note at a Time

Think of each note and build your phrases; one note at a time as you come to them. When you listen to music you hear phrases, but the person playing builds those phrases one note at a time.

You don't want mediocrity because everything is habit forming. Show off a little! Sound great! If you got it, flaunt it! Dare to make a few mistakes, but keep your inspiration. At times you might sound bad, but remember that those moments are like a rough diamond. When playing with a bad sound, go for the diamond. Remember that it's as easy to sound bad, as it is to sound good.

Singing the Entry Note

Change the tone of your instrument by using your imagination. Imagine a rich tenor tone. Start making music from the first note you play. Remember that the first note after the rest in the one in jeopardy. You must protect those entry notes by having a clear mental picture of how those notes sound. Take chances with this. Your solos will become yours. As a result of this type of approach, your playing will become easier and more efficient.

You should never play with anything less than your greatest sound (except if you have a musical reason for it). What separates a great artist from a lesser artist is the ability to play with excellence at all times. You can't have anyone sound better than you. This is a great attitude to have in our business. Use your imagination often because we all have great brains, but we are not close to using their full potential.

We must become very conscious of our results. Because of various reasons, some people get excellence most of the time. Maybe a conductor has asked them to produce excellence for an extended period and the player has formed a habit out that experience.

Don't blow and listen to what comes out of the horn hoping that some miracle will happen. You must give your brain examples of great artistry. You flood the brain with beautiful sounds so as soon as you see a note on the page, you'll hear the sound of that note with all the pitch and sound qualities you need. For brass instrumentalists, this is important because you have to send a perfect partial into the instrument (so you get the full spectrum of sound and dynamics out of your playing efforts).

This study can be very frustrating because it requires high levels of mental efforts. This mental effort is important because brass instruments are stupid pieces of brass. They can't give you the pitches—like a piano would—so we must put "perfect notes" into them.

Avoid putting the areas of the brain that deal with pitch recall to work in directing individual muscle tissue. Just order a product and get out of the way. If you go blank in the head, you might miss notes. Instead, *sing* in the brain. Your horn will always reflect your artistic thoughts.

The Physiology of Breathing

We have about 659 muscles in our body and 654 of those are set in antagonistic pairs. In other words, they have a great potential for shortening to exert great power (the same muscles also have the potential for stiffness). However, you can't teach a person about breathing by telling him what to do. Instead, you have to provide the correct stimuli and the brain will activate the correct muscle groups. A good example is blowing out matches. In this instance, the blowing out muscles activate while the inhaling muscles deactivate.

The abdominal muscles are expiratory in nature. When they "push in," the diaphragm raises to a certain level and when they relax, the diaphragm is free to come down. The main function of the diaphragm is inspiratory in nature (when it comes down it lowers the air pressure in the lungs and it will also increase the abdominal pressure).

Like a bellows, the abdominal muscles go up and push the air out (the intercostal muscles are also involved in blowing out). However, the abdominal muscles are also involved in two other functions in the body. Those functions are innate "blueprints": 1) pelvic pressures (childbirth, defecation, etc.), 2) combat (tensing up the abdominal wall to protect the vital organs in case of an attack), and an attack), and 3) blowing (brass instruments or birthday cakes). The latter are listed in order of importance from the standpoint of survival on this planet.

These blueprints are part of life and they are quite necessary. However, when trying to blow large quantities of air while being in the "pelvic pressure" or "combat" blueprints, blowing becomes difficult. This misapplication of activity is what the "old school" of brass playing (*circa* 1920's-1970's) advocated.

There is tremendous potential for stiffness (instead of efficient function) in the respiratory system so players have to order the right product. (In the case of inhalation, it's suction at the tip of the lip. For exhalation, it's blowing). In other words, the player could trigger the wrong blueprint with his thoughts.

Breathing Isometrics

Your ribs go upward when you breathe. However, there is a potential for isometrics involved in this movement. During isometric contractions, the ribs go downward and inward. If the isometrics are involved, playing a brass instrument is "hard," but if the isometrics are not involved, brass playing is "easy."

Brass players need to stay away from "isometric" contractions and instead work their respiratory system as a bellows. We want to push the air out of the lungs with the correct efforts. When you have pelvic pressures, you might be fooled into believing that you are playing correctly.

A good exercise to transfer the air pressure to the tip of the lip (where it's needed) is to blow (as if you were blowing a candle), then put your index finger on your lips (to seal the lip aperture), and as you keep blowing, remove the finger from your lips. This exercise will connect the air and the lip. For lead trumpet playing, you'll "blow like a Dickens," but the blowing has to be against the inside of your embouchure and not against the tongue.

Whenever there is a problem with basic respiration, you have to deal with it based on the psychology of playing. Go to the control panel in the brain and forget about the machinery system. For loud playing, you blow more (faster) and for soft playing, you blow less (slower). Keep it as simple as that. The amplitude of breath will increase with air speed.

Lips don't have to cooperate with the air passing through them. To avoid this, you have to make your playing the study of sound and not the study of air. Most players base their creation of sound on blowing and not on buzzing. It's important to know that you can always blow without buzzing, but it's impossible to buzz without blowing. In other words, once you get the buzzing, you get the air with it.

The lips can resist the air as you blow. They don't have to vibrate just because you blow. You have to make them vibrate by thinking of each note as you play—note by note, one note at a time. It's all in the brain. It's like opening a can of worms if we talk about the details and limitations involved.

You must base the psychology of breathing on suction and the use of minimal motors. The sound of a "free breath" is the sound of a volume of air without real opposition. (This applies to the air going in and the air going out).

Various Body Types

Your body type will affect your air capacity. For example, William Scarlett (former assistant principal trumpet with the Chicago Symphony Orchestra) was 5'7" in height but had 6.8 liters of air capacity. In general, people who have long torsos and short legs will have a larger lung capacity. Even though there is a large difference in the air capacity people have, everybody is capable of playing beautiful music regardless.

Players with small lung capacities need to make sub-phrases out of a long phrases. In other words, the player will need to breathe more often. Rules are meant to be broken, but in music they have to be broken with wisdom. For example, a tuba player will need to breathe more than a trumpet player, so the rule of not breaking a phrase in half will need to be broken. Besides, you can waste air because it's free. Don't follow too many rules. Another example is the rule that says, "Don't let the audience see you breathe." This is wrong because you need to expand to fill-up.

To use your lung capacity, you have to breathe in full movements (full length of muscle movement). During respiration we fill-up from about 35% TLC (total lung capacity) to about 80% TLC and that constitutes an enormous change in your body. I want you to make that change—from much smaller to much larger—when you breathe.

Regional Breathing

Regional breathing happens when you inhale using a small part of your lung structure (e.g., if you bend down, you'll collapse the lower part of your lungs and as a result you'll "regional breathe" with the upper part of your lungs). Incidentally, some overweight people will have their diaphragm go up (because of the extra pounds below) making their lungs shorter. In other words, the extra pounds will cost them about .75 (in liters) of their air capacity. [Mr. Jacobs, after his heart attack and hospitalization, lost about 40 pounds resulting in a gain of one liter of air capacity].

Avoid specializing in regional breathing. You must exercise the whole breathing system. You can exercise it by using a "test lung," also called a "breathing bag," or by using a "breathing tube." You have two ways to improve the smooth working of your breathing system. First, by practicing vigorous inhalations, you can load the breathing muscles with work and once they are fatigued, they will let go—i.e., they won't be able to go into isometric contractions.

Another way is by using *Ventilin* (a nasal spray used to open-up your respiratory vents). *Ventilin* will help you take the air out of your lungs beautifully. Sometimes, pollutants in the air will irritate your lungs and make you suffer from asthma symptoms. We call the latter subliminal asthma. *Ventilin* will help you in this case.

When you start to achieve "complete breathing," remember that you don't have to do it correctly right away. Whenever you learn a new skill, you always start from the crude to the refined (in other words, out of crudity you develop skill). Sometimes in your private lessons, you get a general understanding of this subject, but then you have to go home to develop it further. In other words, the learning of complete breathing (away from the instrument) will take a couple of years. This is so you develop the necessary conditioned reflexes to "complete breathe" subconsciously.

Expanding Instead of Breathing

The way you order your body to breathe is very important because players can order expansion instead of wind. You must always tell the truth to your body. Always order wind, not expansion. In other words, when you take a breath, you must order air suction from the tip of your mouth. The psychology of wind is at the tip of your mouth.

The greatest intake happens during the initial second during inhalation. After that point, you'll still get air into your lungs, but in a downward curve (at a slower rate). You must order a yawn and not body enlargement because your body can lie like crazy.

Tension in the Abdominal Wall

When you take a breath, the air will go into the lungs (via the bronchial trees) following a trajectory based on what part of your anatomy is expanding at that moment. In other words, it's not like water that fills up from bottom to top. This is why it's so important to sit tall as you breathe. However, if your abdominal wall gets hard, the ribs will be too stiff to move up to create a vacuum (the vacuum is necessary to lower the air pressure in the lungs so the air in the atmosphere—outside the lung—can rush into them) and not much air will get into the lungs. To alleviate this problem, you can exercise your breathing with the "breath builder."

Keeping Simple Things Simple

We must keep simple things simple. The human body is, perhaps, the most complex "machine system" on earth. Nonetheless, complex machines have simple controls (like an automobile). In the human body, the simple controls are in our brains so we can be free to cope with life outside ourselves. To deal with life inside ourselves, we can study Yoga so we can influence our internal body by using mental concentration and emotions.

A player's breathing has three simple blueprints: 1) pelvic pressures (where the musculatures are fighting each other and as a result your lip will not get the 'thick air' it needs), 2) combat (your abdominal wall goes into an isometric contraction to protect your internal organs in case of an attack), and 3) blowing (the preferred blueprint for great brass playing).

Your brain is already "wired" so when you order one of these blueprints (or products), your body will perform the "action sequence" involved in that particular blueprint. Incidentally, the benefit of knowing this information is that you'll protect yourself from the "pitfalls" of the performing profession. Of the three blueprints, one is usable for great brass playing. You could use the other two blueprints, but you'll be working too hard.

Taking air depends on what you are going to do with it. For example, flutists have a higher airflow rate than oboists. Take enough air so you can waste it because we must always play with *Song and Wind*.

The musical message is the most important element for performers. You can't wait for the musical message to come out of the horn by itself. Instead, you have to put the message into the horn. You have to conceive a message in your head (using your emotions and musicianship) to communicate it to an audience. You have to create a pattern in which you order a product [a brass sound]. This way, you create a stimulus for your muscles to follow. This is what brass playing is all about.

You can't bypass that process by trying to directly control the muscles. You have to instead order an artistic product and get out of the way so the regions of the brain, which deal with the control of muscle fibers, can work.

The Use of the Breath Builder

The breath builder was built by Harold Hanson of *Casino Enterprises* (California). It consists of a sealed transparent tube with a "ping pong" ball inside that moves up or down in response to the changing air pressure blown by the user (the user blows the air through an attached plastic PVC tube). It takes about fourteen ounces of air pressure to take the ball up, but only four ounces of pressure to maintain it up there. Always keep the breath builder in a vertical position so gravity pulls the ball down. As you do the exercises, we also want your body movements to go to the extremes because the complete breath requires the whole breathing system.

To use the "breath builder," try to keep the "ping pong" ball up as you blow in and out. You'll notice that the tension in your abdominal wall will stop, but you'll still be able to move large volumes of air in and out. (This is what the expression "use of minimal motors" means. In other words, the use of minimal motors occurs when you achieve an action by only using the necessary muscles).

By introducing a full breath, we make the six units of the lung (six individual layered sections similar to the petals of a flower) into one full unit. If you start a low breath, stop and continue with an upper breath, you'll work harder than if you take the breath in one take (because the low breath will pull the ribs down and they will have to work harder to go back up).

This "bellows system" works best in a standing posture (sitting tall) because in this position all the six separate "little bellows" in your lungs become one. Learn to use your breathing capacity. For example, you can take in a full breath and use it in parts of one-third or one-fourth then three-fourths—just as you would use a violin bow. You can practice this exercise daily.

If you touch around your clavicle, you'll touch where the top part of your lung is. When you take a full breath, you'll have the full organization of the musculatures, its various relationships, and the full function of the breathing mechanism. There are two benefits to taking a full breath: 1) with the extra air, you'll be able to play long phrases and, 2) the organization that comes into your breathing mechanism will make your playing easier and more efficient. Keep in mind that, although you want to be able to take a full breath, it doesn't mean that you have to use it all the time.

Rather than developing strength in the breath, you are working for weakness in the breathing system. That means large movements of air without much effort. You must have the breathing muscles work with each other, not against each other. After working on breathing exercises, it's natural to have your mental focus on the breathing exercises. However, you must put back your mental focus on music — sound, emotions, and phrasing. After all is said and done, many players still manage to create beautiful music while breathing "incorrectly" (with abdominal tensions).

The Use of the Breathing Bag

The use of the breathing bag allows for a visualization that helps players take larger amounts of air. (One of the ways to use the breathing bag is to fill it up with your own breath, cover its end so the air stays inside the bag, empty your lungs, and inhale the air inside the bag. You can repeat this inhalation-exhalation process many times without suffering from hyperventilation). If the player takes a full breath with the breathing bag and he plays his instrument immediately afterward, the player's sound (and general technique) will improve. The improvement in sound and technique is due to the increased ability of blowing more wind at lower pressure.

The entire breathing process (with or without the breathing bag) must be natural. When you think about it, human beings have been breathing since "day one" and as result, we have developed an efficient breathing system. In other words, when it comes to breathing, your body knows what to do without your conscious interference.

Breathing is a natural act, not an intellectual act. If I [Arnold Jacobs] were to play using my knowledge of air, I probably couldn't play a note. Instead, I play by my knowledge of music and by ordering air as a product. [Jacobs knew human anatomy and physiology well, but he also knew how to play music well].

You want to play your instrument with the "relaxation pressures" (positive pressures) that occur when you breathe. At this point, the elastic nature of the lungs (and intercostal muscles when relaxed), help you blow easily (almost by itself) using minimal motors. (This action compares to filling up a balloon with air and once it's full, you release its air).

When you play, you want to stay within the positive pressures because in the negative pressures there are problems (mainly muscle tensions). Some players reach the negative pressure point and don't get out of it because they keep taking shallow breaths. As you stay in the negative pressures, you'll have to play with more muscle activity in the intercostal and abdominal regions (trying to push the air out of the lungs). At this point, pressures increase in the lungs and the little airways going through the trachea. In other words, while one pressure (the one produced with the muscle activity) is trying to help you play, the other pressure (the one being raised inside your lungs) is harming your playing. You'll be fighting yourself and in that process, the capillary beds in your lungs will start to fill up with blood; becoming heavier and harder to move. (Also, the blood vessels fill up in your lips; making it harder to buzz and as a result, your inner aural pressures increase).

Neural Inhibition

If you are playing with abdominal tensions and you want to solve that problem, you have to visualize a "big bubble" (like the ones used to write the script in cartoon strips) filled with air. Your job is to suck all that air in. At this point, the brain will deactivate the internal pressures by using "neural inhibition." You just have to give the order of air suction. If you don't give the order properly (as when breathing with a tensed body), you'll keep trying to breathe while having opposing pairs of tight muscles.

Seek weakness in your muscle contractions. To achieve this, you must work with the positive breathing curves—which will help you avoid isometric tensions in the abdominal muscles. (If your abdominal muscles firm up, you'll take a great deal of your air capacity out).

Pseudo-Functions

Watch out for pseudo-functions in your body. You have 659 muscles in your body and 656 of them work in antagonistic pairs. As a result, they will fight each other at the drop of a hat. Strength or weakness in muscles depends on how many muscle fibers you contract (in a specific muscle groups). Muscle fibers will contract based on what you want to do and on how many muscles achieve contraction.

In the cases of "maniacal strength," you find a burst of electrical energy in the brain that will fire most of the neurons and as a result, the muscle systems will contract to levels beyond normal. However, you have protections against the voluntary use of maniacal strength built into your brain to avoid breaking bones and tearing ligaments. The enlargement of muscle fibers through hypertrophy, once achieved, will ease the contracting power—so you'll need very little warm up time. Atrophy is the opposite of hypertrophy.

We can experience over-applications of muscular activity through suffering from fear on stage. A great athlete, for example, has ease of play because her brain has gotten rid of the over-applications of muscular activity. Remind yourself how easily it can be done. Listen to Adolph Herseth to remember how easy playing can be. Give it time to develop because what was difficult to play in 1982, in 1983 might be easier (because hypertrophy and efficiency have increased).

Working hard is a big illusion because you can work hard and not get any results. (Jacobs gives the example of running upstairs and screaming something to his wife and because his abdominal muscles were relaxed, his voice was loud). You don't need all that strength down in your abdominal region. From 40 points of efforts, go down to 4 points of effort. That's all you need to play.

Don't put all your knowledge of human biology into music. The study of breath is simple. You can simply study *Wind* by blowing out matches or birthday cakes. Then apply that to music. You have to motivate *Wind* this way.

Air pressure is always present in expiratory functions. *Wind* is a product in itself (with *Wind* you already have expiratory function without the engagement of the inspiratory functions). On the other hand, when you blow with massive air pressures, you simultaneously activate two functions—the expiratory and the inspiratory. The psychology of *Wind* is always outside the body. About 85% of brass playing should be in the study of *Song* and 10 or 15% should be in the study of *Wind*.

Teaching Large Inhalations

There are various options to help a student take more air. You can use tools such as visualization and other musical challenges. The question is, which one will fit the student's psychology? To find out, you have to talk to the student and investigate.

First, have the student touch his abdominal region, feel the movement in that area, and establish a range of motion. If the student feels stiffness in the abdominal

Appendix A: Edited Lectures

region, provide them with resistance at the tip of the lip. This way his muscles will start to work together against the resistance at the tip of the lip (this works because you can control the resistance at the tip of the lip, but it's more difficult to control it at the back of your mouth). You must always strive to work toward the use of minimal motors.

You can use the sense of touch to teach the student about the wind outside her body. If you just talk to the student about an efficient breath, you might not reach the student, but if you have the student feel the breath, the student will learn much faster. Have the student do a full bellows movement. Then have her put her hands in her belly and tell her to push her hand in as she plays. This way she will start a program of proper air support.

Shallow Breathers

Shallow breathers have trouble playing the end of their phrases. If they take a poor second breath, they will really be in trouble because their reflexes will activate and they will start to tense up (or start to close) their throat. Furthermore, their chest will be tensed and everything will spiral downward from that point on.

There are many more complications associated with shallow breathing. For example, shallow breathers will have playing problems as they age because they will experience a decrease in their breathing abilities. In other words, they will use the same muscular activity with less results. Consequently, shallow breathers find it difficult to continue their profession by age 45-55.

However, if they form correct breathing habits, they will get around that problem by simply taking larger breaths. You develop correct breathing habits in the practice room and not on the job. If you follow through with the study of taking large breaths in an orderly fashion, you'll age gracefully as a player.

Pressurization

If there is breath pressurization before the release of the first note, you might play with a hard attack or miss the note. To avoid pressurization, you should take as much air as you can and start counting aloud, "1, 2, 3, 4." You'll notice that there is no internal pressure as you count. You'll also notice that your body regulates itself beautifully—in between the numbers—as you count.

Very powerful air comes from zero pressure. As you learn to control your breath, you learn to control the breathing apparatus—not the other way around. To inhale, you must have less pressure internally (in your lungs) than externally (in the atmosphere). Point zero is where the inside and outside pressures are balanced. At this time, all the airways are opened. Zero pressure—up to the moment of sound—usually happens when great players play their entry notes.

If you use antagonistic movements in your breathing apparatus (e.g., lungs and abdomen), you'll feel that you are playing with more effort. However, when you experience zero pressure, you'll still have the necessary muscle activity to perform and it will be easier to play.

Playing With Static Pressure

Static pressures in a cylinder go up and down (they also go up and down in the walls of the cylinder). Some players experience static pressure behind their tongue and as a result, their lung sensors adjust to the pressure signal (this pressure can easily move to the throat). The majority of players will accept this fact. Pressure in the lungs is supportive to a downward contracting diaphragm (it gives an additional two or three pounds of downward pressure) and it will always involve closures in the throat region.

When playing your instrument, you must pretend that you are blowing something outside yourself. Blow the air out as if you were blowing a candle and avoid blowing pressurized air. Order motion rather than air pressure! You must practice a few minutes a day blowing out candles or pieces of paper. You must remember that when talking about air, 15% is about air, but 85% is about music.

Breathing Exercises

You have to find the simplicity (childlike) of the function you are trying to achieve and stay away from the complexity of the biological sciences. Breathe in with suction and with minimal efforts. In other words, one level of the brain (the conscious thinking level) will tell the other level of the brain (the *cerebellum*) what you want. In turn, the *cerebellum* will tell the muscle fibers what to do. You always have to go by the "control panel" in the brain and not try to direct the muscle fibers through the thinking level of the brain. Simply, order a product and your body will take care of the rest.

As you breathe this way, you don't have to know what you are doing in terms of physical function. Your only job is to take a full breath and all the necessary breathing systems will work by themselves.

The characteristics of a breath taken as *Wind* are: 1) large air flow, 2) easy work, 3) low pressure, and 4) legitimate function. The characteristics of a breath taken as "friction" are: 1) small quantity of flow, 2) hard work, and 3) pseudo functions. (Jacobs said that as a bass player he found that as he kept his bow straight, the sound coming out of the bass—as well as his body movements—were correct. Later he discovered that as he kept the wind coming in and out of the lips straight, his sound and body movements were also correct. He concluded that the sound of a player's respiration—an "OH" type of sound quality—should be the same as he breathes in and out—this is when doing breathing exercises).

When doing breathing exercises, you should be in front of a mirror (naked from the waist up). You should observe—without self analyzing—your body movements as the air moves in and out. Create a mental picture of yourself. Achieve maximum changes—from small to big—going from empty to full (tip to frog) following no rules (e.g., allow your shoulders to raise). By observing yourself breathe, you'll learn faster because you are multiplying the senses. (Incidentally, by using the sense of sight, while doing the breathing exercises, you'll also cancel out your sense of feel).

You should also aim for contrast by going from black to white. You use this black and white contrast to move the awareness of your body movements far apart. In actual performance, you can compare your breathing movements to subtle changes between shades of gray. However, in your breathing practice you should strive to go from black to white (full to empty).

Another way to help you achieve ease of breathing is by using a piece of tubing (about the length of a trumpet mouthpiece and the circumference of a trumpet mouthpiece rim). You use this small piece of tubing by wrapping your lips around it (it has slightly to pass beyond your teeth) and breathing in and out. This exercise will introduce strangeness to your training (this is specially useful when trying to throw off a negative or old breathing habit).

When breathing with the tube, you'll also be able to feel a "cold spot" in the back of your mouth—that's the point where the air hits, meaning it bypassed your tongue. When taking a breath while playing your instrument, you can also aim to feel the same "cold spot" as you inhale.

Air quantity depends on the clear communication between your brain and your body. You have to tell your body how much air you want and then tell it how fast you want it. Always be specific about it. Most players will order a cup (or a pint) when they should be ordering a full gallon. If you simply order your body to breathe, that's non-specific. (This is the way players get into the negative curves of pressure fast by not taking enough air in).

Practice the following exercises at home to get used to taking large air quantities. Remember to practice them away from music and use a black and white approach (from very big to very small). Only then, you'll have two opposite patterns so you can learn faster. In other words, put your instrument down before practicing them and concentrate on breathing.

Exercise 1: Breathe in keeping your mental focus at the tip of your mouth because this is where you have the most nerve sensors. (You also have nerve sensors in the chest, but they are subtle). Make guesses on how much air you have just taken. Then fill up a "test lung" and see how much you actually took. Repeat this exercise several times.

Exercise 2: Take a full breath "from tip to frog" (empty to full) and watch your body movements. (You can use the test lung or, if you don't have a test lung, repeat only three times to avoid hyperventilation). Then divide your breath into thirds. Each third has to have a sufficient pause for you to be able to self examine. Now, make a guess as to how much air you have in your lungs. The next step requires you to put your hand on your mouth and as you exhale one third of your breath, move your hand forward one third of the way. Follow this by blowing the second third as you move your hand forward one more third. Play around with this exercise and let out two-thirds and take one third back in (all while moving your hand back and forth accordingly). This way you'll learn specific quantities when inhaling.

Exercise 3: In 5/4 time, blow while counting to four and inhale on the fifth beat. (By counting in 5/4 you add the time factor). You can also try this exercise in 8/8 time (breathing out to beat seven and inhaling on beat eight). While inhaling, make sure you keep an "OH" vowel to avoid throat closures. It's important to know that if the opening of your mouth is larger than the diameter of your throat, you will—because of an innate reflex—close your throat. (Perhaps to avoid foreign objects from flying in to your "naked lungs").

Exercise 4: Breathe counting to five while raising your hands to your sides and hold your breath for about two or three seconds. Then let go of the breath. Watch yourself in the mirror as you do this and observe your ribs go up while your diaphragm goes down. This is called the "bucket handle" effect. (With the bucket handle effect you have the greatest distance from rib to rib. The opposite happens when you are out of breath and your ribs are closer together). For the "bucket handle effect" to happen, you have to sit straight up. Only then, the sternum will go up—as the diaphragm goes down—to create a huge chamber in your intercostal area for the air to rush in.

As you work with the "bucket handle effect," you'll notice that you are working with little effort. This is because you are using many muscle groups so each muscle will work a light load. (In addition, the control factor is much better if you involve a wide diversity of muscle groups). [Jacobs also recommended the study of the Alexander Technique to learn the correct body alignment for breathing. The study of the Alexander Technique teaches the player "not to fight gravity"—helping the player release any unnecessary muscle activity].

You want ribs that go high and a diaphragm that goes low. That's vertically, not laterally. (The eleventh and twelfth ribs are not bound by cartilage so they can move laterally. Nonetheless, there will always be some lateral expansion in all the ribs as you breathe in).

Playing Blackout and Hyperventilation

Hyperventilation and playing blackouts are two different things. Hyperventilation only happens when you exchange massive movements of air. Brass players confuse this with "playing blackouts" because their symptoms are very similar. The playing blackout happens when a player gets excited and plays high and loud. Very frequently, the vessels that return blood to the brain are squeezed. In other words, the playing blackout happens because of the lack of blood circulation to the brain.

Hyperventilation is another phenomenon that comes from the large movements of air going in and out of the lungs. The large movements of air lower the carbon dioxide levels in the blood stream. It's not too much oxygen that brings on the symptoms, it's too little carbon dioxide. If the player merely holds his breath for a few moments, his tissues will throw in carbon dioxide into the blood stream and his brain will return to normal very quickly.

The early signs of hyperventilation are visible in the person's eyes and face. If you are about to hyperventilate, simply hold your breath for a few seconds. Always try to find simple answers to complex problems. Stale air can be a signal for the brain to activate the breathing in muscles at the same time you are blowing out. At this point, the muscles become antagonistic.

The Respirometer

When using the respirometer, put its tube in your mouth and blow as rapidly and as completely as you can. The respirometer has a revolving drum and as you blow, the interior of the unit raises due to the air going in. A pen moves up and down writing on a sheet attached to the revolving drum. We measure for the quantity and the velocity of the air.

This is an important subject for one reason and one reason only. I want to explain that when you breathe in there is always enlargement. Your body functions like a bellows. When you yawn, you are simply taking in large volumes of air. Nature is wonderful. It's a fabulous thing that we have parts in our body that can expand no matter what position we are in.

Occasionally, wrong body postures cause serious trouble in brass playing. I had a horn student who came to me with a respiratory problem. This student would press her horn's bell tight against her rib cage. I found one lung functioning and one not functioning. Who can play with just one lung? I found that there was an inadequate fuel supply because her ribs couldn't rise up and she couldn't inhale enough air. Her diaphragm had considerable pressure in this alignment. A combination of a slight tilt to the right and her rib cage being stuck to the bell, made her respiratory activity all on one side.

This is a very severe problem in a small individual. A very large person with six liters of air capacity could get by, but a small person with four and a half to four liters of air capacity couldn't get by playing this way.

We are structured so no matter what position we are in, we can take enough air to survive. For example, if there is pressure on the back of your ribs—like when you are laying on a hard surface—you'll find that your ribs are not maneuverable because they are already in the expanded position. In other words, as you lie on your back, the only way you can inhale is by using your diaphragm.

As the diaphragm descends, you'll see the abdominal area rising. If you immobilize the ribs, the average individual will have about 45% of his total lung volume at his disposal. That leaves 55% of which he is not using.

Medical science uses the case of a newborn child to illustrate diaphragmatic breathing. When the child is born, with his chest in the enlarged position, all he can use to breathe is his diaphragm. This is a small breath compared to the full breath brass players use. As a child assumes the upright position by the age of two or three, his ribs begin to move down and begin to gain mobility.

The diaphragm is responsible for 45% of the breath in some individuals, 40% in others, but it can be as high as 50% depending on the individual's body type. In stretching upward, you'll breathe with the diaphragm in a high position because your chest is already enlarged and it can't move. However, you'll have enough air to sustain life.

Brass Playing and Asthma

I have asthma and I know quite a bit about it. In the high airflow instruments (like the trombone and tuba), it's beneficial to play a brass instrument to alleviate some of the symptoms of asthma. Actually, playing is not going to harm a player because the high airflow required in brass playing involves low air pressures.

However, if a baritone player or a bass trombone player has a small lung volume and he has asthma as well, he might not have enough air to play well. He might need four or five liters of usable air. In fact, you'll find that he won't be able to play at *fortissimo* levels as well as not being able to tongue as he should. His air will be too slow and you'll hear the difference in tone.

The good news is that medical doctors can treat this problem. As a rule, there are various treatments available and you can get a certain amount of relief. I'm now using some of those treatments. Today there are air pollutants that are becoming a rather severe problem and more people are coming to my studio suffering from distress in their respiratory system. I wouldn't take them off a brass instrument as long as they have enough air to get by. Besides, playing a brass instrument is actually good for them.

The Relaxation Pressure Curve

We have working potentials in the tissue of our breathing musculatures. As we expand, there is a gradual increase in muscular resistance that can cause, you might say, a work potential as the muscles relax.

In a spirometric test, a person puts a tube in his mouth and blows into it as rapidly and as completely as he can. It might take seven seconds to take the usable part of your air out of your lungs. I say "usable air" because we have residual air that can't be removed from the lungs. I know there are teachers who teach how to use residual air. In actuality, their thoughts are right, but their terminology is wrong.

Residual air is the term used in the old legal test to find out whether a newborn was born alive or dead. In other words, if there was an insurance problem and there was doubt as to whether the child was born alive or dead, they would perform this test. In the test, they would remove the lungs of the dead child and if the lungs sunk to the bottom a water tank, it meant that that newborn had never drawn a breath. On the other hand, if the lungs floated, it meant that the newborn had drawn his first breath. There is always a certain amount of air that stays in the lungs, which you can't exhale by blowing.

You start blowing the air at high velocity and no matter how hard you blow, at some point it will start to slow down. In some individuals, it will slow down drastically. In a healthy young person, you figure 80% of the air can be removed within the first second, and in the next three seconds he will be able to remove the rest of his usable air.

In many of the professional players, you'll find that as they grow older their expiratory reserves begins to get a little smaller. This is a very important subject and for that reason I am going to talk about it. It has a great deal to do with many of the physical problems involved in brass playing.

When an average person sleeps, he has about five liters of available lung capacity. With the residual air, we would have our lungs 1/4 to 1/3 filled without taking a breath. Incidentally, in a fresh cadaver you would have enough air that if you pushed down on its abdomen and chest, you could measure the air coming out. What I am trying to say is that there are physical problems that occur when you play with that residual air.

When you take a large breath, you move further into the positive curves of your total lung capacity. As you go further into the positive curves, there is a constant increase in the elasticity of the work effort. The elasticity, in a large man like me for example, may be as high as 3/4 of a pound of air pressure. If we measure a sigh—which would start out anywhere from a 1/2 to 3/4 of a pound of pressure—it would fall rapidly to zero pounds of pressure. It could also be as high as 3/4 of a pound of positive pressure. The air pressure would fall gradually, but constantly, all the way down to zero pressure. At the point of zero pressure, we start to descend into the negative curve. In the negative curve, the symptoms reverse. We lose the elasticity factors and our work efforts increase.

The elasticity that was helping the air get out of the lungs is now doing the very opposite. You have to overcome that state of lack of elasticity in order to get air out of the lungs. During the negative curve, we have some unpleasant things happen.

What I want to get across is that there are unpleasant consequences in the extreme negative pressures. As you increase your air pressure, you begin to collapse the airways. You actually begin to collapse the small tubes in the lungs. It's a compounding phenomenon because each breath cycle tends to make it harder to get the air out—as well as taking the next breath. That's a problem because on empty lungs, if you take a limited breath, you'll take a 50% inhalation from empty. You'll start out very comfortably in the plus curve, but within two seconds you'll be entering the negative curve again. You might also start out by taking half a breath, but with a second breath you can get to the positive curves quickly. However, if you have a long phrase with no chance for a second breath, you'll be entering a region where it gets harder to get the air out of the lungs. In other words, to be safe, every breath has to be large.

You won't sense when you are running out of breath because the brain doesn't pickup those signals. However, you'll feel it as stiff lips, sluggish tonguing, a closed throat, and sometimes irritation in the larynx. You'll get signals that can indicate that you are out of breath, but unless you are familiar with the subject, it might be a little difficult for you to read those signals. I find the signals very quickly because I am used to them and I have the material and the knowledge to analyze them.

The negative curve in your breathing chart is a source of great problems because it comes near the end of the breath. There is another problem involved in playing a brass instrument. Many players pre-compress the air before they blow. If you pre-compress the air, you already have all sorts of air pressures. If you add further pressure as you are playing, it could really cause throat spasms and you could start choking. You could be very uncomfortable indeed.

The negative curve is a constant variable. If you are sustaining a note, you can measure all kinds of physical changes using all sorts of electronic equipment. However, you don't need to know most of this information to play a brass instrument. Let me put it this way, your body is reacting differently every instant of your breathing curve. When an artist learns to hold a sustained note, it's like a computer; it's constantly adjusting the many fibers that have to contract in the body to produce that note. As you are holding a long tone, your body will show—under investigation—all sorts of changes. Therefore, if you play by feel, you'll go crazy because the feel phenomenon is a constant variable.

Your sustained tones, phrasing, and overall qualities of tone are handled through the lower levels of the brain. The function of the brain stem is new knowledge, but we know that it's a marvelously efficient portion of the brain that will fire up the various physical mechanisms as needed. When you get out of its way, the brain works marvelously. You get out of the brain's way by studying music and not by studying the body. You can study breath as function (like blowing out matches, etc.) and benefit greatly, but you won't benefit as much by studying the breathing apparatus. If you go by the study of the breathing apparatus, you may find that you have substituted all sorts of muscular movements, shapes, and changes for a full natural breath. The reason why I stress this point is because this is one of the important reasons why you must stick to the art form of music. You can't handle your bellows system as if you were a machine—by manually handling its various parts.

As a teacher, one of my big problems is that as players get older there is always a change in their vital capacity and no matter what you do, the downward curve will still take place. By the time you are in your 40s or 50s, it becomes quite apparent that the six-liter capacity you had as a 20 year old man has tapered off down to five. In the case of a person who started with four liters of vital capacity, it may be down closer to three. The problem is that as your vital capacity begins to move down and your playing habits start to change, you find that there is much more strain in your playing. Some players might recognize the strain, but some won't. You can overcome this problem if you can retrain your breathing habits.

Air Pressure

Having taught many persons in the various parts of the country (working with many trumpet, tuba, and trombone players), I have found that many professional musicians have artistic thoughts, but they unconsciously block their air from the lips. They were taught to use a "TEE" vowel as the way for moving from the lower register the higher register. Along with "TEE," some players use a pure "EEH." Players will also move to the sibilant "S" without being conscious of it. When you go too far into these reduced vowels, you actually rob the embouchure of air. This is robbing the embouchure of the fuel it needs! Unfortunately, the player will feel it as resistance in the lips and he will try to fix his embouchure.

You shouldn't isolate the sense of air resistance at the tongue because it should be at the lip. "E" will not isolate the air at the tongue. A player can utilize the airway of the pure "E" without running into Boyle's law. (Boyle's law has to do with what happens to air under pressure. However, because in brass playing it's internal, we can forget about the moisture saturation of the air as well as the temperature factors and simply talk about what happens to air under pressure).

Don't think for a moment that because you have air under pressure it will move faster because it doesn't. Air under pressure is present during childbirth and in bowel movements. It's a reinforcement phenomenon for activities within the body and the brain is fully adjusted to it. In other words, it's a reinforcement phenomenon just like a hiccup. During pelvic pressures, the inspiratory muscles and expiratory muscles are in isometric conflict. The potential for movement is not there unless one set of muscles lets go.

The Embouchure

The embouchure starts where the lips vibrates. It always starts at the center of the lip and it moves outward to the peripheries. Other parts of your embouchure, such as the chin, are not as important in the beginning stages of development. (Incidentally, the *mentalis* is involved in brass playing by pulling the lip down or pushing it up. Avoid putting too much emphasis on this right away at the cost of leaving music out of the picture).

Musical Development

The development of musical abilities (by a method of orderly changes) takes time. Go from the elementary to the advanced. Children don't think of the time it takes to develop. On the other hand, adults think of the time it takes to develop and usually don't have the patience to stay with it. Adults must understand what's involved in learning a musical instrument and come to realize that development takes time. The main point in studying a brass instrument is to enjoy making music with it.

It's important that you always work with your brain as a musician. It so happens that as you develop as a brass player you get interested in other things—such as anatomy and equipment—but you must realize that although these are important things, they are peripherals. As a result of over emphasizing the importance of the peripherals, some players forget to work with their brain as musicians.

Along with this, avoid setting rules for physical functions because there are slight variations in neural-muscular patterns so players will come to create different embouchures as time goes by. (If you play only by "feel," you'll drive yourself crazy due to all the physical changes involved).

You have to work with the student's mind because in most cases, his playing problems are not in his muscle tissue, but they are in his brain. In other words, the student's psychology has to be altered. You can do this by altering the stimulus in their brain. (If you want to alter the response pattern in the tissue—the priority is not in altering the tissue, but the message that goes from the brain to the tissue).

Paralysis by Analysis

Don't concentrate on the wrong aspects of your playing because you won't improve. You have to work with the challenges of performance in terms of music making. You should get away from the analysis on how to make this or that note happen. Our concentration should be on the storytelling aspects of playing—not on the mechanics involved in playing. It's like wearing different hats because at one time you are the performing storyteller at another time you are the teacher or the scientist. However, you must wear the right hat at the right time.

While playing, avoid getting too much into the mechanics of tone production. Do indeed get into the study of tone, but from a musical standpoint (e.g., imagine of how beautiful your tone can be). There is always some awareness of tone as it comes out of the bell, but it should be about 10% of your mental efforts (90% of your mental efforts should be toward the mental image of the sound you want).

The easiest way to learn the storytelling aspect of music is by the imitating a great artist (such as Adolph Herseth). You can also study acting because it correlates to music performance as a form of extroversion. In acting, you portray another person and in that process there are physiological changes that you use to influence (impact) the outside environment. (This is what is meant by the phrase "influencing the outside environment through the use of psychomotor activity").

Always avoid self-analysis while playing, but if you want to analyze your playing, you can record yourself play and listen to the recording later. When you practice, you should play as a painter paints on a canvas. That's painting from your head (mental images) to the paper, but in music you instead go from your head to creating beautiful sounds with your instrument. This is more difficult to do than it appears because intelligent people—especially adults—have to know what's going on as they play. This habit will surely get them into playing problems. To get an "intelligent player" out of the habit of analyzing is simple. First, you get her to start a new habit based on the imitation of a great player. Don't try to fight the "old analyzing habit" because you'll be stressing it. (Just like as you diet if you think, "I can't eat food," you'll be stressing the image of food and you'll probably get hungry).

Music is indeed a stressful occupation in terms of the psychology involved in performance. The psychological process of performance is simple. The horn simply reflects your thoughts by treating your lips like vocal chords. If you miss a note, it most likely was not in your brain—like a light bulb going off in your head. This is why it's so important to *sing* first in your head before you play.

The Mind-Body Connection

I don't know about the spiritual aspects of playing. In other words, I can't make statements. There are many things I don't know. For example, the good Lord—or whatever designed us—has given us tremendous mind-body relationships. Our body is wonderful so you go through life expecting health as a norm. Think of the machines we make. There is always something going wrong with them, but think about the human body and how it rebuilds and protects itself. We don't get to use many of our brain potentials simply because we don't know how to order what we want. Work on what you want to do and don't get in the way of the chain of commands. Develop by ordering a product and you'll go very far.

Conditioned Reflexes

Advanced players have conditioned reflexes—which are as valid as natural reflexes. If you want to alter any conditioned reflex, you have to do it by altering its stimuli as a musician. For example, many positive changes happen when you challenge a brass musician with playing tunes on the mouthpiece. If more changes are required, then you can introduce "knee bends" while playing the mouthpiece because when the big muscles of the legs are used, the brain will take the effort away from the small embouchure muscles (which were malfunctioning in the first place) to protect the big leg muscles. Perhaps you can buzz the mouthpiece or you can play simple melodies while jumping on one leg, but whatever you do, play good music.

Rim Buzzing

Don't buzz without a rim. It's so close to being right that it's dangerous. You see, the lips form as a little oboe reed so there is a space between them. The vibration will be around the oval space in between the lip's aperture. When you buzz without the rim, you can't form the lips to make it function as a buzzing unit. Instead, the lips become a closed unit. Most players will try to blow harder to move their lips apart, but as a result their breath becomes elevated (this is turn will activate all sorts of pseudo-functions in the respiratory system). The act of buzzing brings focus to itself, but the rim must bring shape to the lip.

The lips are quite complex in structure. The lower lip starts back in the upper part of the cheek area. The top lip starts in the lower part of the cheek area. Interwoven in between the large muscle groups you have feeding up—like a basket weave—all sorts of muscle groups (quite small) that have to do with the protraction and retraction of the lip. You must have a fresh cadaver in order to study those small muscles because after the cadaver dries out, the small muscles are very difficult to define. The small muscles are outclassed by the mass of muscle fibers of the *obicularis oris*. To put them into function, you have to use a rim as isolation pressure. (Hence, there must be mouthpiece pressure). [According to Jacobs, the trick of playing a trumpet hanging from a string is non-sense because you end up developing a muscle mass that will overpower the protractors and the retractors. If you give those able players something to play that moves up and down, they won't be able to do it].

Use sensible mouthpiece contact, but isolate the small muscle fibers. You can't do that by buzzing without a rim. You have to work too hard to keep the lips apart and you'll run into the danger of transferring that "hardness of blowing" back to your playing. (Also, you'll have a tremendous resisting power in the embouchure). Remember that the lips have more power to close compared to the wind's power to open them up. It's an unfair contest between the two.

You must go by the tone production properties of your instrument. You want an embouchure that wants to vibrate, not one that is forced to vibrate. When you play a brass instrument, you must think *buzz, buzz, buzz* and not *blow, blow, blow*. In an automobile, the engine moves the wheels. (It's not the gasoline moving the wheels). Your buzz is like the automobile's engine.

Embouchure is important because we function based on motor skills. The seventh cranial nerve (the facial motor nerve) is similar to a wire hooked up from the brain to the lip. It branches out into the trigeminal nerve (facial sensory nerve) for various functions. If you touch your lip, you can feel it because that's a message going inward. That's felt through the fifth cranial nerve (trigeminal) that has nothing to do with actual performance. The ability to perform is tied into your sense of sending a message (as when you use your lips as vocal chords). That's the job of the seventh cranial nerve.

Find out where your mouthpiece works best and through the years you'll cut out the extra changes. People move their lips in many different ways to talk so in brass playing you must let players find their own way. Don't over teach in this area. What you must teach instead is to play music with maximum amplitude (*forte*) and minimum amplitude (*piano*). Do it by the study of sound and not by the energy of pushing air through resisting lips. Do it as a musical endeavor and not as a scientific endeavor. Practice with great *fortes* and decrease into great *pianos* while keeping the same great tone. Practice *decrescendos* and hold the *piano* at its softest point. Stop and start at that soft level again. This way, you'll develop a beautiful command of soft entrances. Do the opposite with your *forte* playing. By practicing your dynamics, you'll develop a beautiful embouchure.

Double Buzz

Double buzz is a segmented sound. In it the embouchure buzzes at different speeds. Its cause is the insufficient thickness of your air column. As a result, your embouchure is set to vibrate at a faster rate than your given air speed. Your embouchure simply gets too small, but it will start to relax where it vibrates in the center—not above or below, but right there in the center around the aperture—and that will start the segmentation.

Mouthpiece Playing

While playing the mouthpiece, you must search out for music without thinking of technical rules. (Just use the musical rules of sound and music). Think that you forgot your instrument at home and you still have to entertain your audience. You'll see that as you play the mouthpiece, the storytelling aspects of your playing will increase. (This has some to do with the introduction of strangeness inherent in mouthpiece playing). When you add the mouthpiece to the instrument, your sound will sparkle. Mouthpiece training will connect your musical thoughts to your muscle tissue so I recommend to some players to do one hour of mouthpiece playing a day—in ten minute segments—to start the training aspects of storytelling in music.

Conceive the vibration of your lip the same way you feel its vibration when you buzz in the visualizer. (This way, the buzzing of the lips will become the challenge). Keep buzzing at all dynamic levels. Also, keep using air as a fuel and buzz your lip like a little engine!

When you play softer there will be less vibration, but the quality of your tone must continue into the *pianissimo* level. We call this way of playing *veil pianissimo*. (It's a thinner *piano* that sounds beautiful; it's created by a small surface that vibrates minimally). To achieve this kind of *pianissimo*, you can start with a note at full volume and *decrescendo* keeping the same quality of sound (just like turning the volume down in your stereo). *Veil pianissimo* is like putting a small reed into a big instrument. You can carry the *veil pianissimo* to all the registers of your instrument. Both, *veil pianissimo* and regular *pianissimo* are good and useful under different musical circumstances.

Remember that you *sing* with your lip and the instrument serves as an amplifier of whatever comes out of your mouthpiece. Your instrument increases your mouthpiece buzz by 20 dB (if it's in pitch). You always have to provide the mouthpiece buzz and your instrument provides the amplification.

The Study of Sound

We must be versatile and change our motivation. You should put on a "soloistic sound" often. The power of tone is not the *major*, but the beauty of sound is.

Woodwind players have reeds and they work with them. Brass players have to know how to work their "flesh reeds." Lips can fight back the breath. When you have a strident sound, that's a symptom of an embouchure that's starting to fight back against the pushing power of the breath. There is no way you can blow and pull your lips apart with your wind because it's an unequal struggle. We can't encourage this at all. We have to encourage increasing the vibration of your lip instead. Take a middle range note and give it a great tone and a beautiful singing line. Maybe play it with *vibrato*. Then you can large dynamics with a beauty of tone. The *vibrato* will throw your instrument into resonance (pitch average) without forcing it. Increase your sound, not your effort.

Develop your sound based on a mellow approach. Use your intuition and figure out how to get results. Get to the point where you say, "Bravo, that was good!" And not, "God, I can't stand it!" Find the *norm* (beautiful tone) and just like the volume of your stereo, play louder or softer with the same quality of tone. This way you are putting the rough sound quality farther and farther away into the outer peripheries of your dynamic levels.

You can also play the big excerpts with a mellow tone or a strident tone. You can change the instructions a conductor gives you into a mental image of sound that your body can use when performing. Be willing to be wrong. Get a big-beautiful tone based on your mental concept of that tone. Don't spoil it by thinking how you do it.

A great ability for symphony musicians is to be able to convert verbal instructions into a form of stimulus in the brain. If the conductor says, "You are too loud," and you think, "I must play softer," you might get all "screwed up." If you, however, think on how it sounds to play it softer, then you'll have the proper stimulus to play. Play as a soloist! The intensity of your approach has to be that of a Jascha Heifetz even in the accompanying passages. Practice this way!

Nobody has to be perfect. We are all allowed a quota of mistakes. However, you must be perfect in the brain even if you are rotten in the lips. You must have accurate thoughts. Depend more on your thoughts and less on your lip. In other words, don't get caught up in the physical structures. Come down in the scale of complex thought and self-analysis and turn up your musical communication.

Rim Buzzing: Benefits and Hazards

There are benefits and hazards when buzzing the rim. However, with mouthpiece buzzing there is benefit with no hazard. You can go on vacation with a mouthpiece and you can play anything you want. The problem is that the rim is not an acoustical device. The pressure relationships are different when compared to playing the mouthpiece. There is a little more effort on the rim than on the mouthpiece. The danger with playing your high notes on the rim is that you might transfer the increased pushing of the breath—as well as your embouchure's decreased ability to vibrate—

back to your instrument. This way, you might harm your playing. On the instrument, you must reduce back pressure but if you are not familiar with buzzing on the rim, you might transfer the high pressure back to your instrument. If you know what the danger is with rim buzzing, you can avoid it. I don't recommend too much high range playing on the rim. Lower register playing is fine.

Players With Facial Damage

This really depends on the extent of the damage. First, you have to recognize that the player is worried (which is quite normal because we are human) like when you think, "What's wrong with me?" Also they might be constantly thinking, "My face feels bad!" These are common thoughts for these injured players. They are working based on sensory nerves.

Bud Herseth's accident in 1951 left tremendous damage, but he came back playing better than before. His success was based in his ability to send signals to the reflexes available to function. You can still function up to your tissue potential, but if you play by the feel of your embouchure, your playing will stop cold.

The loss of movement on one side of the face—paralysis or partial paralysis—where the strong muscles will pull the weak ones over also affects some players. You'll often find that there is, in this case, little wrong in the tissue, but you will surely find something wrong (worried) in the head.

If there is collateral damage in the lip, simply move the mouthpiece over to the other side and hypertrophy will set in after a period of practice. However, you must still be a great musician in your brain. There will be a loss of range, but that will come back. Lips are not delicate. There are few ailments that strike them because there is such a healthy supply of blood going through them. If there is nerve damage, it has to be fixed by a neurologist.

To study the psychology of playing, I recommend the following books: *The Inner Game of Tennis* by T. Galwey and *Psycho Cybernetics* by M. Maltz. Anything that focuses the mind is beneficial if it's focused on the right thing. For example, you can't overdo positive thinking. I was brought up in a family of pessimists and I had to learn to have positive thoughts. Positive attitudes will give signals to many levels of the brain, so you have to make sure you order what you want. Your body works so much better when you think positive thoughts, and you'll feel much more comfortable as well.

Appendix A: Edited Lectures

The truth about any book is that you are going to get good information, but its application might not be there. You have to apply the information so it works for you. For example, if you want to play, you not only need the will to play, but also the stimulus for each note.

We need to produce results, but you won't find how to produce them in any textbook. When you walk and breathe, we take it for granted that we have so many natural and learned reflexes. When we play, we have to work the same way. Playing is based on thinking on what we want to sound like (i.e., music as an end product).

Mouthpiece Pressure

There is no such thing as a fine brass embouchure without mouthpiece pressure. In vibrating surfaces, you don't have fine vibration in relaxed surfaces. If you examine a brass player's face while playing, you'll invariably find contraction (we call it a "dead pan" expression). You'll generally find that dead pan expression in most fine brass players.

This is important because it does immobilize some of the phenomena that happen in the external regions of the embouchure and it permits internal functions to take place. You can still have this same function, but have an unorthodox looking appearance. If your embouchure is off centered, you may not have the same appearance, but you might have excellent function.

Neck Bulging

What I am describing is several things. One is the bulging of the neck as well as tension in the facial musculatures. The bulging of the neck has to do with whether or not the air is going to meet with the sibilant "S" when you try to play loud.

If you reduce the airways, you may have to go up to 2-1/2 pounds of pressure to have one pound at the lips. You'll blow harder and that's how you get the broken connective tissue to where you may actually have a huge bulge in your neck—as some trumpet players have.

If an obstruction is put in the way of the airflow, then you are going to blow hard and you won't have much vibration. To solve this problem, you have two choices and the quickest way I know is to put the instrument down, take the mouthpiece, and start making music on it. The strangeness of it is such that—if you are musically motivated—you find you can play again. Then you suddenly find that you have lost much of the bulge.

Removing Excess Pressure

It's very difficult to play on the mouthpiece when compared, you might say, to your instrument. As you play on the mouthpiece, you may find—particularly if you get up and walk around the room—that you get away from excessive pressure. When slurring a great deal—rather than tonguing—you also get the obstruction of the tongue out of the way. I would go to the slurred passage on your instrument as a dominating factor for quite a while and then I would go to the lower range for a while. I would temporarily abandon the region where you find the greatest malfunction.

I have always believed in taking a problem that exists and finding the back door to sneak up on it. You find something the student does well and you work on it. Once improved, you transfer that back to the area of difficulty. This is preferable than confronting the problem head on. It's just like learning to come in on a high "C" or any high note as an entry attack. I listen to players who want to just attack the same note many times thinking that they are going to improve that way. They are trying to improve the attack on the high note. The part of the brain that doesn't judge from right or wrong just learns from the repetition. While one part of the brain says, "I need this, I need that," another part just says, "Well, you are doing this all the time, it must be what you want so I'm going to learn it."

There is a much better way of learning the entry attack and that's simply— no matter how bad it starts—sustaining that note (maybe play with *vibrato* and add the pulses of your heart to make it beautiful). At first, it may not be so great, but you always do it from the sustained note or from the slur. In other words, you learn how to come from a bad sound into a beautiful sound.

You hold on to the good notes. Learn about the note and then you come back to it. You see what I am driving at, it's sort of a back door approach so you don't confront the problem head on. I would say, if I had to pick the three most damaging phenomena that I know for a brass player, the first is isometrics, the second is the inadequate ventilation of the lungs, and the third is the inability to have a thick air column that moves directly to the tip of the lip.

We must understand that we are structured for survival on this planet and not for brass playing. We have syndromes that the brain knows full well and we utilize these in our art form. We can't fight nature. Instead, we must go along with it. One of the things involved in brass playing is that we must have a brass sound in our head and a brass instrument in our hand. It's very important not to fight that piece of brass "head on" because you can't win.

Now you recognize the power of lip closure. You can close your lips even to the point where you can't possibly—no matter how hard you blow—squeeze any air out through them. Even with four pounds of pressure, you couldn't do it. The power of the lips in closure versus the breath power to open them apart is an unequal contest.

Equipment and Overtones

If you use the right equipment for the right job, you'll avoid frustration. Otherwise, you'll be ordering more volume potential out of a small mouthpiece. The overtone characteristics will also be altered by using different equipment. Big instrument equals big fundamentals, which equals small overtones. Small instrument equals big overtones, which equals small fundamental.

You have three variables in your playing: 1) player, 2) instrument, and 3) mouthpiece. You can initiate change by changing either three. All of these changes affect the relationship of overtones to their fundamental.

With small instruments, you'll have more high overtones, but you can bring them to a balance by getting a bigger mouthpiece. However, you can never change the amplitude the instrument can give. An instrument can't make up for its size.

I often played on an adjustable cup mouthpiece. If you are playing light music, you could choose a small-shallow mouthpiece (instead of changing the instrument). The small mouthpiece will lighten up the tone.

To play Anton Bruckner's *Symphony No. 8*, you have to use a bigger cup because you need a big fundamental. However, if you forget your extra mouthpieces at home, you can do your best by using your mental concepts of sound (letting the embouchure make the changes).

As you get louder, you'll tend to change the overtone content in your tone. At this point, you'll have distortion. To fix this problem, you have to play a bigger mouthpiece and play softer.

Work by changing the mouthpieces and avoid changing leadpipes (because they are fixed items). Leadpipes have very much to do with the ability to resonate a horn as well as the ability to establish intonation. A leadpipe is extremely important to your horn so make sure you get one that gives you what you want. Usually, you lose something as you get something. (Step sized leadpipes are excellent because if there is a change in length, there will be a change in overtones).

There are men who are artists at building instruments. You get a fine player and a fine maker and you come up with something excellent. Vincent Bach was a good example. The gorgeous Bach trumpet is the product of great players stopping by the factory and trying them out. You can never make a good instrument just by using pure mathematics. You can, however, standardize the measurements of the instruments, but you must have great craftsmen making those instruments. Machine instruments are fine if you have a good "first design." However, if you have to change anything in the design, you have to go through the whole factory changing things.

Mouthpieces

The thinner the wall of the mouthpiece, the more dissipation occurs in the energy of its sound waves. Much less sound comes out, but it's a good quality sound. It reduces the entire dynamic range. For example, I had a Schilke "thin mouthpiece" that I used to play in the brass choral section of Gustav Mahler's *Symphony No. 2*.

This adjustable cup mouthpiece was made by Renold Schilke circa 1951. I used it for the first time in the Chicago Symphony Brass Quintet. It's like a small trumpet cup. It's good for brass quintet but not for orchestral playing because it's got the overtone range of a trombone and therefore it would get crowed out.

There is nothing wrong with experimenting with mouthpieces—different thickness and lengths. This way you'll have a great control over your spectrum of sound. Switch around depending on your musical requirements. However, all of your mouthpieces should have similar rims (either all flat rims or over-rounded rims). This has to do with the development of the protractors and the retractors in your lip. I used to change mouthpieces to keep things interesting in the orchestra in terms of variety of sound.

When you change mouthpieces, you don't get as dependent on the feeling and familiarity of that mouthpiece. If you play by feel, you'll limit yourself because then you'll always have to have the same equipment and acoustics. Be versatile and try to get the same tone on different instruments.

Once in a while, you should change mouthpieces because it brings strangeness. Think of Maynard Ferguson changing from trumpet, to trombone, or to the slide trumpet. Keep in mind that there are limitations in doubling so if you are a player in a major symphony orchestra, you might want to do your work on your main instrument.

Teaching

There is a factor in teaching you should know about. You have to be very sensitive to your student's needs and be able to equate with them. If necessary, you try to think like the student. That means that you have to study their background a little bit. For example, study his use of language so if you use the word hypertrophy and the student doesn't know what you are talking about, then you have to use another word. We have to find words that have meaning and that the student understands. We can issue messages from here to doomsday, but if the student can't receive them, the messages have no meaning.

I would say the individual is involved in the choice of what you teach. In other words, you go by what the individual wants to know. There are people who think along different lines in relation to what I do and you have to steer those people into a heavy dominance of the musical thought. I frequently have to be technical in the sense that I am responding to some of the student's needs. For example, there are teachers who come to see me. They have inquiring minds that will not stay with me unless I can first answer some of the technical questions. In other words, I gauge the student who comes to see me based on our first words together and then I try to establish some way of a "two-way" communication.

Many times I have to over teach because whomever I am teaching at the moment feels that that's what he needs. At that moment, I can pull rank and say, "No, you do it this way," or I can cooperate, especially if it's somebody I am going to see for an extended period and say, "All right, we can start with the subject of anatomy and physiology." Then I tell them, "You are not going to use this in your playing, but you can use it in your teaching."

If you want to help a person, you'll find simple answers to complex situations. The complex answers don't fit the picture. If you talk about complex machine systems and find the "anatomy" of a machine, you have to also find a fine mechanic to fix the machine when something goes wrong.

To heal the human body, we have physicians who can do wonderful things for us when something goes wrong. It's not necessary to know your own structure unless you are planning to repair it yourself. It's like a car that has simple control panels. I have studied people in various situations like athletics, like the Australian aborigines, and untutored people in parts of South America and I found that they all do tremendous physical feats. They dance, they play flutes, they play drums, they use their bodies for tremendously complex things, and they have no Ph.D. degrees.

I have studied and I have put many factors together. I have used myself as an example of a fairly trouble free player, I had people with problems, I have people in other fields with whom I consult, I have studied the human structures, I have studied a great deal about the brain, and I have followed the research that's going on in various disciplines. As a culmination of many years of investigation, I want to stress that the answers are all based on simplicity, not complexity. The study of what we are has become very complex. I would have to live various lifetimes to finish the study. I came to realize that whoever designed this machine of ours has put in us magnificent brains. I don't think any of us begins to use our brain with real efficiency. What I am trying to indicate is that the answers are in the study of motivation, the study of what people are like, the study of how to use our brains efficiently and not in the study of mind control over moving this or that muscle. Why spend hours studying how to lower your blood pressure—as in the study of Yoga—by conscious thought when you have built in ways to lower your blood pressure (like when you are happy and you have wonderful thoughts). To use your brain efficiently, don't waste time trying to control something you can't control (e.g., an embouchure). When you control the music, you control the embouchure. You don't control the meat to control your sound; you control your sound to control the meat [embouchure]. This can be checked out. It's not just my statement.

As a brass player ages, there are physical changes—mainly the decrease of lung capacity—which makes his playing change. I recommend to the aging player to take "surplus quantities" of air to stay away from the negative curves of his total lung capacity. In other words, the aging player should take more air than he would normally take.

There are psychological changes as well that influenced the lowering of performance quality in aging players. The aging process not only includes a physical deterioration and the lessening of some of our potentials, but there is an attitude change where enthusiasm tends to lessen. There is a change in perspective. When you are young, you can't wait to demonstrate what you can do with difficult music. There is no worry about anything that could go wrong. As you grow older, there is a sense of caution that starts to come in and you begin to ask, "What if? What if I miss this note? Gee, I missed that note ten years ago and I hope I don't miss it today." The first thing is that you start to think negative thoughts instead of positive thoughts. This is what I am talking about. In other words, if you fail to provide the stimulus in the brain, you won't have the physical response. If you play perfectly all your life, the filing cabinets will have automatic responses that are good. If you want to take charge, you have to sing to your audience. The deterioration that we are talking about is an attitude change that comes with the aging process. Of course, there is physical deterioration as well.

To me, the love song is one of the basic factors in tone production. I prefer to hear tone production based on lyricism where we have the finest qualities. To me this is like tuning up an engine in a car. You get your finest performance based on motor activity and the response of minimal use of gas with a finely tuned engine. You can detune the engine and the car will move slower, but you won't save gas. In other words, you have lost efficiency. The love song—or the lyric aspect of brass playing—acts just like the tune up in a car. With the love song you get your finest tone production and you maneuver it into other emotional states. You maneuver it into the fanfares, but with quality. You maneuver it into a variety of interpretations of styles. Then you'll have the artistic tools you need. If you want stridency, or you have an emotional state where the music calls for someone to someone's throat cut, you don't want a wonderful love song. At that time, you'll deliver stridency based of conceptual thought. However, the basic emotional state should be lyrical. Always sounding good.

APPENDIX B

MENTAL ASPECTS

Preview

- *If Bud Herseth could put his brain into your skull and you play with his brain, your lips would do a much better job. It's how you think when you play that's going to help you improve.*
- *In your brain, you have to be a master musician. You have to be master interpreter of style and phrase as well as one who communicates a message to somebody else. The rest is just minor stuff. In other words, I don't want you to play right, but instead I want you to sound good.*
- *The lips become the vocal chords of brass playing. Sing with them! Put the notes into the cup of the mouthpiece. By the time it reaches the throat of the mouthpiece, it's success or failure because everything on the other side of the mouthpiece is acoustics. Put perfect notes into the mouthpiece!*
- *Perfect your thoughts and you'll perfect your lip.*
- *The meaning of singing to me is simply that there should be two voices: one in the head and one coming out the bell. The one in the head always directs what's coming out the bell.*
- *If you play a thousand notes a day but 800 are mediocre and 200 are magnificent, the brain will say, "God! Those two hundred notes were great and I am happy." Unfortunately, the 800 mediocre ones form the habit. Make sure you have 800 great ones!*
- *It's always a matter of starting the student at his level. If they can't run, you have them walk. If they can't walk, you have them crawl. You start where they are—even if all they can do is play a single note.*
- *You can be a kind teacher and still get a "hell of a lot" of results as long as you get the student's cooperation. Most people will tend to cooperate when they know what they are asked to do is for their own good and it's something that's not unpleasant.*

Psychology

Don't hesitate to use personal psychology on yourself because it's amazing what it does in terms of mind over matter. I was brought up in the Christian Science Church and my mother was a very good Christian scientist. During my younger years, the mind over matter concept opened a lot in my imagination. I say that because the way I think is so different in so many ways when compared to most people that I think somewhere along the way, I might have been influenced by something. I wonder if Christian Science was the influence. Later on, I became an avid science fiction reader and I ran into other pieces of literature of that sort.

I mention this because what has to improve is the player's concentration. It's not about the embouchure or about muscles—they are already developed. If Bud Herseth [Adolph Herseth] could put his brain into your skull and you play with his brain, your lips would do a much better job. It's how you think when you play that's going to help you improve. The more you think about the psychodynamics involved, the better you'll do in this art form.

However, find out what works for you because I don't have all the answers. All I have are some breakthroughs. The physical applications may vary a little bit, but the main point is when there is buzzing in the lips, there is tone in your instrument. That's a principle! We are just making it come much faster by focusing on it.

Your brain can be marvelous in math or logic. It may be ahead of mine. Bud Herseth, for example, is good in math and he has a degree in math. I love science and I studied it for many years. Otherwise, I wouldn't know what I know. Do you understand? There is great variety of excellence in the human brain. It's like a graph. Mine peaks on recall and pitch. Somebody else's in the sciences would peak on logic. My wife was a splendid dancer and a painter on the canvas and brush so hers peaks in the arts.

However, I have one thing that I haven't found in any textbook. That's that we all can go from the point where we can cope and improve simply by challenging ourselves. Pretty soon the low points will come up to where the high points are and if we keep it up, we don't know how far you'll go. You never give up on people because they all have tremendous potentials, but sometimes they use them in the wrong places. I've never found a second-class brain in a healthy and well-nourished normal person. Illness might affect the brain, but that's another case.

Again, the psychology of what you do is very important. You already have proven that you have the tissue development. You have the reflexes, but now you have to provide the stimulus. To do that, can you begin to simplify your activities so that there is more of a childlike approach? I need the adult mind for interpretation and for the qualities of musical styles, but I want the child for the brass playing applications. Although a little of it is all right, I don't want your knowledge of muscles and feel phenomena. Instead, think sheer music!

Song and Wind

You are a musician and things have to be always worked out based on music. The final arbiter in everything is sound, phrase, and style. Now, the words *Song and Wind* are very important. *Song* has to do with the biocomputer and wind is your motor force. Just like the bow is the motor force for the string family. The bow is just a bow without a string. Our string is our lips. You can't associate your lips with the reed family because it's a different principle. Theirs is a piece of wood. The lips are part of you, and they are tied into your nervous system. The woodwind reed is not. As a result, you have to associate your lips with your vocal chords. Then you get the picture. You *sing* with your lips!

Meaning of *Song*

A cup-mouthpiece brass instrument is the closest to the human voice. The three basic elements of tone production must always be motor force, a source of vibration that involves pitch, and a source of resonance (amplification). Of those three, a singer has all. They are part of his anatomy. The brass player has two. Most other instruments have one. For example, the factory sends out a piano with pitch-vibration and resonance built in. The only element needed is the motor force. Brass players have within their own body two of the basic elements of tone production, but they don't have amplification. As a brass player, you don't have a sound board built in and this is why you need an instrument. However, the pitch-vibration and the motor force (a wind column) are up to you.

Most other instruments are not like that. For example, instruments like the oboe, clarinet, or violin have all sorts of perceptions regarding what the fingers are doing. The nervous system involved in playing them gives us certain knowledge of functions (like finding the pitch based on what you do with your left hand). Therefore, the violin—as well as other instruments—involves more mechanics and awareness. Brass players don't know what they are doing in terms of mechanics. If you would treat a brass instrument like if it were your voice, you would have tremendous success. You simply can never get into the analysis of anything you are doing. Deliberately, recognize that your playing is very much like a voice when singing. Playing a brass instrument and singing are very close because instead of the laryngeal nerve going down to the larynx, you get the seventh cranial nerve going to the embouchure. It's the same identical treatment in message. If you don't sing with your voice, *sing* while you are playing! Most players who get in trouble try to use their lip as a woodwind reed. You can't play by treating your lip as a wooden reed. Instead, it has to be used like the vocal chords of a singer. Then you have success!

The Musician in the Brain

In your brain, you have to be a master musician. You have to be master interpreter of style and phrase as well as one who communicates a message to somebody else. The rest is just minor stuff. In other words, I don't want you to play right, but instead I want you to sound good.

Children who whistle and sing a lot usually have an easier time working on ear training. Singing is what develops the music centers in the brain. Those centers continue to develop regardless of age. You could start to develop your ear training at the age of sixty and you'll develop beautifully. However, you just need the patience to do it. The simple fact that you sing will create neural pathways in your brain. However, don't rest on your laurels once you attain some success. Instead, keep singing every day. This type of training pays dividends in a week, but you'll hear a great difference in six months. Ear training is something that I have worked on all my life and I continue to work on it to this day.

The other type of study that will develop your ear is mouthpiece buzzing. A serious brass player developing her playing should buzz an hour each day. If I wrote out prescriptions, I would suggest an hour of buzzing of music you already know. (You could divide that hour into four 15 minute segments or six 10 minute segments).

At the early stages of development, I am more interested in testing the student on ear training than on brass playing because the problem is not in the instrument. Instead, you often find that the problem is in their aural skills. Not every player has the same problems, but in everybody's development weak points can become strengths. In a brass instrument, the player depends very much on the ability to conceive music in the brain. In a three-valve instrument with over a three-octave range, you have to give the pitches to the horn by putting perfect notes into the cup of its mouthpiece. The horn simply provides the valves to adjust the lengths of its tubing to amplify the pitches the player is sending. Most advanced players' embouchures have undergone tremendous developments. However, some of their inconsistencies are not tissue problems, but instead they are mental problems. Eventually, this is something players have to address by themselves.

When doing ear training, you must have a word or a syllable associated with it so eventually the word becomes the stimuli for the pitch. That's the purpose of the study of *solfège*. You can give the note any name you want. At first, the player might not experience a rapid improvement with this study because there are variables in pitch recall and recognition among people, but most players will gain confidence with repeated practice and success.

There is no way or reason to do the advanced technical work with a brass instrument before doing the ear training work. You must always get the "double sound." By "double sound" I mean the sound of the voice in the head and the one out the bell. The one in the head is the teacher. The teacher is the source of stimuli for the conditioned reflexes you have developed through years of practice. Your body is like a biocomputer that will read out music as you conceive it in your head before sending it as a command to the muscles. Your goal is to constantly develop the mental aspects as a musician so you are not blowing a brass instrument at all, but instead you are singing. You must understand that a brass instrument is a stupid acoustical device with no brains of its own. It simply resonates what you send into it. In other words, you must *sing* with your lips into the cup of your mouthpiece.

Greater Mentalizations

You must have greater mentalizations as you play. Your mentalizations are competent, but they don't cope with your performance challenges. You need stronger mentalizations than Bud Herseth does. That is, a stronger magnifying glass on the proper interpretation of music in your brain. This is to increase your musical tension that really belongs on stage during public performances. You are too comfortable right now, so I don't feel a sense of excitement when I hear you play. Normally, I like that but it's simply that you are not strong enough in your brain signals for the muscle tissue in your body to recognize what you want. Turn up the volume in your head! I need you to create phrases by concentrating on each note. On wide intervals, think of the note half a beat before you play it so your lip knows what you want.

To improve your orchestral excerpts, you can play music that is similar to those excerpts or make up exercises that include, or exceed, the difficulties involved. However, you must always have a connection with the music by mentalizing it first in your head. You hear that approach with Bud Herseth. He always adjusts to what the music wants him to do.

This is always the difference between a full-blown artist and a lesser player. However, what has to change first? The first change happens in the studio where you accept the challenge of the music and you begin to respond to it. There will be days when you seem to get worse. That doesn't mean anything. You have to go on as an artist and find out what makes playing your excerpts easier.

Accept your music as an artistic challenge. Bud starts to prepare something like the post horn solo in Gustav Mahler's *Symphony No. 3* weeks in advance. He prepares everything and takes nothing for granted.

A Voice Coming Out of Your Instrument

Can you hear a voice coming out of your instrument? The voice of a wonderful singer singing "OHHHHH"? Changing your lip shouldn't take you from note to note, but instead you change from note to note by *singing* each pitch in your head. If you try to play by changing your lips, you are very apt to miss. You have to play from your reflexes in your brain, and you are almost guaranteed results.

I have been working on this in recent years because I'd like to put some papers out on this subject, but it looks very much to me like brass playing is really a reflex response. We are so used to handling our embouchures, but in this case if you let go and handle the brain instead, you get better and easier results.

You have to start each tune with great quality. Prepare the qualities of tone in your head before you play and you'll be better off. Prepare the sound and not the mechanics. Your body will respond as a result. Then we go back to what my thesis is, "brass playing is a reflex." If I am right, you'll see that many things in your playing will change for the better. All of this has to do with your ability to mentalize your music before you play it.

I have taught mentalization my entire adult live, but I have never looked for the text and the ways to prove it. However, I am doing that now. The more I do it, the more I am convinced I am right.

Motivating *Song and Wind*

Always motivate *Song and Wind*. *Song* is always vocal chords and buzz. *Singing* into the mouthpiece. That's what you must motivate. The fuel is the *Wind*. You should motivate the musical message like a singer. If you order *Wind*, you don't know what's going to come out. It's pot luck. Maybe it will be good maybe it will be bad, but you are not in charge. You have to order *Song*! Don't order *Wind*. Order the sound directly as your main product. There is no buzzing without blowing. It doesn't exist. You can't buzz without blowing. You don't have to worry about blowing. You have to instead put your money where it pays off. Vibration pays off. There is no sound without lip vibration. Just because you blow air, it doesn't mean that you are going to have lip vibration. Blowing by itself creates silence so if you want sound, you have to order *Song*.

Make sure the singing is the first thing you do—not the lips and not the blowing. Like a singer, there are habits you have to form that have to do with taking charge of your music. In other words, you have to treat yourself as a vocalist. By that I don't mean in terms of breath applications or specifics of vocal techniques, but in terms of using the *voice* in your head.

The lips become the vocal chords. *Sing* with them! Put the notes into the cup of the mouthpiece. By the time it reaches the throat of the mouthpiece it's success or failure because everything on the other side of the mouthpiece is acoustics. Put perfect notes into the mouthpiece! Don't depend on a three-valve instrument to give you three or four octaves of chromatics. You've got to *sing* perfect notes into the horn so it can resonate according to its acoustical laws—primarily based on sympathetic resonance.

During the beginning stages as a young player, you need the awareness of embouchure and the applications of what you are doing. At an advanced stage, however, you don't need that awareness because you have conditioned reflexes galore. At that advanced stage, you have to work on the stimulus part of your playing as an artist. Your lips will respond based on the readout from your brain. Trust me, this is the easiest way to play.

Going by Your Meat

Don't go by your meat [muscle groups in your lip]. The meat is under the direct control of the subconscious levels of your brain. All you have to do is tune your mind and you'll automatically tune your lip. This is based on the reflex responses to the stimuli coming out of the brain down the seventh cranial nerve. Perfect your thoughts and you'll perfect your lip!

I am trying to get your playing to a highly competitive level when compared to the fine artists who have played so well for so many years. They have all sorts of habits and—like a biocomputer—they have memory banks stored with examples of excellent playing of all types. You are starting to fill up your memory banks now to make up for it, we make sure you constantly use every trick in the book to stimulate your excellence in phrasing music. The use of speech forms—such as lyrics, *solfège*, or numbers—to sing music gives you great mental power because you have had speech all your life. The singing will help you play better. You have to *sing* loudly in your brain even when you play softly because there is a mental threshold you have to overcome.

Feeling and Sounding Good

Playing by feel it's not a trust worthy way to go. When it feels good, it always sounds good, but you don't have to get the *feel* to get a good sound. Instead, you get the good sound to feel better. Make sure your playing is under your mind's control.

Singing While Playing

You are taking to blowing your instrument as something that's separate from you. Your instrument should be like an extension of you—as if it belongs to your body. You should *sing* and blow air out here—outside yourself—and forget about your instrument. I want you to think less about playing a brass instrument and more about *singing* with your *vocal chords* [lips]. This way, when you divorce the brass instrument from its player, you are very close to a singer. For you, this should translate to being much more vocally oriented and much less mechanically oriented. Always start with the sound in your head and not with mechanical preparations.

The habit of *singing* while playing has been an interest of mine from before I started teaching. As a kid, I used to sing when I was a vocal student. I intuitively used my voice and I was lucky because when Fritz Reiner [then teacher at the Curtis Institute of Music in Philadelphia] would ask for orchestral parts a certain way, he would usually sing them. I couldn't hear what he said, but I would pay close attention to his vocal interpretation. That was what I really copied. It was much more successful than trying to interpret words. When I interpreted words, I usually screwed up. I noticed that when I copied his voice, it was only once through and he was satisfied.

I'm impressed by the closeness of singing and brass playing. The quality of vocal teaching is sometimes terrible. The average vocal teacher doesn't know which way is up so I can't send a student to a singer because they might acquire bad habits from bad teaching. However, the training for the brain in terms of interpretations of music and styles is marvelous. Mentally, a brass player is much closer to a singer than any other instrument. The more vocal your brass playing becomes, the better you'll sound.

Now, don't confuse using *vibrato* with *singing* because the meaning of *singing* to me is simply that there should be two voices: one in the head and one coming out of the bell. The one in the head always directs what's coming out the bell. In other words, we want the stimuli in the head to be pure song!

Playing with Inspiration

To play well, you have to be inspired and at the same time dare to be wrong. Then, your playing will sparkle. Take chances! Be enthusiastic in the way you play music so you become an interpreter of music.

Don't play as if you are putting your toe in the water. That would be as if you were listening to yourself as you play. Instead, you should go into show business and play as an artist. Imitate great artists! Pick great role models and use the power of imitation. Don't prepare your muscles to play your instrument, but instead prepare the sound in your head. Play four "G's" in a row, pick the best one, and put it at the start of your phrase.

Be an actor and pretend to be someone else for a moment. Use imitation (or create your own model) and hear the different players in your head. Put great examples in your head and demonstrate how a great player sounds. Imitate Maynard Ferguson, Adolph Herseth, or Doc Severinsen.

People in universities try to use their brain too much to figure out what they are doing. You have to recognize that your body needs stimuli for a specific response. Put great sounds in your head and be willing to make mistakes. The mistakes are not important because I don't want your brain to begin asking questions. Instead, I want your brain to continue to issue statements. It's as if you were talking to somebody else. When you play your instrument, you imagine an audience out there and you sing like Luciano Pavarotti.

Asking questions is not undesirable. I do it too because that's the way we learn many things. However, when you play your instrument I have to get you to be a storyteller of sound so you avoid self-teaching.

You need to play with a "show business" attitude to compete with players like Adolph Herseth. Sing with your voice and use body language when you study music. Don't be too careful when you play. We need more "show business." Hear your voice when you play and don't hear your instrument. You should bring in body movements because every time you bring in physical phenomena—along with your musical thought—it will enhance everything you do.

Cheat a little bit! Sound great even if you are feeling rotten. Be like a "used car salesman." It's simply that in order to use your nervous system properly—to influence the external environment using your motor systems—you have to issue statements.

As you start to practice each day, play music that you already know. You must awaken your sense of artistry so you don't play like a student. I would have young students take a year of acting lessons so they can express the various moods of life just by pretending to be someone else. When you act the physiological changes are tremendous. You could feel love or anger and your body will respond accordingly. You have to recognize that your brain is as good as mine, but you have to use it properly to succeed in this art form.

As you issue a musical message, other areas of the brain will organize the tissue required. It's similar to a magnificent computer that I call a biocomputer. This biocomputer has areas that control and coordinates motor functions (tissue movements), but it has to be instructed by other areas in your brain. The ability to hear sounds in your head is important because that's what directs the lower areas in the brain. Take fifteen minutes a day and study, in a formal way, hearing music in your head.

Each ink spot on the music page should represent something in your head—just like when you read the written word. Some of that is missing in your art form. Form the music in your head before you touch the horn. Think of how that music would be played by a rotten player followed by a great player.

If the musical statement is not clear in your head, then your lip won't know what to do. Each note requires specific stimulus from you. Remember that you don't play simply by pushing the keys down. Train yourself to *sing* in the head. Remember that out of weakness you must develop strength. It doesn't have to happen right away. It could take a couple of years, but you'll be better off if you treat yourself as a singer and not as a brass player.

Keep *Singing* in the Brain When Discomfort Comes

Can you discipline the brain to continue *singing* when discomfort comes? The human brain won't want to do that. It won't want to cooperate because it likes to always be alert to whatever dangers surround you—so they can be avoided or corrected. It's a survival instinct. In our art form, however, we must overcome that. I want for your survival in this profession to get the results. I want you to *sing*! At the very instant you think you should be feeling, I want that *voice* in your head to flood out any other thoughts. Can you sense the direction in which I want you to go? This approach will produce a sort of purity in tone production where enough airs gets through the lips so you are not pushing them apart. In other words, you don't want your lips holding together so tightly that you have to pull them apart with your wind to make them vibrate. Instead, they should move in the direction of the flow of the air very much like the singer's vocal chords move upward in the direction of the wind. However, without *singing* in your head, your lip doesn't know what you want. The lip will simply be a shape that might, or might not, function properly.

Remember Your Sound

You have to remember how you sound and not how you feel. There is a tendency to remember the organization of the "feel phenomena." I want the simplicity of remembering the product [how you sound]. Then you begin to see the importance of your mentalizations. You must have more music and brass sounds in your head and less thinking on how to play a brass instrument or about your embouchure.

The more you get into the art form of music, the more the instrument becomes a stupid piece of brass governed by acoustical laws. Some students tend to adapt themselves and play their instrument like a piano—by simply pressing keys. The acoustical principles between a brass instrument and the piano are so vastly different that the acoustical relationships are altered. A brass instrument is an acoustical amplifier with strange laws based on "sympathetic resonance." The piano's acoustical laws are based on "forced resonance." The piano has one sound board that resonates all pitches. A brass instrument has a sound board that resonates specific partials with all sorts of gaps in between. That means that coming from the player must be the motor function and pitch vibration. All the horn can do is amplify. You have to play a brass instrument as you would play a megaphone by putting a message into it.

If you want to be a good brass player, you have to play with the brain of a singer. Use your voice to sing or whistle often. Sing using *solfège* syllables or sing simple songs. When you sing, you should put pulsations of energy in the music so people listening to you will want to get up and dance. You must succeed in telling a story to an audience. In other words, the psychology should be psychomotor all the way, so you are teaching other people how your music sounds.

If you imitate a better player than yourself, you'll instantly sound better. Everything you do is habit forming. If you play a thousand notes a day but 800 are mediocre and 200 are magnificent, the brain will say, "God! Those two hundred notes were great and I am happy." Unfortunately, the 800 mediocre ones form the habit. Make sure you have 800 great ones! Then you'll become a competitive player. If there is someone listening to you outside the room and he has a $90,000 a year job waiting for a competitive player, you want to sound good so you have a good shot at that job.

Having Two Voices: One in Your Head and One in Your Instrument

Your notes have to be more in your brain and less in your lip. You are missing notes in the same place where there is not enough singing going on in your head. There should be two voices: one that comes out of the bell (which is not too important) and one you conceive in your head (which is very important). Can you let that voice grow more inside your brain? I won't be able to hear it, but you'll be able to hear it. Make sure you play a beautiful first note. That will set the pattern for the rest of the notes that follow.

This way of playing will keep slipping in and out and you won't know it. The unfortunate part in that you'll suddenly feel that you can't control the notes. When you feel that way, don't blame your embouchure, or try to correct your lips or your breath. Instead, correct the *song* in your head and "she" [your playing] will correct itself quickly. You have good conditioning behind you now. You'll start growing as soon as you start to mentalize your music. You've got to train yourself so that all the ink spots on the page of music are converted into sounds in your head.

Singing Loudly in Your Head

Make sure you go for the high notes in your brain and chances are your lip will obey and follow. It might let you down, but I doubt it very much. If you miss the note, at least you would have done your part. Otherwise, you'll find that you are reaching for a high note without thinking of what note you are going to play. Remember to *sing* that high note loudly in your brain because if you sing softly, it might not have the sufficient intensity to act as a stimulus for your reflexes.

Somewhere I need the artist in you to intervene and make a low "c" become a low "C"; like a "C" belonging to a part of Verdi's *Simon Boccanegra* or something operatic like that. Avoid preparing the air and the lips to play a low "c." Instead, prepare to play the low "C" in your head first. The biocomputer levels of the brain will carry the necessary body movements. The simplicity in this process is just beautiful because the part of the brain that keeps you upright while walking also helps you play your instrument. Because you already have the developed conditioned reflexes, all you need is to prepare the message in your head.

There seem to be thresholds and I have noticed them in so many aspects of playing. You see, I am still learning as I am teaching you and I am learning more about these thresholds. For instance, very soft conceptual thought doesn't register in the brain. For it to intervene, it has to be at a certain level even in your thought process. Now, this varies from individual to individual. I don't have codes, scales, or anything I can go by, so this is virgin territory.

Singing Materials

Take materials that you already know and sing them. Then try to get your brass playing as close to your singing as you can. The brain responds so beautifully to these types of challenges that it actually begins to grow areas specialized for music.

The funny thing is that when we say, begin to grow it not only begins to grow in ability, but it also begins to grow in size in your brain. A lot of research goes on subjects related to the brain. For example, in studies done with aging, it was found that areas of the brain begin to get smaller with age, but as you continue to use them, they grow again. I used to keep up with these studies when I was able to go to the libraries.

Hearing the First Pitch of a Phrase

I used the idea of hearing the pitch in my head before I played long before I taught it to anybody else. This was one of my techniques from when I was a kid. Once I knew you had to hear the notes before you play them, I started to play with authority. My first year at the Curtis Institute of Music in Philadelphia was a disaster in a way. They put me down to play in an orchestra during a production of Leopold Auer's opera *The Spanish Hour*. I remember that I had to come in on a middle E-flat and I couldn't hear the pitch. I had no idea where I was. I was a kid, just sixteen years old, so I took a chance and fortunately, I made it. That's a terrible feeling to sit there not knowing where anything is. You can put the valve down and anything can come out. I learned that when I was sixteen years old and I thought, "This is no way to live your life." I started to study these things and the result is my career and the way I teach today. It's not hard to play when you can hear a note just by looking at it on the page. It can get very hard to play if you don't know the note and you have to guess what pitch it is. That way, you are half dead before you start to play.

The Study of *Solfège*

The greatest study that will advance your playing is the study of *solfège*. As you become proficient in *solfège*, you'll get the quickest training for the musical brain I know. When you look at music and you can hear it, you guide your embouchure right away. If you look at music and you don't hear it, you are not getting much information to the lip.

One of the most stabilizing influences in playing is counting in the head aloud and in pitch. That sends a signal down from, you might say, the motor cortex. It has to be a *voice* up there in your head as if you were going to sing with your vocal chords, but instead you *sing* with your lips.

Get Pasquale Bona's *Rhythmic Articulations*—or any other *solfège* book—and practice fifteen minutes a day of *solfège*. There is no short cut to excellence, but there are shortcuts to maximum efficiency. This is the closest thing I know for brass players as far as a short cut goes. The quickest pay off is the training of your brain in pitch and rhythm independent from your instrument. Don't be discouraged if it goes slow at first.

The Pasquale Bona studies are tone studies. Do them on the mouthpiece because it will do you a lot of good. People who are having trouble with pitch recognition usually set up the physical mechanism to produce a tone before they mentalize the music. There is no way you can do that successfully and play at a highly competitive level. You have to actually imitate something and that something is the pitch *sung* loud and clear in your head.

The one thing that will slow your playing down is getting into nervous situations—which you'll get into. At that moment, your playing will start to revert to old habits. The *solfège* study will start to reverse that. To do this, you must have pieces of music that you repeat many times over a long period.

The study of *solfège* is a long-term proposition. In other words, the pay off is very apparent right away, but it has to be constantly renewed and made into a way of life and that takes years. I am still working at it even now. So many good things diminish when you are in your 70s. For that reason, I have to keep perking up my ear training just like when I was a kid. I have to do that! In other words, it's like being on a ladder and you keep going down so you have to do something to prevent yourself from going down too fast.

Solfège is a type of specialized training in pitch and rhythm. This is not like ear training, but actual singing of music using *solfège* symbols. This is a wonderful training for any brass player. Adolph Herseth, Dale Clevenger, and Jay Friedman are experts at *solfège*.

The Human Brain

For all of us, the human brain is a magnificent tool. There are no second-class brains. When you get down to the magnificent potentials of the human brain, none of us comes close to using the brain to its full potential. We have wonderful tools in the brain and we must use them. For example, in brass playing you have to be a storyteller of sound. That's one of the tools.

Avoid comparing your improvement to someone else's improvement because people's brains are different. I was born in a musical environment, my mother was a professional pianist, and I grew up in a period where there was very little home entertainment—except playing the piano and singing. As a result, my mother played the piano and we sang. I probably heard my mother play music when I was in my mother's womb. Everything I played was by ear. You see, the development of the regions of the brain used for pitch recall and recognition started with me at an early age.

You can start ear training at any age—or level—and develop it to any level you want. I received a phone call from one of my former students who is retiring from a professional symphony orchestra after 35 years of successful playing. When he studied with me, he was as tone deaf as anybody can be. We worked hard and he got his ears going.

My wife is like that student. She swears she is tone deaf, but I tell her she is not. I figured out what her problem was the first time I heard her sing. Simply, she is in this category where she sets up her singing mechanism first before hearing the musical message in her head.

You have a good ear. It's just that your brain wants to use another methodology that's not as good. You'll notice that you'll produce a better tone if you hear it first in your head. The big pay off, is that you'll play in the center of the notes where they should be played. The horn will respond beautifully because you are not trying to lip the notes up or down or playing other sounds that don't belong in the horn (sounds that will not resonate properly). Do you see the simplicity of that? You have to simply put perfect notes into the horn.

Do a portion of your practice singing and playing. Much of the singing will start to feed back to your playing all by itself. As it starts to grow, it will become a skill. Keep this training going for now and don't put it away because it might slip in and out for a while. Sing and play all the time! You must always have the voice in your head because that's the signal that goes down the seventh cranial nerve to your lip.

The Simplicity of Teaching

One of the things I have realized throughout the many years of teaching—and that I have only been able to use in my teaching for the last ten years or so—is the simplifying process. Twenty or thirty years ago I taught using simplicity, but people didn't come to see me because I wasn't teaching how to use muscles and they thought I wasn't teaching right. That was until it was proven that playing with simplicity is the most efficient way to play.

It's hard to convince a person until they achieve success playing with simplicity. Your habits don't include some of the concepts and skills I am teaching. At this point, you have to recognize that. Don't undo anything you have done before. You are a fine brass player with what you've got. However, you are not a great artist yet. You just have to add more tools to your arsenal of thoughts.

All the things we are doing in the lesson are to simplify your thoughts—not to complicate your thoughts. I still want *Song and Wind,* but I also want you to recognize that you have the tendency to over change and over do. I want you to be more dependent on your concept of how these notes have to sound and make sure you pay attention to what's going on in your brain rather than in your lips.

Brass players usually don't think this way. Adolph Herseth does. He is a storyteller of sound. I mentioned that to him years ago and he liked that. You have to bring in developmental challenges even if those challenges are not included in your instrument's repertoire. In other words, take some of the violin music and interpret it. Take charge of your music and not of your instrument!

One of the finest forms of teaching is to demonstrate to students so they have a good example to copy. This is beneficial because it forces the students to use their brains and gives them a mental challenge. It helps them copy and emphasize nuances in tone color and phrasing. It connects their thoughts with their embouchures. By performing for them, you are going to benefit as well.

I think a great deal when I teach, but I don't use the same thought patterns when I play. I am very active mentally when I teach. The reason I teach the concepts I do is because that was the way I played. However, I didn't know I played that way until I researched the subject and found that not everybody played as I did. You see, I learned to play by ear. I was just pressing valves until I got the right note.

Starting a Beginning Student

The first thing you do with a beginning student is to play middle "G" on his instrument. Have him listen to you and then have him imitate. Then I would play a little melody for the student to imitate.

You should always give a beginning student something musical to imitate so that he is very much interested in imitation. You always test him for the ability of pitch recognition and recall. You ask him if he can sing something he learned at home or at school. You can also sing a few notes for him to sing back. Now, you don't discard him just because he doesn't have the ability to sing right away. Some students will have that ability and they will surprise you, others will be borderline, and others yet won't recognize what you are doing. It's always a matter of starting the student at his level. If they can't run, you have them walk. If they can't walk, you have them crawl. You start where they are—even if all they can do is play a single note.

Always have periods of silence in between the notes you are asking your students to recall. This is for the brain to have a chance to recall the specific pitch. This process goes quickly in young people. This is why the study of *solfège* is so important at any age, but especially when you are young.

When you start working with pitch and rhythm—based on visual and aural stimuli—it's just marvelous. You do it gradually so there is no big panic or you might scare your students and hurt their feelings. You can be a kind teacher and still get a hell of a lot of results as long as you get the student's cooperation. Most people will tend to cooperate when they know what they are asked to do is for their own good and it's not unpleasant. To have a full conditioned reflex it takes several years, so you have to keep up the training for a long period of time.

The Negative Effects of Teaching

What I sense, although I don't know your life style, is a strong influence from your teaching schedule. Your teaching might be tearing you down instead of building you up. There is nothing wrong with teaching as long as you recognize the fatigue and habit forming factors.

When you teach, you are primarily receiving information through your sensory system going inwards into your brain. When you play, you are using psychomotor pathways where you use messages that are going outward to the effectors. The two systems are opposites in function and direction. Don't let the sensory system take over while you are playing or you'll ruin yourself.

Teaching is fatiguing to the brain. Even though teaching and performing are allied, the constant analyzing a teacher does is habit forming (if you teach many hours a day). The first bad effect of teaching is that you are always analyzing and that tires the brain. You have to learn to bring this under control because I have seen many fine players go down hill once they start teaching heavy schedules. Maybe you can decide to teach when it does the least amount of harm. That's so when you go play, you have a fresh brain.

A Bad Teaching Experience

I had a bad experience today. This student was his own worst enemy. He was so wrapped up in how his playing felt, how to do things, and he always had some crazy gimmick going on. For example, he wanted to play his full register on the rim [visualizer]. All I want is the lower range on the rim so you can get more of a feel of an embouchure vibrating with low air pressure. As your embouchure shortens, it actually becomes a few millimeters long in the extreme high register. Up there, the air pressure will go way up in trying to make an audible sound on the rim. The feel factor will also go way down and you'll have resistance and closure. This is a very unhealthy way to play. He came here today and he could hardly play. All I want from playing on the rim is to get the sensation of buzzing in the low register.

No matter what I told him to do or think, he would still fight the horn. I got him to play well with the Ernest Williams method, but as soon as he played his excerpts, he went back to sounding bad. I know that this is in his psychology. I had people like that in the past, but they were on drugs and I don't like that either.

The Mind-Lip Connection – The Use of the Rim

Make sure your tongue is a small little tongue inside your mouth. This is to allow a thick air column to go toward your lip. Playing with a thin air column is similar to pushing with one finger rather than with your whole hand. If you *sing* in your head, your buzzing will tend to clear up right away. Try to go to your brain first and forget about your lip. Your lip will take care of itself if you *sing* loudly in your head (even if you have to play softly). Find each note in your head and not in your lip.

Buzzing the rim [visualizer] exposes the lack of mental control and the lack of taking charge of your music. It's also a marvelous tool for connecting the air and the embouchure. Make sure you play each note in tune. Don't guide your lip, but instead guide your mind by *singing* each note. Trust your brain and avoid taking charge of your embouchure. Always use your middle range when you buzz the rim.

At first, you might not buzz well on the rim. It takes a heck of a good player to play a lot of music on the rim.

Making Mistakes

Allow a mistake or two to happen, but you have to make the next note better. Not every note has to be better but, of course, you try. Remember that when things go wrong, you must find out what was going on in your brain first and not what was going on in your lip. This is because the brain has to give the right stimuli for the reflexes in the embouchure to function. Don't allow the brain to shut off because you won't have a source of stimuli for the lip. As a result, your lip might go blank.

The Biocomputer

If you start the first 20 minutes of your playing day with something that captures your imagination, that will put you in a highly musical mode that encourages easy tone production. You'll also see that everything else gets easier for the rest of the day.

You must always memorize your tone quality. You must have wonderful models of excellence in your mentalizations. I always like to think of the regions above the brain stem as the biocomputer levels of the brain. It takes orders from you and tries to give you whatever you want. However, you must mentalize what you want because that's the language your biocomputer understands.

All the brain activities concerning muscular adjustments are subconscious, but they are based on the orders you give to the lower brain regions. What I am saying here in that somewhere along the way you have to make sure you don't become somewhat jaded. You have to give orders as an artist in your brain (dictating what you want). It should be like an actor going into a new city trying to sell the same act to a new audience. Everything renews itself. You've got to play that way.

Programming the Biocomputer

When you learn something new, it doesn't have to be perfect right away. It's like programming a biocomputer in that you are adding information to your memory bank. With time, your playing gets easier and better. In other words, things that are hard this Saturday will be easier two Saturdays from now and even easier six months from now. In a year, you'll think nothing of it because it's already in your memory banks. You just have to be patient because you have to do many good repetitions daily. For example, the memory banks in your brain will be empty for playing music that jumps two octaves if you haven't played music that jumps octaves. Later on, when you have had more experience with music that jumps octaves, playing octaves will be easier because it will be in your memory banks. This might take hundreds or thousands of repetitions over the next few months or years.

The big challenges don't have to be done daily, but you have to do them frequently. When meeting a big challenge, don't play by mere muscular strength, but instead play by controlling the music your way. You must always have the tune in your head. You'll use more or less strength as needed, but that's not important anyway. Music is important! The quality of the individual notes is what's important!

Motor and Sensory Nerves

I want you to send the pitch into the cup of the mouthpiece and you do that by first *singing* it in your head. That's the whole point because what's happening now is that your brain is shutting off. In other words, since you are a student of psychology you know about sensory and motor nerves. Today you are predominantly functioning based on your attitude toward sensory nerves. It should be toward motor nerves so it's a message going outward for somebody else. You are playing by reading instead of interpreting. You are reading for yourself as when you read a newspaper. Don't do that! Read for the audience. Teach them what's on the page.

Listening to Your Own Playing

The psychomotor activity in the act of playing picks up some brain activity so you are not only listening to your sound, but you are also feeling your sound. There are many other complications with that. However, as a performer, you'll be different from your audience members because you are on the sending end and they are on the receiving end. When you get a chance, listen to music from the perspective of an audience member. Maybe you can record yourself and listen to the tape later. Once you listen to the tape, you'll quickly know what you like or dislike. You want to have your interpretation at the same level or above as that of your competition.

Mental Fatigue in Practice – Improvement to Higher Stages

Sometimes it's not only lip fatigue as it's mental fatigue. It's also a muscular disorganization that gradually sets in. The main point is that your playing requires stimuli from the brain to innervate your muscles. As the stimuli start to lessen in the brain, there will be less stimuli for the lips. In other words, your lips don't have to work just because you blow. They are like vocal chords and they need a constant renewing message in the brain—just as if they were a speaker reproducing from a stereo. You just can't do these things by the mechanics of brass playing alone. The human brain works best in small groups of all types. The best thing you can do is to take single phrases and repeat them to improve them. (So you don't play an etude or concerto from top to bottom). You need sections that you repeat. In other words, play your etude or concerto through once and on the second time play it repeating small sections. This way you'll enter into competition with the great artists. The repetition and the building of neural pathways are the things you really need. For you to get better, you don't need to acquire more materials, but instead you need to enter into competition with the great players using the materials you already know.

Artistic Thoughts

You have to hear a human voice *singing* your excerpts to round up your tone. You do this by using your imagination. You'll hear a difference in your tone right away because your embouchure will readily react to the air it gets. Imagination is a great tool. As a scientist, you might appreciate that once you go to the interior of your body, you must use a completely different type of thought processes. This is especially true when compared to the thoughts you would use for the exterior of your body. With the exterior of your body, you take charge of the details of function, but for playing a brass instrument, you must use your imagination to create artistic thoughts. In other words, your biocomputer will pick up your mentalizations and it will give you what you want, but you have to learn to communicate with it. You must do it through artistic imaginary situations. You must hear a voice *singing* "TOH, TOH, TOH, TOH." By *singing* "TOH," you are getting the space you need inside your mouth to get the thick air you need. Your tongue must get small and out of the way. You don't do that by the study of muscles but instead, you do it by finding a source of stimulus in the brain for the correct reflex response in your tissue.

Imagination and Intuition

Imagination, just like your experiences in real life, is powerful. When you think of some wonderful food, you salivate and if you pretend you have just won the lottery, your heart might start beating fast. You can brighten yourself up with your imagination. In other words, you influence your body tremendously by imagining things or situations. Imagination is indeed a powerful tool.

Intuition is similar to a computer read out. Many things flash in the mind. Very frequently, the first ones are right—not always—but very frequently. It's amazing how much you can depend on your imagination. What you have to get rid of in brass playing is self-analysis. You can analyze sounds, musical qualities, phrase, rhythms, sonorities, but never yourself. Now, there are focal thoughts for your brain, but always 85% or 90% of your playing should be the concept of *Song* in your brain. That's the message you want your audience to hear—like a great storyteller or a great singer. Maybe the other 15% has to do with other aspects such as air flow.

There is always the danger that you are blowing hard to force the air out. Blowing hard summons natural reinforcements where you get additional pseudo muscular movements that you don't want. If you have a good imagination, you can pretend there is nothing in the way—you forget about the mouthpiece and the instrument—so huge quantities of air flow outward as if you were *singing*. *Song* and a mass of *Wind*! Not *Song* and muscular strength! Can you simplify your thoughts and go my way? Try it and see what happens.

Don't control your lips, but instead you must imitate the sound you hear in your head. As soon as you imitate, your playing will be fine. Work your brain out, not your lips. Your lips will work as a response to a stimulus. You must supply that stimulus.

You should form a mental picture of what you should sound like in your brain before you play. Try to formalize this approach so when you look at the ink spots on the page, you convert them into sounds in your head. You must always hear the pitch as well as your interpretation by using your imagination.

Brain Potentials in Learning

Can you see how your playing changes according to how you think? I want you to realize that because this is your deficit. You are an intelligent person so when

Appendix B: Mental Aspects

I tell you this don't think of anything personal. It's just that we all have strengths and weaknesses. There are people who think in different ways and they all have different excellences. There are people who have marvelous abilities to think in terms of shapes, color, and space. These people make great artists with the brush and canvas. There are wonderful people in mathematics who have great relations to symbols and logic. There are people who have wonderful recall and imagination of tonal color. Almost like the taste of food, they have it as tastes of musical sounds. It takes all sorts of people to make this world.

Now, something that is not generally recognized is that everybody has some element of everything. That will depend on your cultural heritage, your genes, and on the challenges that you faced early in life. There is no such thing as being tone deaf. That's a lot of non-sense. Probably it was that the recall and recognition challenges were not met at an early age, but that doesn't mean that they can't be initiated later in life. What I am trying to say is that your brass playing is higher than your musicianship. In other words, you have developed your playing abilities with all sorts of fingerings and techniques. Now, I have to get you to be a storyteller of sound. You have to take charge of the emotions and inflections in music.

As I listen to the state of the art form of music, I notice that each generation learns faster. They learn from what the previous generation has to offer so they can just move ahead and go far. When their time comes, the same will happen with their younger generation. I know that when I was young, I was way ahead of my teacher in just a few years. It was simply that I was interested in many more musical things than he was. I think that was the main difference. Today, the same thing is happening with my students as they are interested in so many things than I. Soon, they will be ahead of me. It always goes this way. I have also noticed the difference in their learning. There is much faster learning going on today. I don't have to nearly spend the time I used to doing remedial teaching.

In general, it's going well. Your tone quality is far better than average now. You ear training is still a problem. Now, weaknesses become strengths. If you just think of progress as a graph that keeps moving up. Bud Herseth is up high and most good trumpet players are a bit below, but you are here (lower) because of your ear training. Your playing ability is far better than your ear training indicates. Now, it doesn't take long to make progress and if you keep this up for years to come, you'll find yourself going higher and higher. If you have the persistence, you can go up right next to Bud and maybe pass him.

Don't try to turn on your abilities instantly, but instead turn on your artistry instantly. That's very important. Recognize that you have to go through a period of conditioning and the whole point is how you challenge yourself in your head—that is, in the way you think. This is the key to the whole thing. Your ability to conceive in your brain is already large, but your recognition and recall is not to that point yet. Think it's like a graph where you have high points and low points. The lower points have to be brought up.

You have made a lot of progress and we want you to go onto the next stage. Each time you make a lot of progress—instead of becoming complaisant—we suddenly increase the challenge. That frustrates my students to no end, but that's not the point. We can't rest on our laurels. We have to constantly go up the ladder of improvement.

Graphs, Challenges, and the Ladder of Improvement

What made you improve so far is that you responded to a series of challenges. Some I presented to you and some others you found as you played in the ensembles or in practice, but either way you always have been able to climb up the ladder of improvement. In other words, what you couldn't do in November you were able to do the following January. The time factor is so great because your graph was down here when you started in November and it's much higher now in January. You always look for the accumulation of abilities.

There are certain skills and concepts that I would expect be occurring in tandem in your stages of development. Your tone has improved (it has thicken up), but it still needs the openness Bud Herseth gets when he plays.

Personality Types

There are personality problems in music performance. You might have a student who has a personality that doesn't get exited and enthusiastic over certain aspects of playing. If that student would use her imagination or study acting, then she would find that if you imitate an extroverted person, even if you are an introverted person, you become an extroverted person at that moment. On the other hand, if you are an extroverted person and you want to imitate an introverted person, you can also do that. You become what you imitate. The human brain is a magnificent tool and you

Appendix B: Mental Aspects

have the capacity of accomplishing what you want, but you must have the ability of approaching it through your imagination. Just as if you were an actor who pretends and makes believe.

Ear Training

Can you hear the notes in silence? It's hearing the notes in silence that counts. It's with the recall of pitches and ear training that you'll begin to sense improvements and become a more stable player.

Challenge precedes development. Think of the pitch and then sing it. Challenge yourself! Stop and think of it in your head. Then play it on your instrument. You'll find that your instrument will always sound better after you sing. You must use names for the notes you sing (that's the principle behind *solfège*). The names you put to the pitches could be letter names or numbers. Like a great singer, you should depend on the *Song* aspects of music making.

I can't think of any other shortcut for improving brass playing than the study of *solfège*. Accept this study to be a long-term goal (for about ten years). It will take you a week to notice positive changes in your playing, but in two years, your playing will sparkle because of this study. That's a promise!

Motivation plus repetition is the important thing in ear training. You must practice pitch recall so the periods of silence are the important ones. By that I mean, can you hear a "D" right now? It's maybe a bit vague in your mind's ear, but that doesn't matter right now. Turn up the volume in your head and make it a *fortissimo*. Like a big bell ringing in your head, hear that big "D."

You'll benefit from doing intensive ear training on your own. Get an electronic *Casio* keyboard because they are very accurate in pitch. As you practice, don't go sharp or flat while you sing or buzz. After a while, your discrimination of pitch becomes very acute. In some electronic keyboards, you can bend the pitch and recognize the pitch differences.

Using Fingerings – Advanced Ear Training

As you sing, finger your instrument because that's part of the connection between your mind and your playing. That will also tend to recall the pitch. Play a high "A." Do you think you could have sung it? Sing it. Do you hear it now? The trick is to actually hear the sound in your head before you play it. You'll benefit from doing this exercise. It's not 100% success because there is always a little fluctuation between how you sing the note in your head and how it comes out the bell.

This is not a simple subject. It's very complex but as you challenge yourself in singing, you'll bring many of your playing problems to the surface. They will clear right up as you repeat this exercise. Avoid having a conflict between what it feels like and what you expected it to feel like. Go by the pitch in your head instead. Turn up the volume in your head!

Missed Notes

Missed notes are poisonous. They spoil everything so you shouldn't miss them because you have control over this. In other words, you should hear each note as you play it so your muscles know what to do. The thing about accuracy is that the player who has good pitch recall and retention can be very accurate. That's why I suggest ear training for brass players. Use a keyboard and sing along in *solfège*, but do it in your own vocal range (i.e., you don't have to match your instrument's range). Learn the various intervals using familiar tunes (e.g., Use the *NBC* Logo Theme for learning the major sixth). You know so much music by now that you can find the appropriate tune to learn your intervals. It's important that we improve your pitch recall and recognition by singing. It's an unfortunate mistake for schools not to offer *solfège* classes.

The Use of Syllables for Singing

The use of a word (or syllable) is going to enhance your brain activity when playing music. Because it will take more brainpower to pronounce that word as you play, you are going to make the whole excerpt stronger by the simple diction of each note. Use numbers or syllables and you'll find out that you'll be more successful. This is especially helpful in fast passages.

Having One Instrument in Your Head and One in Your Hand

Can I get you to be more of a singer in your head? Play down your instrument quite a bit, but play up the *Song* in your head. So again, you are dealing with reflexes

APPENDIX B: MENTAL ASPECTS   173

in your embouchure that respond to the stimuli in your head. Can you increase the stimulus? You do this by creating each phrase by its individual notes. Remember, there should be two voices: one in your head and one coming out your instrument's bell. The voice coming out of your instrument should be a mirror of the one in your head.

This runs throughout the whole brass family. Don't let your old habits and methodologies return anymore. Can you instead get more into the art form? The important thing is to sound good! In other words, I need more of the musician and the storyteller and less of the brass player.

There is always a feedback factor coming back through your sensory system of about 10% or 15%. That is, you can hear yourself as you play. It's better if instead you play by sending messages outward—like when you are talking to somebody else. Go as far as you can with this approach. I would much prefer if you exaggerate this aspect of music making. Recognize that you are a human being. The human body is a magnificent machine and, in your brain, it has a whole set of buttons to make it function. Your task is not to be caught up in the feel of the machine, but instead you must find the buttons that cause it to function. There is simplicity in this process and the simplicity is in how you work with your message in your head. When you keep your thoughts simple and directed toward what you want to accomplish, it will be easier for you to play

Receiving and Sending Information

You must realize that you don't play by listening to yourself play. That's playing by asking questions. We receive information by asking questions, but we impart information by issuing statements. Then you'll enter into show business the way you should. We need to issue musical statements with enthusiasm. Use your imagination and think of how great you can sound. This way you become a storyteller of sound.

Fascination with the Acoustical Device

This whole business of performance can be tricky because there is a strong tendency of becoming fascinated with the acoustical device and making that your focus because it's fun. That's all right, but let it fall into place very quickly. Once you get past that, you get to the part of our profession where you play for your audience members and you watch for their facial expressions as you play. Again, that's based on psychomotor activity. We learn through sensors and we impart information through motor activity.

We don't want massive learning experiences to begin when we are transferring knowledge. That's musical knowledge is this case (e.g., playing music for somebody else). We want to make sure we stay within the guidelines that govern our mind-body relationship. That's the basis of my teaching; finding out what we are in life and transferring that to our work in music.

I cooperate with nature in the sense that I study long and hard how our bodies work in many ways—in sickness, in health, and in music—as well as in other areas. You'll soon find that you don't have senses in your muscles, but instead you have divisions in the brain where muscle sensitivity exists at subconscious levels. People think that muscle sensitivity starts in the lip, but it's not there. Muscle sensitivity works at various levels in your brain. If you learn to use your head by honest simple thoughts, you'll learn to communicate with your body. You have to communicate in a language your body will understand. In other words, if you want to touch your nose, you simply touch your nose. Your body understands that because it's a clear goal you want to achieve. If you start rationalizations and peripheral thinking, you'll lose the mind-body communication right away.

Playing with a Sense of Authority

Even when you are wrong, I need to ask for more authority in your interpretation. In addition, you should pay more attention to your attitude. A positive attitude is very important for a musician in terms of confidence even when you know it's not deserved. However, you've got to play music with authority. If you miss, you miss, but you'll find that you'll miss much less if you play with authority.

You are beginning to play music too much like reading a book at home, "Once upon a time in a far off land there lived a little boy, and his name was Joe." In front of an audience that becomes, "ONCE UPON A TIME IN A FAR OFF LAND THERE LIVED A LITTLE BOY AND HIS NAME WAS JOE." There is a big difference between words interpreted for you and words interpreted for an audience. With a lot of teaching, there is chance that you are playing for yourself. We must be in an art form where we work for audiences.

Positive Attitude

Can you clarify your thoughts more and pay less attention to your embouchure? If you miss a note, the next note has to be better. That's one thing that Bud Herseth has that's remarkable. If he does something wrong, the next thing is better.

You must have a positive attitude because everything in your playing depends on stimuli for conditioned reflexes. That means that if your brain is worried because something went wrong, at that moment you'll fail to give the stimulus for your muscles to function. Then you have old habits lingering in and you won't be able to be predictable anymore.

With a positive attitude, you are in charge. As long as you are in the music profession, you must secure your mentalizations and not your physicalizations. I coined the term mentalization because I don't think it exists. The idea is that you should play as a singer would sing. The vocal chords receive the message from the brain based on what the singer is communicating to someone else. The embouchure must act like the vocal chords of a singer.

Psychomotor Activity

If you were an actor and you had to act on stage—playing different roles and portraying different emotions—that would be the type of training necessary to play a brass instrument in front of an audience. The idea is that it doesn't have to feel good, but you have to be able to talk to your audience with your instrument. That way you'll become the teacher teaching your audience how your music sounds. It's a matter of allowing your nervous system to operate and the only way it can do that is by you imparting knowledge to someone else.

When you are nervous up there (on stage), you'll be imparting information to yourself because you'll be feeling what you are doing. Your blood pressure will go up and your heart will start pounding. You can't do that. You have to tell a story to someone else. It's not a matter of relaxation. It's a matter of *singing* for your audience. So if your lip feels bad, so what!

It's all psychomotor so we use our nervous system to impart knowledge like when talking to somebody. It's very much like singing. Once you get that attitude, your playing will go very well.

Artistic Attitude for Performance

Right now, if you set a challenge in the brain, it will go directly to the lips due to your conditioned reflexes. You are afraid of the upper notes, but you don't have to be afraid anymore. Your confidence will grow with repeated successes. You've got to trust the stimuli you are creating in your head. You tend to avoid it because of the feel factor. Don't do that. As an artist, *sing* in the head! Then *sing* while you play. It's going to be hard work, but who said it was going to be easy anyway?

Remember that brass playing is not what you are after. Musicianship and artistry is what you are after. Your instrument is just a piece of brass with no brains. In other words, you are the artist so you have to keep developing as a storyteller of sound. Your instrument is just the medium that you go through to tell your story. Don't keep fighting it.

Achieving good mental concentration is difficult if you are nervous. The "run or fight syndrome" will tend to take over and take your musicianship with it. One of the things Adolph Herseth told me about the players who have auditioned for the Chicago Symphony Orchestra trumpet openings is that they had a general lack of musicianship; too much forcing and crudity in their playing. It's almost as if they are having too much of a student approach. Instead they should think, "How would a great violinist interpret this music?"

The big thing about music, or any other art form, is that you can enjoy what you are doing, but others must also enjoy it. Its orientation should be like drawing a beautiful picture on canvas for others to enjoy. When you are playing a solo, you are not playing for yourself, but for the people who are listening.

Performance Consistency

Performance consistency always comes from consistency in the brain so anything that tends to knock your thinking off will affect you. If you can simplify your thoughts, you can keep your consistency. However, if you are *foggy* in your mind, then you'll have a problem. If you have a chance to sing a little, you'll have a chance to start up your brain. (You can carry a pitch pipe with you to get the pitch you need). This will get your brain "pepped up" because this is where the help is needed. You don't need the organization in your embouchure, but instead you need the organization in your brain.

Higher Levels of Development

You must take charge of your new musical concepts each time you play. Don't rely on your old playing habits. Play with your new musical concepts when you play your daily drill forms (e.g., Max Schlossberg's *Daily Drills*). The drill forms are necessary to fill in the technical and artistic gaps in your playing that come from the imbalance found in the orchestra repertoire you are practicing. The health of the player depends on a healthy musical diet. Keep your new positive habits by playing your drill forms daily. It only takes minutes a day.

Some players don't have a musical life that will lead them in a steady progress toward becoming the great artists most of them have a potential of becoming. Without certain advantages in terms of ensemble playing, you might not have enough experience. This is because you are not doing the sufficient amount of playing in professional ensembles where others are making judgments about your playing. If that's the case, you have to rely more on your own insights because you are not being guided by a brass section or by a conductor. You have to set high standards for yourself and recognize that there might be *plateaus* in your playing. You have to understand that every time you take a new piece, there will be new challenges you need to overcome.

Keep raising your standards and keep competing with great artists like Bud Herseth. Don't be afraid of mistakes because you won't discover anything if you are afraid. Do whatever you have to do to find these answers. Find out what works for you. A lot of things that Bud did when he was young he did because he didn't give in to the fact that there were difficulties involved. He earned his stars doing things the hard way for his own education.

You must take new challenges slowly at first for the sake of understanding the music. Once you gain that understanding, you can extrapolate your music to what, for example, the Chicago Symphony Orchestra would do with it. You have to imitate players who have already arrived. Then you have to set their standards as yours. Playing all isolated in your practice room won't do it. You can also play recitals or play in a good brass quintet.

If you are challenged with music—so you stop thinking about the mechanics of your instrument and instead you put emphasis on your sound, the emotions that go with your music, and the colors of tone—you'll improve much faster. You have to always tell a story. You must be a storyteller of sound.

APPENDIX C

MUSICIANSHIP AND INTERPRETATION

Preview

• *I need you to imitate artistry. To do that, you have to pretend to be a great artist.*
• *When you have a story associated with your music, it's much easier to phrase.*
• *The small details make the difference between a good player and a great player.*
• *Think of an accompaniment for each tune you play.*
• *If you are around great musicians, all the interpretative nuances are much easier to pick up than if you are alone at home practicing.*
• *Playing out of tune is more important than missing a note because playing out of tune is an indication that you are not aware of it, while missing might be an accident.*
• *Most of the top-notch players are in the center of the pitch all the time; where they get the most amplification for the least effort possible.*
• *When you are in an ensemble situation and you are not the boss, even if you are right, you have to follow the ensemble.*
• *While sight-reading, you still have to interpret the music for your audience.*
• *You must make sure you are interpreting the music just as if you were reading a children's storybook (animated to entertain your audience). Don't just read the music as if you were reading the daily news (as if when reading to yourself). You have to develop as a general storyteller. This will pay-off big in our profession.*
• *You have to play in rhythm because the embouchure has to work in rhythm, the breath has to work in rhythm, and the tongue has to have the rhythm. When everything is in rhythm, it's easier to play.*

Developing musicianship, interpretation, and aesthetics sometimes takes the experience of being on stage while reading many types of "stories" to an audience.

You always have to "ham up" your stories so you become entertaining when you read. That is, dramatic when you need to be dramatic, funny when you need to be funny, and sad when you need to be sad. If I could just get you in one walk of life to be like that, you could then transfer that sense of storytelling to music. Take a chapter of a book at home and make it come to life. As the creative part of your mind awakens, you'll find that it will make your brass playing easier.

I was always a ham. I was in the movies when I was a little boy. I don't know anything about those movies, but I remember that I was paid five dollars and was given an ice cream cone. As you see, I was brought up in show business. My mother was always playing the piano in movie theaters and I used to see the movies for nothing. (She played for the silent movies in Hollywood). There was a lot of show business in my family so I came to realize that much of what we do in performance is based on extroversion.

I need you to imitate artistry. To do that, you have to pretend to be a great artist. For example, if you have to pretend that you are dying, you can't do it by really dying. However, you have seen enough films of people dying so you can imitate the actors. Those actors have studied how to pretend to die with doctors guiding them through the dying process. If you want great joy, you don't have to jump fences or eat an ice cream cone to attain it. All you need is to respond to a feeling of joy. This approach will pay off in our art form.

If Adolph Herseth would put his brain in your head—given your current physical structure—you would be a magnificent trumpet player. You have the development for very fine playing. We have to recognize that your musicianship has to be brought up now. That means that you have to study artistry by listening to great artists. Study the subtleties of their phrasing, their sense of rhythm, and how they interpret music at different levels. Listen to fine violinists, fine singers, and all other fine interpreters of music. In other words, learn all about stylistic playing in all genres.

Make sure you become a fine musician and an interpreter by becoming a storyteller of sound. Play ethnic music from one country and then turn right around and play the ethnic music of another country. This is marvelous because it keeps your brain working and it connects your brain with your tissues—yielding beautiful results.

You must make sure you are interpreting the music just as if you were reading a children's storybook (animated to entertain your audience). Don't just read the music as if you were reading the daily news (as if when reading to yourself). You have to develop as a general storyteller. This will pay-off big in our profession.

The Art of Phrasing

I went to a class at the Curtis Institute of Music in Philadelphia that taught us many suggestions on how to phrase. They didn't teach us rules of phrasing. Instead, we studied the *crescendos*, *diminuendos*, and the changing of pulse between down pulses and up-pulses to give us ideas on phrasing. Real phrasing has to come from the performer. If it helps, you can pretend you are singing the lyrics of a song. I studied voice for many years so my phrasing is more from the vocal school. I studied phrasing instrumentally as well. The idea is that you can have various versions of the same phrase. You take a set of notes and you do them in many styles.

In phrasing, there could be a consistent use of small *crescendos* and *diminuendos*, which lead from one note to the next. You can put a little lift in some of the notes or you can smooth out some of the others. Put some *vibrato* in one section or take it away for another section. There are many tools you can use when learning to phrase. You can experiment with phrasing when you are learning a piece of music. In the orchestra, I phrase depending on the part I am playing. For example, in Gustav Mahler's *Symphony No. 6* there is a tuba part that whenever I played it, Georg Solti used to smile. A number of other conductors used to come and congratulate me on my phrasing after concerts. I just did it for myself since I thought nobody would notice the tuba part. These little details in some of the major orchestral works are very important. For instance, in the symphonies of Mahler there are ethnic flavors in some of the parts so in one beat you might have to go up and down in dynamics— little *crescendos* and *diminuendos*. Those details keep you mentally focused and very close to the character of the music. You must keep up the study of phrasing along with the other things you are doing in your playing.

Whether I was playing solo or *soli*—like when I used to play with Bud [Adolph Herseth] two octaves apart—I would adjust my phrasing to his. Whatever he would do, I would try to adjust to it two octaves lower. If it was my own part, I would phrase it according to my own concept, but I would usually create a phrase. I would try not to play a straight line.

If you hear a singer, you usually hear wonderful story telling and phrasing because she has a story to tell with her music—she has lyrics. For example, you can hear the subtleties when a singer sings a love song. When you have a story associated with the music, it's much easier to phrase. The idea is that words have meaning. You can put lyrics to your solos and excerpts as you *sing* them. You can emphasize some words more than others depending on their meaning. The idea is for you to experiment, record yourself, and then listen to the playback. For example, you can play *America the Beautiful* as a march or as a choral piece and see what you think once you listen to the playback. It might be a bit embarrassing at first and you might not know what you are doing, but after you listen to the playbacks a few times, you will start making decisions about your phrasing.

You can also imitate other people's phrasing; although there might be people who criticize you for doing so. So what! It's like programming a computer. You've got to have something in your brain first before you can draw it out. So imitate, learn from it, and gradually create your own phrasing.

As a brass player and musician, if you hear another brass player's phrasing you might be able to analyze it. You might also be aware of what he is doing differently from the norm. There are few people who are able to analyze phrasing, but you could find many who simply enjoy phrasing. By imitating others, you are getting the raw materials so you can work on your own artistic ideas. Take one portion of your practice—perhaps 15 or 20 minutes—to work on phrasing. You have to find, however, the appropriate music to study phrasing. You can play love songs or some music that has some sadness or sorrow. You can make music that makes people laugh as well.

I would first take songs because the meaning of the words can carry you along. Take some children's songs and later take some show tunes. Take small sections and begin to establish how a singer would phrase and how you would copy that on your instrument. Listen to a wide variety of interpretations because the various artists will phrase in different ways. If you know the words, you know where the phrase ends as well as the nuances involved in the song. As a singer, I studied phrasing for three years in school. As you get more into the profession, you start to think about these things naturally.

Building the Musical Phrase by the Individual Notes

Don't play by the phrase, but instead play by the individual notes. As an artist, you must play by the individual notes so audiences can hear the phrase. You must narrow down your mental focus to the note you are playing now so there is a stimulus for a reflex. If you are playing by the phrase, your mind is playing the whole phrase the same way the audience hears a phrase. Don't do that! Create the phrase by the individual notes. Each note as it comes! You put each individual note into a series, but your brain has to put in the stimulus for each individual note—one note at a time. You can't do it by listening to yourself play, but instead you have to do it by conceiving of each note individually.

If I let these aspects of your playing go by without correcting them, I would be doing you a disservice. The small details make the difference between a good player and a great player. It's not the large details. It's important to take great care of the small details. The details need high quality of pitch, sound, and rhythm. The shorter the duration of the note, the greater care you must use. Great playing is in the details!

If I get the feeling you are absorbing the motivation I am giving you, then I trust you can work the rest of it at home. My task is to try to get the understanding required to guide your thought process.

Now, playing music is like telling a story to somebody else. If I said, "I brought a rain coat with me just in case when I leave the building it rains. I don't want to get soaked because I have to use the same clothes tomorrow." When I talked to you, you can visualize the rain and you have my reasoning for it. I had to build all that out of individual words.

As this point in your development, you are used to listening to other musicians play the same phrases you are playing. As a result, you know these phrases from having heard them. The tendency then is to play them back based on the phrases you've already heard. These phrases are lines of tone. When you start with a line of tone, there is a great danger that you'll lose the source of stimulus for the individual notes and somewhere the tone will stop—then you'll lose control. Your playing will break down and there will be all sorts of puffs. That won't happen if instead you build the phrase by the individual notes—just as I am building phrases out of individual words.

A sentence is a phrase made out of words. This is important because every note in here builds the phrase. The big danger—I know after 60 years of teaching—is that you are going to focus on blowing, feeling, and looking at the music, but playing music requires a reflex response to a stimulus. Now, if your reflexes are in good standing, you'll get by, but if they are "border line," you can lose control of the song.

It's very important for somebody in our profession to know that all human beings work by habit and by prior conditioning. You have built your conditioning by listening to other musicians. That's fine. Listening is the acquisition of knowledge coming in through the ear to the brain and we all need that. Your tone production doesn't depend on your blowing, your buzzing, or your fingering. Your tone production depends on your ability to *sing* each note with your lip. That's especially true because you could blow from now until doomsday and never have it right. You can also look perfect and play incorrectly. For you, half hour a day on concentrated practice on this subject will change your playing for the better. It's a way of thinking that will pay off in this profession.

Up Impulse Followed by a Down Impulse – Marcel Tabuteau

When I was studying phrasing with Marcel Tabuteau [former principal oboe of the Philadelphia Orchestra and teacher at the Curtis Institute of Music], he had something called an up impulse followed by a down impulse. Can you think of that excerpt as an up and down start? The little change of inflection has a lot of meaning. The upbeat should be "up-downnnn." Can you sense the style of the attack? It's the way the notes begin. Even in the soft passages, put in the rhythm of the phrase. There must be rhythm to the entrance, "up-downnnn."

Do sing the entry note of your solo before you play it. Make a habit of this practice. This way you'll develop a fine pitch recall. Remember that the note that come after a rest is the most important. There you pay attention to the beginning note in terms of quality and pitch.

Dynamic Control in Phrasing

You have to figure out how fast you want to come down in your *diminuendos* or how fast you want to come up in your *crescendos*. You can scale your dynamics as you do with your pitch scales—e.g., from *piano* to *forte* and back to *piano*.

When I studied with Fritz Reiner [at the Curtis Institute of Music], he would ask for a *decrescendo* and I would hear what he wanted in my head. This approach will work nicely with the psychology of playing a musical instrument. Study other people, see how they phrase, and imitate them. This is how you learn to interpret fine music.

Nuances in Phrasing

I want you to go home and record yourself playing the Franz Joseph Haydn's *Trumpet Concerto* and compare it to Bud's [Adolph Herseth] version. Make sure you include all the *crescendos* and *diminuendos* involved in the piece. The subtleties of playing have to be there. When I sang just now, I had the nuances of interpretation. I might be criticized for over doing it, but it's easier to come down from over doing than to come up from under doing.

There are details young players miss in their phrasing. It's just little things—like the up and down impulses taught by Marcel Tabuteau—that make the difference. If you are around great musicians, all the interpretative nuances are much easier to pick up than if you are alone at home practicing. You must study the multiplicity of styles available to us today and notice their nuances in phrasing.

You must also have enough of a change of dynamics for people to notice your interpretive nuances. You must interpret and stylize. Make a big issue out of your sense of artistry. Overdo some of the interpretation. Go ahead! You can always bring it down later. Demand great interpretation out of your music making. As you interpret a larger variety of music, you are making a stronger bridge between your thoughts and your muscle tissue. Get a tighter grip of your music with your brain and not with your lip.

Introducing a Sense of Authority in the Student's Interpretations

I want to introduce the psychology of playing with authority in the student's interpretations. Some students have had too much grounding over the years in insecure playing. Everything a human being repeats is habit forming—even insecurity. Then the brain will accept insecurity as a norm.

You need to have more preparation in the *Song* aspects of brass playing. The teacher can play a pitch on the keyboard and the student can play back the pitch on the mouthpiece. With this exercise, you make sure the student goes more by the pitch than by the lip. Make each pitch authoritative in your brain. If the student is not confident with his pitch, it will show in the student's over all recital, concert, or audition preparation.

Increase the strength of your mentalizations. Make sure you don't get distracted. The messages to the lip must come from the brain. Always protect that.

Make sure you are less aware of the feel of the embouchure and more aware of your mentalizations. Then all you have to do is take enough air so you have a surplus and *sing*!

Sometimes, the application of your mentalization is insecure in terms of quality of tone (it lacks resonance). Put yourself on the stage of Orchestra Hall [Chicago] and imagine that you have to play a solo right after Adolph Herseth. He has just played your solo beautifully and the audience in clapping. Can you hear him playing? Now you go play and compete with him!

In some of the concertos you've learned, you've prepared as a student. Your preparation has been by the individual notes and not enough on the overall interpretation of the piece. You should hear recordings of great interpreters playing your concerto and then you should imitate their style. As you imitate other people's styles, you'll soon find that you can create your own style. That is similar to learning to play jazz. You must have a model from which you work.

There should be diversity in your approach so you can play in various styles. Learn a little about the commercial style by listening to commercial recordings. A beautiful ballad like *Body and Soul* or *Stardust* would do. You play them as if you are on the job. You pretend you are in the bandstand and you are playing for your audience. I was in that business for a while, so I know what they do.

Sometimes I need over interpretation from the students who play here in the studio. They can always back off later. I'd rather have the music over-phrased than under-phrased. Make the little changes more noticeable so the audience can tell you are changing dynamics.

When you play a lyrical passage softly, you have to play it with a positive sense of pitch. You have to play almost like if you were an actor and you were going to cry, but at that moment, don't let it go too far into mush. If you over do it, there will be a change in the qualities of your music. Instead, you must always suit the style and character of the composition. On the other hand, you must keep more of the brass playing aspects when playing fanfares so you get more into the brass family. A musician has to expect to be excited. There is no way you can be a fine musician and just be placid and dull. Life involves many exciting experiences and you express those experiences in music—just like an actor would.

Interpret your music based on a story line. Once the emotions of the story start to unfold, find out what the piece is about. Then your interpretation will make more sense. Even if it doesn't, you are still interpreting your own way following a story line. We are storytellers of sound. I think that's what Bud [Adolph Herseth] has in mind too. As you study a piece of music, you might find that you want to make a few changes. I would also try to look up the story line of some of the pieces you are playing to know what the singer is singing about.

Put lyrics to your music. Treat your music as a singer and not as a brass player. Be conscious of your mentalizations. The minute you change instruments (e.g., from Bb trumpet to piccolo trumpet or from B-flat tuba to F tuba), there is going to be a different feel and as you know, feel can be disruptive. One of the many nice things about playing different instruments is that you can't depend on feel. It allows you the freedom of more creative thinking. Think of a day when you lose all of your instruments and you have to entertain an audience with your mouthpiece. Whatever you do, you must always approach your music as an artist.

You have a graph with some low points and some other points of high improvement. You have to bring the low points up. I must have the sense of virtuoso brass playing when I hear you play. I need you to do a little more in your personal practice with your imagination of musical styles. You can pretend you are on stage playing with the Long Beach Municipal Band. Put yourself in competition with Herbert L. Clarke. Surprise yourself because soon you might start sounding like him. Don't play in monotones with a brass instrument. Put meaning to your playing and add a sense of storytelling.

Tone Colors and Interpretation

I want you to be able to play around with tone colors. Move your sound into areas of more roundness and less roundness. I don't want you to play around with pitch. I want you to sound fatter or thinner with lots of fundamentals and overtones. Sometimes, you must associate your playing with the big instruments (like the B-flat trumpet or the bass trombone) even when you are playing the small instruments (like the piccolo or the alto trombone). It's simply a different way of playing, but because you are an artist, you can play all sorts of different ways. There are times and places for all these tone colors. As you experiment with tone colors, you'll also become more comfortable and flexible in your musical interpretations.

A sure way of interpreting music well is to put rhythmical pulses in the right places. If you don't do that, you could be making comfortable music sound difficult. Some players put the pulse on the upbeat and make the music sound off. Some other players play the notes equal [with no accents], but their audience might not want to stand up and dance to it.

Interpreting Music in Context

Think of an accompaniment for each tune you play. If it's a waltz think, "UM-PAH-PAH" and blow a rhythmical "HA" into it. Then you'll begin to feel a stronger rhythm coming into your whole body. In the privacy of your practice room, I want to feel the wild rhythm of a waltz. The rhythm that goes into your muscles will begin to tie many things together in your playing. We need the multiplicity of styles and we need the smoothness of playing.

People who don't have this developed need to do this kind of work at some point in their career. This kind of study will also bring physical changes to your body that can't be developed any other way. To "stiff players," this study will bring relaxation and it will bring the ability of doing all the "bowings" and sudden changes required for playing music.

Playing Soprano Arias

You should hear soprano arias sung by a soprano because you get a different musical perspective. Usually, brass players that have heard the song performed by a soprano follow along the lines of the opera. If you don't do this, you might play a different interpretation that's not legitimate in accordance to the composer's meaning. The goal is to have a musical concept and to play it with authority. If the conductor doesn't like it, then you can change it accordingly.

However, keep in mind that when you interpret music you have to go by what the composer had in mind. There are times when music should be ugly and not beautiful. If you want to frighten somebody, you don't play a love song. Instead, you want to play music from a battle scene.

Virtuoso Playing Focal Points

As you go into the more virtuoso playing, start looking for the focal points of rhythm. As it gets to a certain speed, you won't be able to think of the individual notes, but instead you have to think of the downbeats. The "follow through" notes will come anyway if you know the piece. For example, the last variation of J. B. Arban's *Carnaval of Venice* needs the use of focal points. Who is going to think of all those notes at that speed? You have to know where the "1's" are. I always had focal points when I performed that piece.

You can practice the 1's (first beats) alone to get control and then add the other notes. Your reflexes will carry the rest of the notes through, but you must know where each first beat is. You'll see that your reflexes will bring the other notes in. The 1's will "save your neck."

You'll find that when you focus on the downbeats, the notes that follow will fall in place much easier. When you get to know the excerpt, your subconscious will start to pull the music together so you don't have to count every note if you focus on your downbeats.

Stabilizing the Rhythm

When you stabilize your rhythm, you suddenly find that there is an instinct that brings in your notes strongly. If you let all your notes go together, they will begin to rotate and scramble. However, if you stabilize one aspect of your playing (the rhythm), you find that your whole playing improves.

You have to play in rhythm because the embouchure has to work in rhythm, the breath has to work in rhythm, and the tongue has to work in rhythm. When everything is in rhythm, it's going to be very easy to play. There is always trouble if those three elements—embouchure, breath, and tongue—are out-of-sync. The answer lies in coordination. However, you can reduce your practice to one element at a time. In other words, you can practice your fingers by themselves or your blowing by itself and then put the two of them together.

I want you to listen to the small details so you improve them. As a result, your general tone production standard will stay high. That's the difference between a good player and a great player. The idea is not to play by just pressing the valves anymore, but instead play by the song in your head. The notes should be loud and clear in your head.

Repeat excerpts many times so they become part of your technique. You need the pitch recall of each note. You must turn the notes on the page into sound so they become the audiotape in your mind that tells the biocomputer what to do. That's where your concentration has to be.

Loud Playing

You don't need to play very loud to play the brass repertoire in most orchestras. Here in the Chicago Symphony Orchestra we can play with a wide dynamic range because of Bud's [Herseth] capabilities. When I was in Philadelphia, I would go to the concerts and the trumpet players would play big, but it was a comfortable bigness. I listened to some of the European orchestras and they rarely come through with loud volumes. To be able to play loud is great so when the conductor wants it you are able to do it. In general, your interpretation and musicianship should come first and loud dynamics should come second. Volume can be a terrible nuisance value when it's too much.

To play with large volumes, you must open your embouchure a little bit so your lips become slightly longer. Longer surfaces give much more impact to the sound waves. A larger mouthpiece makes it easier as well since you are getting the amplification of the original sound in the cup—while being concentrated and amplified by the shape of your back bore.

When playing loud, don't lose your musicianship. As you start to increase the "violence" of the wind with much higher velocities—as if you were going to destroy your instrument with it—use great imagination. Bad sounds can be made into good sounds. As long as you go back to music, you win.

When you start new physical skills, you won't have the skill. In other words, you'll have crudities during that period. You must convert these crudities into a refined skill by the use of repetition and motivation. The same occurs when you practice the extremes. You'll never have the proficiency in the extremes that you have in *the norms*. What you do is retrace your footsteps. For example, ask yourself, "What made you good in *the norms*?" Then you redo that in the extremes—e.g., you can play little melodies, or sustain notes, or play scales, but whatever you do has to be musical. You don't exceed 20% of your practice time in the extremes. Be willing to have crudeness at first, but increase the quality for greatness.

When you experiment, guide yourself by imitating a great artist or by your creative thinking. Then put all the physical effort you need. It doesn't matter if you fail because it doesn't have to be right all the time. However, you should be properly motivated. You should constantly strive for a great big sound rather than a great big effort. In your practice at home, go for a great big sound. That big sound might include a great big effort. The danger, of course, is to keep going after the great big effort trying to get a great big sound. Do you see the difference in the psychology involved? Simply motivate a great big sound and the great big effort will be part of the big sound. I don't mind excursions into motivating a great big effort to get a big sound, but they should be brief excursions.

Loud playing is somewhat tiring to the chops, but it's different from high playing because it doesn't interfere with the circulation of blood to the lip. It's better to rest a little when playing loud, but it's not as necessary as when you play high. Loud playing will tend to disorganize the muscle fibers in your embouchure because—if it gets out of control—there is a lot of feedback that goes back into the brain.

I want to hear the beginning at maximum volume like if it were four trombones playing at once. Really, *sing* it out, but don't force. You have to take a familiar phrase and play it through various dynamics. Just like the scales you play from low to high and high to low. Do the same with your dynamics. You have to get used being a musician when you play loud. Don't just blast! As your dynamics spread out, everything inside your extended dynamic range becomes easier. This is very healthy for your playing, but it's good to do it in a musical way.

Intonation

Don't worry about your intonation until you first get a clear musical message in your head. Once you have your musical message, then you can tune it. Can you think pretty trumpet when you play lyrical passages? Exaggerate now in the early part of your practice and later on, you can refine it. You can't let the music stand still. Instead, you've got to "milk each note."

Now, playing out of tune is much more important than missing a note because playing out of tune is an indication that you are not aware of it, while missing might be an accident. You've got to be in control of the notes all the time because the seventh cranial nerve transmits that right down to the lip for the reflex response to work. There will be no reflex response without its stimulus. Players take that for granted to—instead of thinking of music—pay attention to how their embouchures feel. This is what the so-called "naturals" avoid all the time. While the naturals are sending clear musical messages down their seventh cranial nerves, the other players are trying to learn fingerings and embouchure and don't play as well.

Most of the top-notch players are in the center of the pitch all the time where they get the most amplification for the least effort possible. In addition, your

Appendix C: Musicianship and Interpretation

pitch shouldn't rise when you *diminuendo*. If you are holding the embouchure by the strength of the breath, as you back off the breath, the embouchure might get smaller on you. If your lip is firm, then the pitch will stay put. The point is to always keep tuning the pitch in your brain.

Using the Strobo-Tuner

Whenever you find there is something wrong with your intonation, make a study out of the principle of pitch recall and recognition. While you are getting the readout from the strobo-tuner, see if you have the same pitch. See if you can get the strobo-tuner to stand still on one pitch. When I first got my "strob," I was playing a solo with the symphony that had a "high A-flat." I had gotten so used putting extra effort going after that "A-flat," that I was playing it sharp without ever realizing it. My breathing suffered because of that too. Finally, I was re-learning it to bring it down and a bonus, it was much easier to play. I swore that "strob" was wrong, but it was I who was wrong.

A tuner is a marvelous tool to get you to play in tune. Use your voice and make sure you put in the correct interpretation. Sing and listen in silence. Then play the same notes you sang without looking at the "strob." You'll find that you'll play those notes in tune. You should do this a few minutes a day and it will pay off big time.

The Sound Quality of the Short Notes

You can't keep playing bad high "G-sharps" and then suddenly expect to play good high "G-sharps." The shorter the duration of the note, the greater care you have to give to make sure that note has the same sound qualities as the long notes surrounding it. Short or long, it has to be the same quality note. Just take a "time out," play some sustained tones, and imitate that sound. That's all.

Round out your sound like a wonderful voice up there. You have to think of the high notes as words in your head so you are not thinking of trying to control your lip or your tongue. Instead, you do it as speech so the reflexes of speech control the meat [muscles]. You have to provide the stimuli like a singer and not like a brass player.

Don't round up your sound by studying of muscles, but instead do it by studying of language. When you were a baby, you learned to speak so now the reflexes of language will control the muscles as you speak. All you have to do is *sing* in the head while you are playing and your singing will control your muscles as you play.

The note preceding the top note always has to have a great sound quality because it leads you right to the high note. You have to even up the high range a bit more. You should have the quality and color for each note in your head. I want you to purify your notes in your head and not in your lip.

A new habit will start to form soon and the high notes will start to sound like the lower notes. In treble clef, the "G" above the staff is not a high note. It's just four notes above the "C." It's in the middle range. If you play the "C" above the staff, then you start getting high. You have to get the feel of the lip vibrating and the air passing through its aperture moving the lips forward. Play some tunes you know well early in your practice so you attain the excellence of which you are capable.

When you are doing a large amount of piccolo instrument work, your general tone will tend to deteriorate. Don't let that happen. Keep renewing your tone playing your big instrument—rather than playing the piccolo—and find *the norms* so you sound your very best during the first 10 or 15 minutes of your practice. Also, buzz your mouthpiece often and make it sound as good as when you play your instrument. Mouthpiece buzzing will tend to normalize your thinking and start to connect your thoughts with your lip.

Extreme *Staccato*

Extreme *staccato* is like extreme high notes in that it's the last thing you do in your development. *Staccato* notes are like the slices of a loaf of bread with wonderful ingredients. You simply slice off the length of that wonderful loaf. Once you get the good sound, then you begin to shorten it, but retaining all the elements of that loaf. Otherwise, you'll be getting poor tone production. When Bud Herseth plays short, it's a full sound.

Ensemble Playing Adjustments

When you are in an ensemble situation and you are not the boss, even if you are right, you have to follow the ensemble. It's terrible being the only right person out of a hundred players, but you have to do what the conductor wants. I have done that all my life. I also have the philosophy that you do what he wants and you gradually educate him. Before you know, he is back your way. I would sneak in my own concepts here and there and, because they were good concepts, the conductor would like them. You see, conductors come used to listening other players from other orchestras. For example, Artur Rodzinski came to the Chicago Symphony Orchestra from the New York Philharmonic where Bill Bell was playing. So here, I am in Chicago playing with a big tuba and Bell used a small one. Rodzinski wanted me to change to a smaller horn. This was right after the Second World War. I tried to find one, but the factories where not making them. Later that week, I brought in a half dozen tubas and finally one day, I brought my old big tuba back. I went in to apologize to Rodzinski for bringing the big tuba and he said. "Oh, I like the one you are using now." I didn't say anything and kept using the big tuba.

The Positive Effects of Playing in a Symphony Orchestra

You always put your money on controlling the phrase—your end product. That's what the audience members get after the "candy" is wrapped up in the box and you sell it to them. You don't sell the methodologies that you used to make the candy. The same thing should happen with your playing. The candy is the tone. Sell that! Don't try to figure out what you are going to do because you already know how to do it. You've known for years and you've known very well.

I have seen people improve their playing in three months after joining a good symphony orchestra. When you play for people like Fritz Reiner or Georg Solti—where you can't fool around and you have to get results—you improve. Once new symphony players start listening to their colleagues playing so beautifully day after day, before you know, they are sounding beautifully as well. You have to live the life of a musician.

Sight Reading

While sight-reading, you still have to interpret the music for your audience. You have to go by the story telling aspects of music as much as you can. It might not be all there, but you try so your standards are always high. When you sight-read, be patient with yourself.

Limitations in Teaching the Trumpet Repertoire

There are certain style factors that if you were studying with a guy like Bud Herseth, he would be playing the music for you and you would be getting tremendous guidance that way. I can't do that. I am not a trumpet player and if I play your music on the Tuba, it wouldn't have that much meaning.

I listened to Timofei Dockshizer when I did this thing with the Summit Brass this last summer, and he was a very musical trumpet player. He simply is an extremely musical trumpet player. In his playing, I very much heard what I teach—a buoyant and singing quality all over the horn. That's the type of playing you should imitate.

APPENDIX D

PRACTICING

Preview

- *You are a product of the music you play.*
- *The parts of your playing that you don't use, you lose. Each day you must have excursions into all the facets of your playing—including songs and drills.*
- *If you only play easy music, you'll see that many performance skills will leave you.*
- *You have to play a variety of music in all the extreme speeds, dynamics, and entire range of your instrument.*
- *You need the extremes, but only as 20% of your practice. Spend 80% of your practice time in the norms.*
- *Don't give me second class notes. Give me notes worth $50, not .50¢! In other words, if we analyze each note, each must have your best sound.*
- *It's important to repeat what you practice. You enhance the learning process when you try to do it perfectly a second time. I would do at least three repetitions.*
- *Take old music (music you already know) and work it up for excellence in tone phrasing. Then you'll be competing with players like Maurice André and Adolph Herseth as well as with great singers.*
- *One fourth of your practice should be on your audition preparation, but the three other portions should be on your love for music. The main point is not to focus your playing on auditions, but instead focus on a multiplicity of styles.*
- *After you know your music well, you must start to work for perfection. That's where your real learning starts.*
- *Music is a happy profession. It's a serious art form, but there is a lot of pleasure involved in it. Don't get frustrated with it.*

Jacobs's Personal Practice

If you can sit down with a clear mind and really enjoy music, you can have a wonderful and enjoyable practice session. That makes all the difference in the world. Whether I was using the practice session as therapy because I had some personal misfortune or I was preparing some specialized piece for the orchestra, I always had a high intensity level. It has been a long time since I just sat down to simply enjoy practicing. If you don't feel like practicing, maybe you can use some of the *Music Minus One* recordings or play some ballads so you can still get plenty of benefit out of your practice session.

After I stopped playing—following my retirement from the Chicago Symphony Orchestra—I felt a loss in some aspects of my health. For that reason, I am going back to playing the tuba now. The increase in blood circulation that comes from playing a brass instrument is very healthy. The days I don't feel well, I start playing and I always feel better afterward.

The Need for Challenges

If you only play easy music, you'll see that many of your performance skills will begin to leave you. You have to always challenge yourself. Those of us in the profession, and I am speaking for myself and I know Bud [Adolph Herseth] does the same, keep our practice much harder than the music we have to play in our jobs. That's why I would always have a wide reserve beyond the "call of duty."

You should play softer or louder than they will ask you in rehearsal. Therefore, when we train a person, we like them to have the ability to play louder than they have to and softer than they have to. In other words, you need a little reserve on both ends. To do that, you have to play in those dynamics. These are the extreme ends of your instrument. However, the most important part of your practice is the interpretation of song based on tone colors, rhythm, pitch, and emotion.

Another example is J.S. Bach's *Brandenburg Concerto No. 2*. The *Brandenburg* is difficult, but if you practice a variety of music around the same notes, then the *Brandenburg* is not so hard. You just can't prepare for just one work. Instead, you have to be able to play a great variety of music in all its extremes—i.e., dynamics, tempo, and range.

At first, you'll have less ability in any of the extremes than you have in the normal register of your instrument. However, you'll need to build your abilities in the extremes until they match *the norms*. Frankly, the extremes will never match *the norms*, but you get as close as you can.

Weaknesses Becoming Strengths

I have often seen that weaknesses become strengths. In other words, if you keep working on your playing problems for a long time, you'll soon surpass those who never had playing problems. As you add challenges, the brain will pick them up. You have to work by climbing a series of stairs that lead you upward. You'll see that you'll become more comfortable playing your music as you climb because the improvement won't happen in your instrument, but instead it will happen in your brain.

You grow in response to challenges. It doesn't matter if it takes a year or two—that's my philosophy. For instance, I take Walter Smith's *Top Tones* and if I play those etudes for a long time, I am adding abilities to my playing. Remember that you are a product of the music you play.

The idea is to also keep playing simple music when you are practicing your new challenges. I was seventeen years old when I had my first student (who retired as a baritone soloist of the Air Force Band some years ago). My second student was Abe Torchinsky (former principal tubist of the Philadelphia Orchestra). Now I am 73 years old and in all that time I have seen that if you keep the melodic aspects of your playing alive, you'll always sound beautiful.

Young players are always looking to play higher, louder, or faster. You need the extremes, but you put them as 20% of your practice and spend 80% of your practice time in *the norms*. A good part of your daily practice should be on wonderful sounds—so you ensure that you don't lose that.

So many players get in trouble because they spend too much time in the extremes and before they know, *the norms* disappear. That is, they are working high all the time or loud all the time. The first thing is that the air won't be there in volume and quantity. Then they keep substituting air pressure for air quantity and they won't recognize the difference because there is a pressure relationship between airflow and static air. To avoid this, keep your tone production up. This is the easiest way to keep your air quantity up.

The problem is that after playing high, there is always danger that you'll start to minimize the quantities of air and maximize the pressures by keeping a small throat and small airway. We have to do the exact opposite. That is, transfer the sound qualities of the low range to the high range. To do this, use thick and quantitative air instead of thin air at high pressure.

The variability of the embouchure is also important. You should allow your embouchure to be a variable. Don't stabilize your embouchure, but instead stabilize the music. Do a little research to see what you sound like when you specialize in the low register. Don't protect the high register, but instead protect the note that you are on. Let the lip re-adjust and soon all the notes will be one. Your embouchure will do it by itself without your conscious control.

Now, when you are playing along and you feel that your tone is getting away from you, stop playing. Get your tone production back and continue. It's not important that you play from the beginning to the end of an etude or solo. Don't try to develop your endurance by playing continuously all the time. What I want you to develop is the perfection of tone and style. You'll be developing the endurance as a result anyway.

What I want is for you not to give me second-class notes. Give me notes worth $50 not .50 cents! In other words, if we analyze each note, each must have your best sound. Practice your etudes in separate sections so at times you start at the end section and other times you start in the middle section. That way, you'll get adequate training in all sections. Do your learning until you perfect your music. Don't stop before then and don't allow a single bad note. Your standards have to be very high all the time.

Remember, your lip responds to stimuli from your brain so don't give the importance to the fingerings or to the embouchure — instead give it to tone production. You base your tone production on the study of long tones and of lyrical playing. As you go into the difficult etudes and solos, chances are that your tone will shift more towards closure. If this happens in the extreme high range, I don't care, but if it happens in the middle range, I do care.

Quality of Performance

At a certain point in your development curve, your audience won't notice the ups and downs in your performance. You'll always notice the changes, but your audience won't. As you keep improving, your colleagues will notice your changes in performance quality less and less. This happens to everybody. Some days your playing is not as good and some other days it will be great. However, most players mix much of this in with what they feel rather than how they sound.

Practice Many Successful Repetitions

It's important that you repeat what you practice. You enhance your learning process when you try to do it perfectly a second time. If it's perfect the first time, then you get it even better a second time. I other words, as you get to know a piece, you enter into competition with players like Maurice André and Adolph Herseth as well as with great singers. I would do at least three repetitions. You see, if the first try was perfect, it might have been just an accident.

You understand the word "conditioning," right? Conditioning is very important in this process. If you play your excerpts through once today and then you play them through once the next day with inconsistent quality, you are not getting the same benefit of playing five times today and five times tomorrow. In other words, not just play the excerpts once through with a second rate quality, but instead repeat them five times; each time trying to sound better than the last. I want you to slow down your excerpts, slur them, give them your finest sound so that your standards go up. The least important factor is velocity. Velocity enters into it at the end, once you have normalized all the other factors (e.g., rhythm, pitch, and sound).

You simply can't stop at the first successful repetition. You must have more successful repetitions than wrong ones to improve your playing. The next day, you'll draw on what you did the day before. The benefits come over time, but you must have many successful repetitions. Only then the neural pathways in the brain become permanent so any similar music you play in the future will become easier right away. For example, don't treat the Schlossberg's *Daily Drills* as music that's going to just develop muscular strength and flexibility. All we want out of the Schlossberg is a simple approach; playing perfect note after perfect note. [Think of the Schlossberg as a slow ballad or a love song]. If you go by sensory perception, it will disturb you, but if you go by the quality of each note, it will help you.

You get great benefits from repeating great playing. For the memory banks in your brain, it's good to play orchestral excerpts five times in a row. If you get three excellent tries out of five, you are in good shape to perform the piece. If you get five excellent tries out of five, it's even better. However, if you only get one or two excellent tries out of five, then you know there is potential for trouble.

Openness of Tone

Some of the etudes give you plenty of exercise in high-pressure air, which is rigorous and somewhat forced (e.g., Walter Smith's *Top Tones* No. 15). You must make sure you can counter that by playing music that stays in *the norms* (e.g., Theo Charlier *Etude No. 2*). You simply study the lower notes and transfer their tone production, freedom, and its various characteristics of roundness back to the upper register.

Find a closer relationship between the middle register and the lower register rather than finding a relationship between the middle register and the higher register. In your mental approach, don't go to the high range too soon. Instead, you should bring the high notes down to the middle range where they belong. Avoid the habit of preparing for the high notes way ahead of time. In other words, you'll find two ways of approaching your middle range—with the roundness of coming up or the thinness of coming down. I want you to give your middle register a dual identity—one that's thin and one that's thick. Then I want you to use the thick one.

Study the syllable "A-LAH-TAH" to open your mouth (lower your jaw). You can use ballads or lyrical studies, but whatever you play, you have to spend part of your daily practice searching for roundness of tone.

You have the habit of thinning out your sound, but this is not totally a bad thing to do. Gerard Schwartz and Robert Nagel thinned out their sounds more than they had to and their careers were very successful. However, it's better if you can play with the whole spectrum of sound.

You should produce your basic tone production with a larger embouchure. When I talk about lower pressure and more flow, I'm actually talking about your lips. Your lips tend to hold as though they were still playing in the high range. I can't tell you to open your lips more, but I can tell you that by having lower pressure and more flow, you'll have a larger embouchure—that is, the lateral width of your embouchure. You have width, thickness, and tension in vibrating surfaces and what you tend to do is to keep your embouchure too short. As a result, it won't buzz as freely in the middle range and in the lower range. Your embouchure will be much easier to control if you let it be much shorter in the "highs" and much longer in the "lows."

You don't have to discard the thin sounds because they could be useful in some areas of music making. However, I want you to be proficient in the open tone. Always have two thoughts: the *Song* in your head and the *Wind* blown from the tip of your mouth going outward. However, if you are rationing a small quantity of air, it will have to be forced through a much smaller space. Instead, take a large quantity of air and waste it. Your tone production will be better right away.

The Study of Tone

If you want to protect the high notes, make sure you have a very easy middle and low range and save the high pressures for notes above the high "C." Make sure you play with very little embouchure resistance and with thick air.

Let one great note teach the next note. When playing Theo Charlier's *Trente-Six Etudes Trascendantes Etude No. 2*, go note by note. Play your high notes in a lovely manner. That's how you protect them. Study the lower notes, have them teach the upper notes, and use a great deal of mental preparation.

You have developed your playing reflexes so you can depend more on your mind and less on your meat [lips]. You must protect your middle range by using a thick air column. There will be changes way up in the high range, but you have to try to play with a rich sound anyway. Play three "G's" in the middle range and then jump up one octave. Make sure the top note is a mirror of the lower note in terms of tone quality.

Learning Brass Playing Concepts

You don't have to play a large quantity of notes to learn some of the brass playing concepts. Instead, you have to develop some expertise in short groupings. In other words, the human brain works best in short groupings and not in long groupings.

It's not necessary to keep playing up the point where you lose efficiency. It's better to keep a high standard for a few notes before repeating them with the same high standard. After a few days, you can start to add a few more notes. You must have success first before you repeat it. Bad notes can be made into good notes, but silence can't.

A Balanced Practice Routine – You Are What You Practice

You want to keep up a certain amount of "entertainment" pieces as well as drills from Max Schlossberg's *Daily Drills and Technical Studies*. You want to keep your register and your dynamics going. The advantage of the Schlossberg is that you play the same music for many years. This will give you training in varieties of music that are so well memorized that will tend to organize the computer in your head [biocomputer]. You draw on those memories and they will fit the various musical situations and styles you'll play for years to come. You'll soon be able to sight read better and hear intervals clearly. In other words, the parts that you don't use, you lose. Each day you must have excursions into all the facets of your playing—including songs and drills. The more advanced you get, the more time it takes to practice. I much rather have a player who practices lots of music and a few drills. Many of the orchestral studies make for good maintenance material as well.

Practicing Schlossberg

An exercise is complete when you go up and then come down. In other words, you must work out the muscles that help you go up as well as the muscles that help you come down. Do the Schlossberg type of slow study (*Daily Drills*, pages 5-6) at the beginning of the day to round up your tone and to open up your airways. You have to play the Schlossberg as if it were a *vocalise* so the air column gets to push, not with one finger, but with the whole hand. This way your air will thicken up. As you thicken up your air column, you'll find that you have to pull in your tuning slide. Nonetheless, as an artist you'll use both thick and thin air depending on the musical situation. It's just part of your "playing palette."

When practicing the Schlossberg, try not to conceptualize the drills as high notes or low notes. Instead, strive for an evenness and roundness of tone from the lower to the higher register. Let the round tone of the low notes teach the high notes.

Appendix D: Practicing

Take charge in your brain so you are dealing with mental stimuli based on *singing* [as if you were singing]. Your sense of authority will come right back if you do that. Use your voice a great deal. Carry a "pitch pipe" so you have the authority of pitch. Depend on your singing voice and if you have trouble singing in pitch, then you can also expect to have trouble playing the horn.

This is the type of ear training that you have to undertake to improve your brass playing. You must use the Schlossberg studies to develop fluency in your playing. You use the Schlossberg for the rest of your life—it's a lifelong assignment. As you begin to memorize the Schlossberg drills, you'll begin to form memory banks in your brain that you'll use to influence similar music in your repertoire. This will give you a greater sense of authority in your playing.

Playing Lyrical Etudes

When you develop a player based on the singing line, that player never develops a flexibility of breath to quickly change dynamics or to suddenly speed up and slow down his tempo. You play these musical changes with parts of your body of which you can't be aware. However, you have to be aware of the musical changes you are introducing to your playing. The physical changes will be subconscious, but your choice of practice materials has to be conscious.

We have to counter the high type playing with lyrical playing each day. Yet, we need the high playing as well. It's like putting a fountain of water so the tone sits on it like a ball. It's amazing how much lyrical material you can find in J.B. Arban's method book.

You can start the study of Gustav Mahler's *Symphony No. 3* or Ottorino Resphigi's *Pines of Rome*. On some of the music, I want you to play very loud and on the same music, I want you to play very soft. It's like a volume control on the radio—when you turn it down and still you hear the same music.

Make sure you spend the first fifteen minutes of your practice on the soft side—looking for the most beautiful lyricism in your playing—so that approach runs throughout your practice for the rest of the day. You can always return to that sound as a norm. Don't let the "big excerpts" become too physical. Get your tone quality and musicianship going so over time you become the master musician who happens to play a brass instrument. I want your musicianship to increase. Don't worry about your brass playing. You ability to be a storyteller of sound is very important.

Lyrics for Excerpts

Sometimes the interpretation of an excerpt improves if you add lyrics to it. You can approach something instrumentally, but if you approach it as a soprano aria, there will still be further improvement. Can you consider adding lyrics to your solos so they become more like vocal lines—more like something a soprano would sing? The first time I heard Bud [Adolph Herseth] play the off stage solo in Gustav Mahler's *Symphony No. 3*, he played it like a beautiful aria. I can picture a beautiful soprano singing that solo. Add lyrics to the notes and follow the lengths of the words. You can do, "I love to sinnng" or "it's much too cold here for me now," or whatever. The point is that the length of the words should match the length of the rhythms in the solo.

Show Pieces

The idea is to take old music (music you already know) and work it up for excellence in tone and phrasing. Then you'll be competing with players like Maurice André and Adolph Herseth as well as with the great singers. Your must always keep your standards high. Play the important solos for thirty years. Those are the pieces you'll use to demonstrate your great playing to other people.

Get some practice starting at different spots of the piece. In other words, start the middle or end of the piece while you are fresh and not when you are fatigued. Whenever you are counting rests, what's going to come out next is unpredictable. However, if you are constantly *singing* while there is silence, you'll guarantee the success of the next entrance. When the music goes down, you have to make sure you sing down with it. The sense of authority has to come from your head and not from your lip. Make sure you are training your head and not your embouchure.

Memorize your pieces. I think Bud Herseth has the *Top Tones* (Walter Smith) and the Theo Charlier etudes memorized. One day, Bud played for me *Top Tones No. 23* from memory and it was just beautiful.

If you practice the pieces you already know from memory over a long period of time, you'll be programming the computer in your head and that will influence all sorts of playing. Once you stop reading the pieces, you'll start playing them for phrasing and style. I want you to formalize the aspects of visualization so you can anticipate the changes of pitch and dynamics in your head. When you play orchestral parts, you can relate them to this type of memorization work.

When I teach the subject of tone production, I run into the problem with people not being able to start and stop the tone properly. People today are practicing too many of Joannes Rochut's *Melodious Etudes*—where they play with continuous blowing—and as a result they don't develop the ability to start and stop the tone at fluctuating velocities of breath and other changes that happen at subconscious levels in the brain. As a result, they never have the chance to develop the ability to start the tone correctly. In other words, you must have a good playing diet with all sorts of styles (songs, dances, and marches).

Benefits of Playing Walter Smith's *Top Tones*

Walter Smith's *Top Tones* is very well written and it's more musical than many of the other etude books. I like Theo Charlier's *Trente-Six Etudes Transcendantes* and I like Walter Smith's *Top Tones*. The results are excellent and it keeps you well in advance of the requirements of brass playing. They go higher, lower, faster, and slower than most of your repertoire.

Each etude in the *Top Tones* has a difficult spot right in the middle. That's the reason I like the book. Those spots are challenging in how you have to hear the intervals. It's similar to programming a computer. The difference is that the human computer takes longer to program. You must have slowness and repetition to program it. You also have to sit in silence and hear yourself play (or sit at the piano and play the pitches as you sing them). You have to have a stimulus for each pitch you play, otherwise your embouchure will slide from note to note. You'll find that the problems are not in your lip, but in your hearing.

Keep working on Walter Smith's *Top Tones* to keep up your general conditioning. The *Top Tones* will tend to build your lip up for the high *tessitura*. You should do this practice on and off for the next year. This training has very much to do with settling down your embouchure in the high register so it accepts the higher *tessitura* more. The Schlossberg (*Daily Drills and Technical Studies for the Trumpet*) is good, but the *Top Tones* is written as a continuous type of playing. I want you to play for pitch accuracy and excellence of sound. I don't need the etudes to be played fast, but I need continuous playing except when you are tired. In that case, stop, rest, and continue. Always play these etudes as an artist. This is a very important book for all brass players.

Velocity

You need a certain amount of extreme fast playing. In other words, you want to keep up with cornet solos like J.B. Arban's *Carnaval of Venice* and other solos that keep you moving. Velocity is a very important part of playing. Wynton Marsalis plays with great velocity. You can also develop that. You can do it, but you have to work towards it. What you do is take materials you already know and you start to take them faster. In other words, you can't think of the individual notes when you go that fast. Instead, you have to think of groups of notes and of their focal points. You can play as fast as you want, but you can't do it suddenly without first learning the music well. Strive for a good tone and then try it faster and faster. At your stage of development, you need to introduce massive virtuosity this way.

We all have nervous systems that are somewhat alike, but some players will be able to fire up a little faster than others. However, it's not going to be a hell of a lot of difference.

You want to make sure that you keep up with all your tonguing and articulation. You have to also keep up with some velocity work, otherwise those skills will disappear. That's why you have to balance a series of challenges in your practice—e.g., etude books and cornet solos.

Don't let some of your skills go. Your graph in your general playing has passed many of the fine professional people. In other words, it's quite high. We want your articulation graph to come right up there with everything else. All you have to do is 15 minutes of articulation every day. You can also play etudes like Walter Smith's *Top Tones* and cornet solos to keep the virtuosity in your playing. Practice the finger drills in J.B. Arban's *Complete Conservatory Method for Trumpet* (e.g., pages 92-93). They are like a boxer's punch bag.

Cleaning Up Fast Passages

You can clean up fast passages quickly if you focus on the down beats. Your subconscious will give you the other notes because you already know them. However, if you try to consciously play by directing every note, you might get crossed fingers. If you stress the "1s" (or first beats—downbeats), you'll have the passage under control. Allow your instincts to take over (this only works if you know the music well) and keep the sense of rhythm alive.

Strive for graceful brass playing using the high standards of a fine violinist. To do that, you have to think gracefully about the music you are playing. As a soloist, you have the privilege of being creative. This makes you a better player because in order to be creative, you must have ideas and when those ideas come, you are connecting your thoughts and your tissues much more acutely.

Slow Practice

Practice your difficult solo or orchestral parts slowly, but with precise rhythm and within the meter you are playing. The study of rhythm is very important because it has a coordination factor on various parts of your body.

In slow speeds, you are more comfortable and you can concentrate to be a better musician. You can play with proper rhythm, intonation, and all the other qualities needed to be a fine storyteller of sound. I need this more than I need the velocity. As you work on slow playing, do the most difficult parts where you can cope with the problems of interpretation. What I don't want is for you to try to rush through the easy notes while sneaking in the bad ones. I want you to be in control of everything you do. Your development will move much faster in this art form if you always sound great.

Get the wonderful control of *singing* in the brain. Every note has to be in your head so you play based on *Song and Wind*. Come down in the scale of the adult thought complexity. Take out the thirty or so odd items of brass playing thoughts you have in your head and just use two focal points: *Song and Wind*. Pass the other ones out and you are going to still play beautifully. *Song* is 70% of your brainpower and *Wind* is 30%. Don't make them equal. What will expedite your improvement at this point is to always work on your musicianship and not on how to play. You have brass playing conditioned reflexes galore already.

High Register Practicing

A trumpeter should be able to go to a high "G" above the high "C." For the trombone that would be the "F" above their high "C." A professional embouchure has to endure a considerable amount of high register playing. You can go above that high "G," but there would be a required embouchure change. To keep this register viable, you should play music in that register and it shouldn't only be the piccolo repertoire. Instead, play general music (taking tunes an octave higher). This will help you keep those high notes alive.

Don't spoil a good lower note for a high note. Only go for the high note when you go for the high note. In other words, don't spoil the low notes before the high notes by starting to change your embouchure too early. The lip will act automatically because the computer activity of the brain will direct it. The idea is to constantly work for excellent notes so if you have an excellent "E," you transfer that excellence to the "B" above it. Try to hear a beautiful note before you play it and you'll have good results. That's the way I play, and I believe that I practice what I teach!

In the lower register, I heard more of the musician trying to play for an audience. Can I get more of this approach in the higher register? Can you find a few songs that are not too difficult and play where you can begin the professionalism of which you are capable? Can you put that in your high range as a challenge? In other words, play the same music, same interpretation, and style in the low and high register. I want most of it to be in the high *tessitura* where you can sustain lines of tone. You have to sound good on each phrase wherever you go. At least your audience should be under the impression that you are in charge of your high register.

Perfecting a Piece of Music

Once you know a piece, take it on tour, and play it frequently. The more you know it, the more you can begin to put little inflections and patterns. It will become your song and you'll be able to do whatever you want with it. Even when you are just learning the notes and struggling to produce the tone, you should still maintain excellence of tone in your brain. (This is until your tissues have achieved hypertrophy and can readily obey your orders).

Practicing the Small Horns – Piccolo

Make sure your larynx is not way up high when you play the piccolo. To help you achieve this, go back to studying your vowel forms like "AH" or "OH." Stay open and you'll be fine. Then you return to playing the big horns with a thick sound. You have to make this conversion when you go to the "big horns" so your sound stays clear.

While you are learning a phrase with a piccolo instrument, you should move to the lower octave or to a more comfortable key often. You don't always need the repetitions in the upper extremes where you are going to be easily fatigued. You don't have to play as loud either. This way you'll always practice with success and authority instead of practicing with mediocrity.

I recommend to play many jazz ballads or Christmas Carols on your piccolo. In other words, I want piccolo playing to be generalized so that you play many styles. The practice of the piccolo instrument will improve the register of your other instruments right away. Your regular horn will sing up there as you clear up the response problems.

Don't limit yourself to your piccolo repertoire. In other words, you have to be a more complete musician up in the piccolo range so that you have a ballad style, a technical style, or a folk song style to draw upon. You want a variety of styles so your lip doesn't stay in the one pattern. You should take the music you play well in the big instrument and replay it up high on the piccolo instrument. Music is music and when you hit a certain pitch, you should be able to fatten it up or thin it down depending on your particular concept. In other words, you shouldn't be locked into one style all the time. If you were not as advanced in the high range, I wouldn't be suggesting this. In other words, if you were lucky just to get the notes, then we wouldn't be doing this training.

You can play the middle range studies — such as scales — in the high range. The high range is just the middle range an octave higher. You'll develop yourself artistically just as you did in *the norms*. However, you don't do it as extensively.

There is a problem with piccolo playing that most people don't consider. People who say that you should take small breaths for playing piccolo are considering the fact that you don't use as much air to play the piccolo. However, they are not considering that the air is under greater pressure and as a result, it's actually giving you about a 10% or 15% in lung volume reduction. You should take a good size breath so that you have your reserves in the high range. Actually, I can see reasons why the reserves should be larger in the higher range than in the middle range. Sure, I know you are not going to use a lot of air with a tiny little embouchure, but what happens is that the air is squeezed and put into a smaller chamber. You'll be more efficient if you have more air reserves at that point. The ones who say, "Don't take too large a breath," are the ones who squeal up there and have a hard time getting a nice round tone. If you want to get a nice round tone, you must have good air reserves.

Develop the high range the same way you would if you were a beginning player. Play many long tones in the high register because you get more results by holding a long tone for about eight seconds or so. You can also play some slow ballads. Play them first an octave lower to get the sound characteristics you want and then imitate them in the high piccolo register.

The work you do in the piccolo range, no matter how excellent it is, will start to close up your airways unless you formalize the study of the open vowel forms. Study the "open vowels" so you get used to playing with a "big space" in your intra-oral cavity. You may need that openness in your bigger instruments.

Make sure you order your sound at the proper levels of the brain by mentalizing what you want. Otherwise, you might be ordering it through embouchure shape changes that are actually not specific in construction. You'll be vague and somewhat in the vicinity of what you want if you work this way. In other words, to get the accurate note, order the sound you want right before the attack by mentalizing it.

When you achieve excellence in everything you play, it pays off big time. The work you do in the piccolo can prevent excellence in the big instruments if you don't handle it right. On the other hand, piccolo playing can augment the excellence of everything you do if you handle it right. Your "major" should be great *Song* (sound and phrasing) in your head and your "minor" should your lip.

You'll soon find that you sound better in those tunes you already know (and which are often more demanding than the traditional piccolo solos). The musicianship has to be dominant over the difficulties of the horn. Otherwise, you'll go into the conscious manipulation of the embouchure.

Don't work on endurance in the upper register. Instead, work for the perfection of your sound and musicianship. Let your endurance come by itself simply because you are playing music and you are resting your lip. When you play in the high register, you'll find that you'll be full of lactic acid almost immediately. Don't go too for long on a single try. Play 30 seconds, rest, and your endurance will start building as a result.

Play a series of ballads (from J.B. Arban's *Complete Conservatory Method for Trumpet*) with lots of *vibrato*. Use a lyrical approach for developing your high range and intersperse some *Brandenburg* [J.S. Bach's *Brandenburg Concerto No. 2*] from time to time. The hypertrophy of muscular tissue will come slowly because hypertrophy requires many repetitions with great musicianship.

Learning always comes best with powerful concentration for short periods followed by periods of rest. As you go into the heavy-duty power training on a daily basis, you'll lose strength instead of gaining it. It takes a recovery period (48 to 72 hours) to gain the strength. If you are patient and you separate your strength workouts to be twice or three times a week, you'll gain strength. However, don't only play to increase strength, but instead play to increase perfection. You are working for wonderful musicianship.

Switching Back from Piccolo Playing

When switching from piccolo playing to your regular horn, realize that you are going to change from a high resistance instrument to a low resistance and a "small tongue" instrument. In this case, immediately allow a small air pressure line and a large airflow line to occur.

Some people play with the same resistant embouchure they use in the higher *tessitura* and as a result, they play the lower register by pushing air through a tight embouchure. That's the danger of doing a lot of work on the piccolo instrument. The rewards of such study is sufficient to validate it, but the danger is that the player learns to play with constant back pressure that goes beyond what the player needs. In other words, a trumpet player should play with a trombone back pressure and a trombone player should play with a tuba back pressure.

High Playing

Allow plenty of rest in between your high excerpts. Recognize that as you play high excerpts you are apt to end up with very small airways that are compatible with very small embouchures, but incompatible with middle range embouchures. You've got to go back to the big oral cavities and the thick air when you play in the middle or low registers. Don't go up to the point of real fatigue when you are practicing J.S. Bach's *Brandenburg Concerto No. 2* or pieces like that. Don't make the mistake—like so many of the players who have come to see me for the past 40 years—that after extensive high playing, their lip becomes a little less responsive so they blow harder and soon they find there is no sound at all. In other words, keep sensitizing the embouchure for vibration so it can respond to comfortable breaths—not pushed breaths. It's the embouchure's duty to provide buzz, not resistance. It's not the breath's duty to force a reluctant lip into vibration. Protect your high playing by going back to mouthpiece buzzing and middle range playing.

Getting Tired During Etude Practice

When you get a little tired, you must protect the high notes by using your mind. Otherwise you'll find that your etudes will get harder and harder to play. You must keep the same standards all the way through an etude. If you have to stop to rest your lip, I don't care.

What's important is that you keep the quality of your playing high so you begin to enter into competition with fine artists. Sometimes, start the last section of the etude first. Other times, start the middle section first.

Make sure the quality of your turns and trills comes through. Make sure that you define those turns and trills in your head first, before you play them. You must have wonderful examples of singing in your brain for every note you play. I don't care about the notes that come out the horn, but I care about the notes in your head—they must be perfect.

I simply don't want you to get a lot of practice time when you don't sound good. If you sound bad, stop your practice or slow it down. If it still doesn't work, maybe try playing another song for a while.

Playing While Tired

You might miss more notes while tired because your muscles are losing control due to fatigue. In addition, you might have been playing with shallow breaths for too long resulting in the increased the levels of carbon dioxide in your blood. This, in turn, will make you suffer from poor and unfocused thinking—making you miss more notes. If you play with large breaths, you'll stay thinking clearly.

Getting Back in Shape

You can take some time off—even two weeks off—and it won't hurt you. It takes about three weeks for a reduction in the size of the arteries to take place. It's like an athlete with a strong arm that will take about three weeks after the ceasing of exercise for any reduction to take place. To get back in shape, you should go back to playing songs and tunes for about an hour. Then go to some very familiar etudes and exercises—things you know well and you have already set to high standards to see if you can reach the high standards again. You can also take your mouthpiece when on vacation and stay somewhat in shape by playing 10 to 15 minutes daily. It's better to let your extremes compress after taking some time off. In other words, avoid going too high or too low, but instead keep *the norms* before spreading them out again. It's not necessary to rush into the extremes when you are getting back in shape.

Periods of High Stress

You should have a program of simple music that you keep going during periods of high stress. You should play easy music with high performance qualities during any period anyway. When an external crisis seems to be bothering you, make sure you revert to the singing lines and a beautiful tone. In other words, don't avoid the big challenges, but make sure you don't lose the singing line.

Playing easy tunes will probably normalize the stress you feel. In other words, you need something that you enjoy doing so your mind doesn't stay focused on problems all the time. Many physicians stay in music because they deal with so much stress. Playing an instrument helps them release pressure.

On stressful days, you have to find music that's particularly interesting to you. I usually use music this way. When I am at my lower end, I like to take a piece of music from my past that I have particularly enjoyed. I start to renew it and see if I can bring back the positive mental states that were associated with that particular piece of music. It really works well.

During periods of high stress, I don't want to play music that I can't really play to add to my frustrations. On simple music, I can compete with all the great players. Don't play any drills or any dry stuff when you are under stress. Instead, play some folk tunes or ethnic music you know well. Anything that has meaning to you will work. Don't take it seriously and have fun with it.

When Reiner was our music director in Chicago, he used to put us under very intensive pressure. I watched musicians break. I even saw suicides from this man's abuse. He was a sadist! A nice guy in some ways, but very sadistic in other ways. I got along very well with him, but every now and then he would turn back on me and put me under pressure. Sooner or later, you would be challenged by a piece of music and that was where he would get you.

Those kinds of pressures are very destructive and occupy your thoughts. Your brain will get to rest only when you die because it is active even when you sleep. In other words, you don't look to rest your brain, but instead you look for something else you enjoy. There should be periods when you read a good book or watch a good movie and laugh. You have to somehow stop thinking about whatever is worrying you. If there is worry, you'll have recurring thoughts reinstating themselves. That will stress out your body and it will tear you down. It's the stress syndrome. Music is one of the nice things you can do to alleviate that. It's very therapeutic. For me, I go into the biological sciences to get my thoughts off the other problems. I don't know if it works that way for other people, but at least it works that way for me.

Practicing with Two or Three Approaches

You should have two or three approaches for everything you do. This is because once you get used to something new, you'll be free to change it, and in two or three weeks, you'll be back where you were. At that point, you have to change your approach again. In other words, we must have the same results tied into two or three different methodologies because as soon as you get used to one approach, you can change to a different one.

Practicing to Achieve Excellence

You don't want to get a lot of practice in mediocrity because you are capable of sounding awfully good. I need your best sound on every note. If we put them under a microscope, each note should be worth 50 bucks.

As a student of psychology, you know that everything you do is habit forming. Anything that includes repetition begins to form patterns (conditioning) and as a result, it gets easier to do. When you play with mediocrity, it gets easier to play with mediocrity. When you play with excellence, it gets easier to play with excellence. It's not harder than that. It just takes more care on your part so you are conscious of the quality you are delivering to your audience. They should hear only your best. If you want to compete with Manny Laureano and players like that, you've got to go for it.

Practicing for Style

You have to challenge the student with "habit forming" affairs in music. So much of the basic ideas of brass playing will tend to stay with you because of the interpretation of styles.

Studying orchestral excerpts is beneficial to a point, but they tend to change in style too quickly—that is, they are too short in length. Etudes, on the other hand, are longer and have more overall challenges. Make a program of music that will help you improve. Include singing-like etudes (lyrical studies) and march-like etudes. Find many different styles. You have to increase your general artistry. Learning to recognize the different styles is a learned ability. You'll find that when you are playing music of various styles daily, you are also challenging your embouchure. As you become fatigued, you still have to keep thinking about music. Ignore your lips and instead *sing* like a great singer. Make sure you are training your brain and not your embouchure.

All the *crescendos* and *decrescendos* in music making involve the study of breath. The study of *crescendos* and *decrescendos* will also give you much more "reserves" in the orchestra so you'll never be caught short. In other words, you'll be able to play the multiplicity of styles in the literature of a symphony orchestra.

All the orchestral music will begin to fall in some sort of general style found in the etudes. You have to realize that orchestral playing is just a partial type of development. Along with orchestral playing, you'll need some Schlossberg (Max Schlossberg's *Daily Drills*), some scales, etudes, and interval studies. The orchestral material will help you in some developmental aspects, but it will leave some other aspects underdeveloped.

Playing the "Norms" – Cornet Solos

I grew up with the Herbert L. Clarke's solos—the old park concert pieces. They contribute in the making a fine and efficient technician. There is so much good middle range work involved—rather than the extremes—that every player should do more of this type of playing. Some Clarke solos go high, but the bulk of the time is spent in the middle register. I spend the bulk of my practice time in the middle register as well. I consider from "G" above the staff (treble clef) to the high "C" the "money register." I spend about 20% of my practice time there. The rest of the time, I spend below in the middle register.

When you play in the high register, it shouldn't be done for just playing the high notes. You should instead interpret a variety of music so you make the love song dominant. I mean, lyricism. Don't limit yourself to playing the high excerpts, but play all sorts of music up there. I often play the *Carnaval of Venice* an octave higher. It's good for you!

Playing Commercial Music

You must have an unlimited musical approach. This way you'll develop artistically and won't have trouble changing musical styles. You don't want be challenged by a musical style that will suddenly throw you off. After you play a program of selected etudes (e.g., Theo Charlier's or Walter Smith's), you'll become more viable as an interpreter of music.

You should be able to do all types of playing. Bud Herseth played some of the Big Band repertoire when he was in the military services and he says that he feels quite comfortable playing that style. I also made my living playing commercial music when I first came to Chicago.

Wassily Brandt Etudes

The Wassily Brandt etudes are good training exercises for playing Gustav Mahler or Richard Wagner. Make showpieces out of those etudes. Do them all with an "OH" vowel using a thicker column of air. This way you'll have a wide range of color you can draw upon.

W. Brandt

Practicing Excerpts

I want your excerpts to become showpieces. There are certain values in your excerpts that I want you to have in your general playing. Play your excerpts at least three times a week. Memorize them so you can play them when you are 75 years old like me. Imitate Bud Herseth, Jay Friedman, and Dale Clevenger because they do a great job. They play their excerpts like wonderful singers. Excerpts are good for your playing and your control of music.

When you go to an audition, you shouldn't need to read your music. You should have the music memorized from repeating it and living with it for an extended period. The excerpts form all sorts of instructions in your head for dealing with new music. You must have some music memorized at the highest standards. Make a program that includes music by Sergei Prokofiev, Ottorino Respighi, Richard Strauss, and Gustav Mahler. Just don't play them through a week before the audition, but instead you absorb them over a long period of time.

If the excerpt is complicated, try to remove some of the complications in order to simplify it. If there are problems with various elements (such as tonguing and rhythm), then practice them separately before putting them back together again.

Listening to Your Recorded Playing

Spend time listening to your recorded playing and criticize it from the standpoint of being on an audition committee. When you listen, don't react if it's not good, but instead annotate the sections that need improvement and conceive in your mind how they should have sounded. You'll begin to gain confidence through success. Success in your practice is very important for achieving success on stage. I need you to become the master musician in your brain and not in your lip.

If you criticize your playing while you are playing, you'll most likely be criticizing how it feels and that doesn't count. Criticize how it sounds, that's what counts.

I want you to start working on great artistry as Adolph Herseth and Maurice André do. I want more of your own initiative because that will always be with you. I can guide you and make suggestions. However, in the developmental stage you are in now, you can do some of this work on your own. Be watchful because that excellence is intermixed with old habits that sometimes put you in a lesser category where you don't belong. Your great artistry should always be dominant. Great brass playing is not as important now, but your mentalization is. When your playing goes off, is not physical, but instead it's mental. Focus on the improvement of the mental aspects and not the physical aspects.

You find that there is great simplicity in the thoughts used to play successfully. Just think of how Bud Herseth would sound playing your audition, and go ahead and imitate him. Human beings don't like simple things, they like complex things.

High Levels of Perfection

You are already at an advanced stage, but to compete with the "top flight" players you must take music you already know and refine it by perfecting it bar by bar. You are already competing with fine players. In other words, once you can play something well, that's when you have to enter into competition with people like Maurice André and Adolph Herseth. That's how you improve your playing.

Brain Saturation

As you prepare for auditions (or recitals), make a tape of the music you are going to play and listen to it for two hours or more a day. This will saturate your brain with great playing. I need students to have more concentration on the study of sound and less on the study of physical function. You must simply live with the music you have to play.

Playing Excerpts in Auditions

You can practice along with a recording of your excerpts so you begin to hear the accompaniment while you are counting the rests. This way, you begin to get more experience based on hearing the orchestra. It's not ideal because you are doubling your part—*Music Minus One* is ideal.

When you don't have a great deal of symphonic playing to do, your teaching load usually becomes large and that becomes habit forming. Somewhere along the line, you have to be able to create the mental state that goes along with symphonic playing. I have to warn you, this is not easy to do. I can do it because I have done it all my life, but I had the challenge of being employed by a symphony orchestra for

APPENDIX D: PRACTICING   219

many years. As I'm teaching you, I have to be able to put myself in your place to try to visualize what this would be like for you.

You should play for your students because it puts you right in the "fire line." It's difficult to do because you don't have the time to warm up properly for the difficult passages—like when you have to demonstrate the trumpet call in Richard Strauss's *Also Sprach Zarathustra*.

There are benefits in making your living playing and teaching music even though you have to "wear the different hats." You are constantly listening to your students and analyzing what they are doing, but you don't want to do the same with your own playing. Instead, when you are playing you want to have a "tape" [music playing] in your head—these are the thoughts you want to transmit to someone else. You must have psychomotor activity and not sensory activity.

Have a mirror and a tape recorder in your studio. The psychology of it is that you are going to play for the tape recorder as if it were your audience (you can listen to it later). When you look in the mirror, you can see a full concert hall (if you have a good imagination) or you can see a conductor and play for him. You can also play a mock audition and think you are playing for a jury panel.

Don't base your playing only on auditions or symphony orchestras, but base it on your love for music. This way, you'll involve the versatility of styles in your playing. In other words, when you can play Walter Smith's *Top Tones* and the etudes from the Theo Charlier book, you don't have to worry about orchestral parts.

When you enter the art form as an interpreter and as a stylist, all the excerpts and solos get easier. You need etude books that will prepare you for the beauty of the *Pines of Rome* off-stage solo or for the excitement of Richard Strauss's music. Bud Herseth is the perfect example of that. He will sit down and go through several *Top Tones* etudes from memory. That's how I learned of the book because I had never heard of Walter Smith's *Top Tones* until I heard Bud play them.

The challenge is to be a good interpreter of music. I could play some good Dixieland Jazz or maybe some marching band music, but I was secure whether I was playing with a washboard, spoons, or a tuba. I had so much music in my head that everything I did seemed to help everything else.

Recital Preparation

Prepare a recital of music you can play well. You don't have to perform it anywhere. However, you'll notice your standards will go up a notch because you'll repeat that music for a long time. When Jascha Heifetz prepared a solo, he would allow two years of development before he performed it in public. Usually, you can play the solo after two weeks, but then the rest of the time is spent on the "refinements"—that's really the thoroughness of integrating everything. When I was with the Chicago Symphony Brass Quintet, I can remember that the first rehearsals were good, but after touring for three weeks, I could hear a remarkable improvement in our performance. That's when you start to compete with great artists in the interpretative stage and not in the learning stage.

You also need an orchestral excerpt program that you memorize and keep up. For trumpet, you can use Gustav Mahler's *Symphonies No. 3* and *5* and Stravinsky's *Petroushka* among other excerpts. You also need an "etude program" that you work for one or two months. Maybe you could sight-read it, but you still need that month of preparation to present it to an audience.

Music is a happy profession. It's an art form, but there is a lot of pleasure involved in it. Don't get frustrated with it. The whole point is not to play at random. Indeed, you have to run through pages of etudes—particularly at the end of the day. However, there has to be a program of progressive challenges you use to build yourself up.

APPENDIX E

BREATH

Preview

- *I base my concept of breath on imagery and the image is always a fountain of water and on top of that is a ball. That ball is your tone. The water is your breath.*
- *It's Song and Wind and not Song and Air Pressure.*
- *You play by singing and blowing. You don't play just by blowing. Otherwise, you'll make mistakes.*
- *The use of breath is nothing more than the use of fuel. It's not music, it's just part of music.*
- *Good breathing function involves your inhalation muscles [group A] going out of function while the exhalation muscles [group B] activate—they move in and out very much like a bellows. That's the way it should be. Its psychology is very valid. Air pressure involves the muscle groups A and B simultaneously so they begin to fight each other.*
- *The relationship between air and embouchure has to be functional. Embouchure makes the music and air is its fuel. If you interject the tongue in between them, your brain will start to work based on air and tongue.*
- *You don't want your breath fighting your tongue. You want to use your breath for vibrating the embouchure.*
- *The violin string always needs the bow to vibrate, the bow means nothing without the string. What we need is for the hair of the bow and the string to move in the same direction.*
- *You have to differentiate between your ability to have high pressure (as when bearing down or during childbirth) and your ability to have high flow at a lower pressure (as when blowing out the candles of a birthday cake). We don't use static air in brass playing because it's always associated with throat closures and other contraction states.*
- *You want your breathing in muscles to work with each other and not against each other.*

Song and Wind

Whatever you do, don't play by just blowing air. Instead, play by *Song and Wind*. *Song* is the major factor in playing and *Wind* is the minor factor. If you make the breath the major factor, your embouchure will just be a shape with no function. Don't do that! The muscles don't have to obey the *Wind*, but if you instead *sing* the music in your head, the muscles will obey that. I have given you the principles of playing, but now you have to go home and experiment with them. Work with your thought processes and find out what works for you. Let your horn be an amplifier as you *sing* into it with your lips.

Always have a "master and slave response." *Wind* is the master and the breathing muscles are the slaves. When you blow, you must order *Wind* as a product. If you study the psychology of brain programming, you blow in order to handle your breathing muscles. You don't handle the muscles in order to blow. In other words, you order *Wind* as a product to have the reduction and expansion in your respiratory system, not the other way around.

I base my concept of breath on imagery and the image is always a fountain of water and on top of that is a ball. That ball is your tone. The water is your breath.

Thoracic Breathing

By using thoracic breathing, you are bringing wide spread musculatures into motion. Diaphragmatic breathing will only bring in the abdominal musculatures. Thoracic breathing brings in the abdominal, chest, and other muscle groups. As a result, it becomes very easy to play. In other words, the large quantities of muscles brought in during inhalation don't have to work that hard. You coordinate all this by the use of the "H" consonant. The "H" consonant should be a constant throughout your entire playing life. You might want to write it down and put it on your music stand at home. You can't feel thoracic breathing, but its synchronized muscle movements happen internally over a large area of the body. That's the beautiful part.

Try to feel the air rushing out from the tip of your lip. Could you change your psychology so you are blowing something outside of yourself? (For example, candles or matches). When blowing, always try to affect something outside your body.

The psychology of *Wind* is always outside your body. As soon as you do that, there is a positive change in your respiratory function. Good respiration involves your breathing in muscles [group A] relaxing while the muscles for the expiratory function [group B] activate—they move in and out very much like a bellows. That's the way it should be. Its psychology is very valid. It's *Song and Wind* and not *Song and Air Pressure*. Air pressure involves the muscle groups A and B simultaneously, so they begin to fight each other.

Think of a golf swing with a follow through that avoids the conflict between the A and B muscles groups. You must allow your main breathing muscles to perform their function and let the accessory muscles work as needed. Allow this to happen naturally. Avoid the positive innervation of the blowing muscle groups as you are breathing in. You must achieve "muscles softness" when you breathe.

Breathing to Expand

Set up a mirror in your room to see the full length of your body as you play. Stay tall and watch yourself play. This way you'll reinforce your learning with the sense of sight. Always breathe to expand and avoid expanding to breathe. The study of posture is very important. The Alexander Method [Mathias Alexander] stresses posture and muscle alignment based on achieving function in relation to the forces of gravity. Your sitting posture (from the waist up) should be the same as your posture while standing.

As you get flabby in your abdominal region, it doesn't take a lot of effort to have your ribs go up and out when taking a breath. That's our goal. We want weakness in the abdominal area.

You can see that the muscles just below the rib cage—the internal and external obliques—have to do with the lateral rotation of the trunk. These all have to do with exhalation rather than inhalation. The obliques might start pulling down, even though they are the rotator of the body, and their combined pull will move downward and inward. In other words, they will make you small. We have to somehow make you big and not small. Breathe without strength so you don't innervate those muscles. Make sure the muscles below your rib cage are soft.

When you simply expand without ordering a breath, you'll have pseudo breaths without taking air in. However, it's impossible to inhale large quantities of air without expansion. I need you to play with pulmonary reserves. There are many undesirable changes that occur as you get to the last third of your lung capacity. I say that because those factors will start to work against your success as you run out of breath—i.e., putting temporary limiting factors to your physical mechanisms. The rewards of taking large breaths are beautiful.

The Use of Minimal Motors

You haven't come down far enough in the scale of static strength. You have 659 muscles in your body and 654 are paired antagonist to each other. You have too many muscles fighting each other. Let's say you have 200 fibers contracting in your blowing muscles, but you have 250 contracting in your inhaling muscles. In this case, you'll barely blow wind, but you'll feel like you are working hard. In other words, you'll have no blowing thrust. I want you to get your conflicting muscular strength out of the way so you can blow freely. To achieve that, you have to first reduce the tension in your abdomen. Take a chance! I want laziness in your body. If you go too far, you'll know because you won't be able to play.

You have to use minimal motors. That is, just use the necessary muscles to blow while avoiding isometric contractions. You can control your dynamics by blowing slowly for soft playing and blowing fast for loud playing. When you apply muscular strength, you'll apply it toward moving your air outward. If you simply get isometric contractions, you won't be able to deflate your lungs fast enough. If the muscles are not fighting each other, you can get great blowing power.

Take a breath and wait. Relax and touch your belly so you are flabby. In other words, let the efforts be the result of your blowing. Blowing power comes from weakness in the abdominal region. How many muscle fibers are innervated? The muscle fibers in the skeletal structure of the body—including the abdominal muscles—are fibers that are grouped and bound by connective tissue. They are not single fibers like the ones in your face. (That's what gives your face mobility of expression). You can have blowing strength, but don't confuse the two into one subject.

Breathing Quadrants

The lower quadrant of your breathing capacity is an area of potential problems so you should take enough air to stay in the higher quadrants. When you play in the lower quadrants, you become a student trying to play right.

What can I give you so you take a deep breath? Look at me breathe. Can you get more upward movement in your body so you look like Dolly Parton when you inhale? Stare in the mirror and exaggerate the movements. I need you to have those large over-changes. Sometimes, small breathing changes are like having two shades of grey where changes of just a little bit are significant, but they are also very subtle and difficult to recognize. I must have you change those shades of grey to black and white changes. Don't be afraid of crudity and exaggeration—allow yourself to swallow air like a big toad. Trust me, it doesn't feel too bad.

You need to take sufficient air in your lungs to solve some of the basic problems of brass playing. You must base your brain programming on maximum air intake and its certain relationships to pressure and flow. Right now, you are building that relationship on the use of moderate inflation [small breath] invariably leaving you in discomfort. Some of your second breaths also suffer from this negative condition and we need to get you away from that. You have to achieve a more efficient situation in which you work as a wonderful musician with a "full tank of gas."

Breathing Curves

Your full lungs start exhaling under a relaxation pressure—due to their stretch phenomena—easily reaching a half or three quarters of a quarter pounds (eventually falling to zero pressure). After that, we have a change toward the negative breathing curve. At the negative breathing curve point, if you were to relax, air would be sucked in whereas in the positive curve, air would be blown out.

Your negative breathing curve increases, as you get older. As a result, you need to get closer to the positive breathing curve so your body doesn't have to work as hard to blow (so large quantities of air come out of the body with ease).

If you don't work close to the positive breathing curve, the first thing you'll notice is discomfort in your neck and your throat. This downward curve in your total lung capacity starts out around your mid-forties. Just simply take extra air to remedy this problem.

Air Reserves

Make sure you play with air reserves. There are factors that go immediately into your favor as soon as you take large breaths. Body compressions tend to reduce lung volumes dramatically without you even knowing it. When you have the larger reserves, it compensates for that. The relaxation pressures will also work for you favorably.

Taking a Large Enough Breath

For a big man, you don't take enough air. Go ahead and take massive amounts of air. It won't hurt you. As long as you blow toward the lip and not toward the tongue, taking a lot of air won't bother you a bit. I need the exaggeration in your air intake. I have my reasons for asking. You know they are good reasons too.

Trumpet is a high-pressure instrument. As you get more advanced and you play the *big bravuras* (i.e., G. Mahler's *Symphony No. 5* or H. Tomasi's *Trumpet Concerto*) taking a full capacity breath is necessary (in soft playing it will not be as necessary). I want to get you there under my supervision because I know what I am doing. There are teachers who don't know what they are doing so they could get you in trouble if they try to help you.

Use the "breathing bag" (a plastic bag used for practicing breathing exercises) and look in the mirror. You get small and the bag gets big. See how your chest gets big. I need that large breath when you play your instrument.

Using the Breathing Bag

After two or three weeks of using the breathing bag, you'll begin to develop a "quantity sense." This is because you have stretch receptors in each lung. They are very subtle and hard to recognize, but they are there. As you do the breathing bag study, within two of three weeks you'll begin to become aware of the air quantities you are inhaling.

Players Who Smoke

Usually, if a brass player who smokes is playing well, he can compensate for the negative effects of smoking by taking in a little more air. In other words, because he has reduced his ability to inhale, he will have to suck in more air to easily get into the positive breathing curve—i.e., the air that easily comes out of the lung without resistance.

Airways in Brass Playing

We want to use "TEE" and we want "TAH" to close or open your airways. You might want to move more toward "TEE" as you go into the high register. In the high range, you might expect some natural biological changes as your air pressure begins to exceed two pounds. (Generally, there will also be a narrowing of the airways. This wouldn't be necessary if you could continually blow equal air volumes). For example, as you use up your air, there will be a smaller amount of air coming up the trachea. As a result, your brain will automatically start closing your trachea to send whatever air is left through a smaller space (to give it more potency). What we don't want is to deliberately play with a highly thinned out upper register.

To work on rounding up your tone, you have to practice Walter Smith's *Top Tones*, Theo Charlier's *Trente-Six Études Transcendantes*, and Max Schlossberg's *Daily Drills* so the "tone building" aspects of your playing are covered. You have to continuously try to round up your tone throughout your entire register. In other words, you must have the same notes under different conditions. I say this because some playing conditions will tend to bring your tone a certain way and other conditions will bring it a different way. For example, coming down from the high range—almost invariably—will start a thinning out process. From my point of view as a teacher, I have to realize that as you come down—and your airways have already become smaller in the high *tessitura*—your lip won't have the thick air it needs to vibrate as it reshapes to play the lower notes. Now, what I have is a constant flow of professional players in my studio whose tone always begins to sound like *prrrrr* as they come down from the high register. What has happened is that their air column has thinned out at the embouchure where the vibration is taking place. You see what I am driving at? The *prrrrr* sound mostly happens because the air column is not thick enough at the lip. What matters is not the power or strength of your wind, but instead how much of it—in terms of thickness—gets to the lip.

The Air Feeding the Tongue

What you want is to have the release of the air toward the lip and not toward the tongue. Otherwise, at the moment the air hits the tongue, the brain will start forming a response pattern based on the control of the tongue rather than of the needs of the lip. When you buzz on the rim, you bypass that problem by getting a strong sense of buzz—immediately setting the correct air-lip relationship. You have to pretend you feel your lip buzzing when you play. The other way of playing—with the air hitting the tongue—will get you in trouble after a few measures.

Thick Air and Air Flow

Your ability to force the air out of the lungs increases when you play with thick air because as you blow, you engage musculatures from diverse parts of your body. You normally lock your abdominal area and you have a certain amount of reduction in your upper torso. As I teach, I look for those signs in the student's physique.

Many players who come to my studio will intuitively compress their air column so it becomes too thin to operate the small embouchure used for playing their high register. There is simply not enough air to make that small embouchure function. You have to thicken up your air so your high playing becomes more functional. The high register will then start have the roundness of tone you want.

Your exhalations should be as if someone pulled a plug from your mouth and a mass of thick wind came out rushing out of you. Can you visualize this? What happens in this case is that you are pushing thick air out of your lungs from many parts of your anatomy. In other words, many muscles are collaborating in your blowing. If something gets in the way—like your tongue—you still need to have thick air at the lip. However, if you have the great reductions in the abdominal region before you blow, you'll have thin air with high air pressures and very little flow at the lip.

Playing with Thick Air

You can play with thick air practically to high "B-flat" or high "C." Then you can thin out your air if you want, but not by much—it will thin itself out anyway as you play the extreme high notes. As you play your piccolo or a lot of high range, the danger is that your brain will start accepting the high air pressure and lower airflow as the norm. This change will happen with no perceptible feel, but soon you'll realize your lip feels uncomfortable.

The tongue at repose takes up most of the space in your oral cavity. When you are playing with a "KEEH" or "TEEH" vowel, the tongue will take most of the space in your mouth and as a result there will be very little air feeding the embouchure. That's why we have to make the tongue shorter and let the air get to the lip where it's needed.

APPENDIX E: BREATH

Empty Lungs and High Notes

You don't want to approach your high notes on empty lungs. Whenever you play in the high register, your internal air pressure increases dramatically. At that point, if you apply more physical pressure by going even higher—and you happen to be down below the half full mark in your total lung capacity—it's going to feel as if you had less air in the lungs.

Blowing and Bowing

You play by *singing* and blowing. You don't play just by blowing. Otherwise, you'll make mistakes. Find out how little pressure you can get away with when releasing the entry note. You don't want your breath fighting your tongue. You want to use your breath for vibrating your embouchure. Like the violin string that always needs the bow to vibrate, the bow means nothing without the string. What we need is for the bow and the string to move in the same direction. Make sure you have the bow and the string. Right now, your air is going to your tongue. That makes no music. Can you feel the lip vibrating?

Low Air Pressure - High Air Flow

You have to differentiate between your ability to have high pressure (as when bearing down or during childbirth) and your ability to have high flow at a lower pressure (as when blowing out the candles of a birthday cake). We don't use static air in brass playing because it's always associated with throat closures and other contraction states. Remember that we play based on *Song and Wind*. You must define *Wind* as the air you experience outside the body. *Wind* is always associated with blowing out matches or filling up balloons. We must have *Song and Wind* because of our biology. Don't fight these basic and instinctive reflexes. *Song* is lip and *Wind* is fuel. As simple as that!

Blowing from Zero Pressure

I want you to take your breath and wait until I tell you to start. Make sure there is no pressure. That is, zero pressure, with no tension, and blow when I tell you. Breathe now, relax your belly muscles, wait, and blow. You'll find that that's very comfortable. You can use this type of zero pressure blowing as you wait for the conductor's downbeat.

The Round Tone

Don't base your normal tone production on your high register embouchure. That's why you have a fine upper register, but a thin sound in the middle register. Many players with a round tone can't get up to the high register. Bud Herseth had the round tone anywhere he wanted. I also had it anywhere I wanted it because I allowed my embouchure to readjust according to the music. In other words, the embouchure is not important, but the music is important. Get used to coming up from the low register with a round sound rather than coming down from the high register with a thinner sound.

Playing the Piccolo Trumpet

Somewhere in your psychology, you are tightening up your airways and as a result, your lip is starving for air. This is the one problem I find with most brass players (trumpet players in particular). They depend too much on closing up their airways with their tongue. It doesn't make any sense. In other words, the lip needs the breath. What are you going to gain by closing down your airways? Obviously, a smaller amount of air will retain its pressure, but a larger amount of air will retain its pressure as well—that is, with the added benefit of having more bulk of air at the lip where it's needed. Be much more functional at the lip. You must add air strength by using a thick air column. Yet, we always go by the tone and not by air strength.

All you have to do is get your tongue out of the way and your tone will come right back. If you keep *singing* in the head, your embouchure will take care of itself. In other words, if you thicken up your air column—which will thin out during piccolo playing—as soon as you pick up the big horn, your tone will come right back. You'll soon get used to doing this. Actually, it's good to practice changing horns back and forth that way.

Work on your tone by playing simple melodies on the piccolo so you gain expertise in all aspects of that instrument. Transpose it up or down as you wish. Play all sorts of melodies using plenty of *vibrato* and have a great time!

Piccolo Pressure

When you are playing high in the piccolo range, the air has to get to the lip. Sometimes just part of the lip vibrates so you don't get the full length of a normal vibrating embouchure. Put it this way, you have to do enough high piccolo playing so you can build ease in the high range. There are exceptions to this. Some very skinny and small people can't play the extreme high piccolo register—like the high "A" in J.S. Bach's *Brandenburg Concerto No. 2*—because they have very little air available to them.

As a scientist, if you think in terms of air pressure, you could appreciate that to achieve pressure there has to be reduction in size. Breath is compressible. Gases are compressible. When you are starting to run out of breath, your body has a limited capacity to compress the air that's left. In other words, the body can only get so small and there is a point where it can't get any smaller.

In players with small bodies, a further reduction is difficult to achieve because their bodies are already reduced in size—not able to reduce further. The problem is that they can't increase their air pressure. To achieve further air pressure, they just need more quantity of air, but they don't have the lung volumes to do that. However, they could get away with playing a very small mouthpiece.

Normal size people with plenty of fuel should be able to play "free style" melodies up there. They must be able to play in conjunction with the rest of their upper range so the high notes are not just "odd ball notes." Those notes have to be apart of your playing for all sorts of styles. I hear Bud Herseth play "C" above high "C" whenever he feels like it. It sounds like a little whistle up there. Simply, you have to find a little section of vibration in your lip that will work at the velocity you need. You must have the high pitch frequency. You might not get this type of vibrating power using large equipment.

Over Pressurization

Think of a bow pressing on a string. Over pressurization will choke that string. The same happens with your embouchure. The middle register should have a freer tone production. I notice that you ride your embouchure too much on air pressure so as you get softer, your embouchure won't buzz and you'll get blank notes. To avoid this, practice the same music at all dynamic levels keeping the same tone qualities. Otherwise, the pushing power of the breath will define your embouchure and once you remove that pushing power, you'll suddenly get blank notes.

University of Chicago Study – High Air Pressures in Brass Instruments

The research I did many years at the University of Chicago ago showed that there always was a doubling in terms of flow rate. Enharmonically, "C1" [Helmholtz System] on the trumpet and on the tuba should have approximately the same flow rate. You must also take air pressure into consideration. For example, with Bud Herseth and I, the pressures have to be practically the same when playing an enharmonic pitch in the same octave. However, in the high register there is always going to be an important relationship between flow and pressure. You are going to use much more pressure and much less flow. As you play in the lower register, there should be much less pressure and much more flow. The problem starts when the pressures in the low register are too high. That usually happens when you come back from playing piccolo or extreme high register parts. You'll lose your beauty of tone and your singing lines if your air pressures are too high in the low register. Simply said, don't over push your breath or you are going to invite excessive pressures. You have to encourage your embouchure to give you as much response with the minimum amount of effort. Avoid encouraging your breath to work harder because your lip is less responsive.

The Trumpet Black Out Syndrome

The trumpet player black out usually happens when players play high and loud. At that moment, the air pressure in the lungs builds up to a point where it cuts off the return circulation through the bronchial trees—which are being squeezed—so you could temporarily black out (i.e., interrupted blood circulation to the brain). You can quickly recover from that by holding your breath.

If it gets bad enough, you might lose consciousness for a moment. Sometimes players play louder in ensemble situations (when compared with the times they play at home) because of all the sound around them. At times, you have to associate the feel phenomena with the volume you are producing so when you play with big dynamics you can guide yourself. In other words, you might find it difficult to hear yourself on a brass instrument. As a result, the tendency is to keep playing louder until you hear yourself. Avoid doing that because your playing will be too loud. As much as I hate to say it, you have to begin to memorize the feel of what's like to play at different volumes. Taking in a little more air and dropping the volumes with which you are playing will keep you away from the trumpet playing black out.

Mental Cues for Better Breathing: Blow in Rhythm

The relationship between air and embouchure has to be functional. Embouchure makes the music and air is its fuel. If you interject the tongue in between them, your brain will start to work based on air and tongue. Introduce a little more "H" consonant and blow in rhythm.

The aspirate "H" brings air out of the lungs and the "A" opens up the mouth. Can you protect the top notes by giving them a little extra "HA" so you get a round sound? Can you hear yourself laughing? Ha, ha, ha! Also, give more "HA" to the short notes. Memorize the sound of it and not its technique.

Can you provide rhythm to your blowing as you tongue? Blow your rhythms using the aspirate "H." Say "who" and feel the wind on the back of your hand. Then add a "T." Your tonguing should be a mixture of "Who" and "T," but the rhythm of the "T" has to be the same as that of the "Who" and vice versa. You can exaggerate this exercise at first.

These mental cues—and how you bring them into the art form—are of great importance now in your development. Much of the struggle and hard work of the past will start to pay off now. Learn these mental applications now. These are "little tricks" that will help you improve.

You can have all sorts of attacks without ever stopping a note. On a graph, you would see the spikes of the entry note and instead of the spikes falling, you would see them staying up. They go up if you have a constant air column. Don't let your sound drop off right away. For some music, that dropping off might be right, but some other music it might not. I want you to become aware of it. These little subtleties of phrasing separate great players from good players.

This is another tool you can use frequently, but use it with wisdom because you don't always play music the same way. In other words, there are many valid ways of interpreting music. As an artist, you need a variety of tools. I learned this from Marcel Tabuteau when I was a boy. He put me in his class when I was fifteen or sixteen years old. Learning about these types of breath impulses have meant a lot in my career. Don't be afraid of over doing it, but instead be afraid of under doing it.

The shorter the duration of the notes, the greater care you have to put into them so they sound good. All notes must have wonderful tone quality, rhythm, and pitch. You have to always translate *Song* into efficient embouchure function. *Song* not only goes to the function of the embouchure, but it also goes to the function of the breath because it's all associated. The biology of sound is based on the *Song* in your head.

Mental Cues for Better Breathing: Blowing Inward

Blow wind outward and then blow wind inward. Study that for a while. Can you feel it when it goes in? Use the "OH" vowel. Feel the breeze [air rushing inward] go into your mouth. The psychology of blowing out and blowing in is important. Lock your lips in the same position for the blowing out and the blowing in. This gives the brain a little boost.

Mental Cues for Better Breathing: Blowing from the Tip of the Lip

Make sure the air comes out from the tip of your lip so the air is not static in any cavity in your body. This is important because the brain can interpret static air in any cavity as static pressure and can cause simultaneous contractions of the "A" and "B" muscles (inhalation and exhalation muscles). If you focus on the air coming out of the tip of your lip, your brain will release the breathing in muscles and it will activate the breathing out muscles.

Visual Learning Process

Some of the learning processes in brass playing go quickly when you do them away from playing. As you begin to learn something new—like correct breathing habits—get a mirror so you don't try to duplicate sensations, but instead you duplicate the appearance of breathing. Watch yourself breathe in and out while touching your belly. You have the sense of touch, you have the sense of sight, and you have the sense of feel. The three of them together make a powerful learning tool if you let them reinforce each other. You must remember the appearance as well as the feel of it when you practice breathing this way.

Breath in Singing Versus Breath in Brass Playing

The implied relationship between the breath taken by a singer and the breath taken by a brass player is not valid. Breath usage during singing is down in the quarter of a pound to three quarters of a pound of inter thoracic pressure. Brass players go up to two pounds to two and a half pounds of pressure. In other words, brass players have enormous changes compared to the minimal changes of a singer. If you understand pressure at all in terms of relationships, you'll see that the changes are much more dramatic when you play a brass instrument. That was what screwed me up when I was a singing student. They didn't take into account that I was a brass player and they were trying to handle me as a singer. They didn't know what to do with me.

Weight and Total Lung Capacity

I think I have more air than I had last year simply because I lost weight. You have to keep your weight within reasonable bounds—then weight is not a big deal. If you start getting a "big pot" on you, then that's going to cut down on your total air capacity. I have picked up almost a half a liter already since I lost weight. As I lose another 20 pounds, I'll probably gain another half a liter. Now I am about 3350 ml (milliliters) and I am more comfortable playing in the orchestra. The blowing of low-pressure air at high flow rate is good for my condition. I have pulmonary hypertension. The doctors tell me that I should stay in the orchestra for as long as I can. I became 69 years old in June and Georg Solti called me because I couldn't go on tour with the orchestra. He told me, "Mr. Jacobs, you must get better because I need you in the orchestra. The Chicago Symphony Orchestra is not the same without you." That was good of him to call.

APPENDIX F

EMBOUCHURE

Preview

• *Controlling the embouchure is an illusion because you can't control the embouchure by using direct commands. Nobody can. You can only control your sound.*
• *The lip will go wherever you sing. You base the form of the embouchure on the pitch you are singing in your head. In other words, if you go by the sound in your head, your lip will follow.*
• *Many times, you'll find that your lip is not tired because buzzing the "rim" suddenly freshens it up. The lip just gets out of adjustment and yours depends too much on the blowing of the air. Air is secondary to buzzing. When you motivate the buzz, you are getting the air too.*
• *You want an embouchure that wants to respond, not an embouchure that's forced to respond.*
• *The embouchure is always a variable. You should instead stabilize the product (music). If you change the musical challenge (music materials), you'll change your embouchure.*
• *There is length, thickness, and tension in vibrating surfaces and to sound great you must have all three variables at work.*
• *The conservation of energy dictates the principle of getting excellent end-results with the least amount of effort. That should be our goal in brass playing.*
• *Remember that the embouchure changes not only for pitch, but also for quality of tone. When you keep the best quality of tone, you make the embouchure's work easier.*
• *In brass playing, don't do anything that doesn't involve the buzzing of the lip. Instant vibration! Instant buzz!*
• *Remember that whenever you lose your sound, you also lose your endurance.*

Embouchure Formation

Psychologically speaking, the embouchure shouldn't radiate in from the rim of the mouthpiece; just like in a bass fiddle your fingering shouldn't radiate from the shoulder to the fingers. Instead, it should radiate from the fingers back to the shoulder. Intuitively, you might be moving toward the rim, forming your embouchure in its outer peripheries. We want the vibrating part of the embouchure to be your endeavor, not the rim aspect going inward, but the buzzing aspect going outward into the cup of the mouthpiece. Simply, set the lip where it's going to vibrate. To do this, you have to use your imagination.

In the middle and lower middle range if you can get your lips a little farther apart so the vibration turns in the direction of the column of air rather than having your lips pressed and squeezed. This is especially important in the high register where you have to allow little lip contact while trying not to squeeze them. Make sure your embouchure is tiny up there by achieving a little more retraction—your embouchure will need to be reduced in length, but increased in tension. Now, in the lower end of the horn you'll have more length and less tension. I also want you to look for that while buzzing the mouthpiece.

Your lip will continue to vibrate if you continue to *sing* in your head. Otherwise, your lip will just become a shape and we don't know if it's going to vibrate or not. If you would simply *sing* the notes loud and clear in your head (like another voice up there), your lip will work. Keep *singing* the notes in your head even if your lip is tired. If nothing comes out of the bell, I don't care. However, if your horn goes blank and your head goes blank at the same time, then I do care.

The lip muscles will go wherever you *sing*. You form your embouchure based on the pitch you are singing in your head. In other words, if you go by the sound in your head, your lip will follow. Always change the notes in the brain and not in the lip. Control your pitches at the song levels of your brain like a singer. When you practice your *solfège* studies, do hand gestures. The hand gestures magnify and emphasize the pitch that goes down the seventh cranial nerve to your lip.

Don't handle a brass instrument like you would a woodwind instrument. In other words, don't put the dominance on the breath, but instead put the dominance on the vocal aspects. As substitute of your vocal chords giving the pitch, your buzzing lips will give the pitch. The tongue or the air won't give you the tone either. The air is just fuel and it won't give you the pitch.

If you squeeze your lips, you'll use them as a closed circuit and the wind will have to work harder to get through. The wind will have to force the lips apart. It's like your lips are vibrating inward instead of outward toward in the direction of the wind. Your lip has to shape like an "oboe reed" so you can blow between them. In the high register, the lips will be closer together, but that shouldn't be the case in the lower register.

Because of your habit of having the wind pull your lips apart, your pressure line is too high. The shaping process in your lip is like having a dozen oboe reeds — one for each pitch. The lip will change according to the pitch and it will do it subconsciously — i.e., your lips become a tiny little reed up high and it gets bigger in the low register.

The changes in embouchure size that should take place over a two-octave range sometimes takes place over one octave. As a result, your tone sounds pinched. There are a few things you can do to solve this problem. One is the simple recognition of playing with a round sound. Always protect the high notes by giving them a roundness of tone. Once the range gets into the upper high range, the round tone changes. You must even out the roundness of tone over your entire register. You don't have to do the manipulation physically, but you do the manipulation mentally. Controlling the embouchure is an illusion because you can't control the embouchure by using direct commands. Nobody can! You can only control your sound. I know of some teachers who teach controlling the embouchure, but I know that's wrong.

There is length, thickness, and tension in vibrating surfaces and you must have all three variables at work. You had eliminated some of the thickness in the lip by having them constantly closed. You gain a lot of range that way, but you run into problems because you'll work harder than you need to in the lower and middle register. Now, this is quite proper for the notes above the high "C," but it's in the middle range that you have to keep your lips apart. Remember that the embouchure changes not only for pitch, but also for quality of tone. When you keep the best quality of tone, you make the embouchure's work easier.

When your lips are closed, your air will work as pressure instead than as wind. Now, the way you buzz is very important. The lip can't shape unless it's isolated by the mouthpiece rim. You won't have the ability to shape the lip to where it shapes like an oboe reed if you don't have a rim pressed against it. You see, the rim will isolate the vibrating area. That's the danger of buzzing without the rim. Buzzing without a rim develops the lip's ability to stay too close.

Appendix F: Embouchure

You educate an embouchure by playing music and not by logic or peripheral thoughts of any kind. You have to actually play the notes. Bad sounds can be made into good sounds, but silence can't. Give your high notes a chance by putting them into the most favorable conditions you can. Let the high notes develop independently from whatever solo or excerpt you are working on. The next time you try the excerpt, the high note might be gone, but the point is that over time you gradually start to develop your muscle tissue. Soon, the high notes will become a reflex response to stimuli and you'll have the hypertrophy necessary to function up there.

Mouthpiece Placement

The same brain signals go down to every part of your lip. Every neuron is carrying the same identical message to every nerve ending across the entire mouth. You've already established the reflexes in your mouth region so it's an unnecessary distraction to direct your attention to where the mouthpiece is going to sit. There is no embouchure where the mouthpiece sits. The embouchure starts where the lip vibrates and radiates out to periphery. It doesn't start at the periphery and radiates inward. I want you to pay attention to the buzzing lip. Don't let your mind pay attention to a minor topic (like mouthpiece placement) while missing on a major one (music).

Playing in the "Red" of the Lip

You have to challenge your students with music and do lots of mouthpiece playing that includes some high notes. Don't call their attention to it, but instead give them the freedom to adjust their embouchure naturally. The embouchure is always a variable, so you should instead stabilize the product (music). If you change the challenge (music materials), you'll change the embouchure. I have done most of my students' embouchure changes by altering their musical challenges, not their embouchures (so the embouchure changes by itself).

However, if you find this is not working and you want to intervene, do it with the mouthpiece in front of a mirror. Let it happen in a parallel situation. Have the students observe themselves in a mirror while playing the mouthpiece. Two pictures begin to form in their minds so they can choose between the two—a visual image and an aural image. Otherwise, they will begin to grow dissatisfied with their aural image and they won't have anything else to choose from. Then you'll have a confused student.

Go into the art form as far as you can when working with embouchure changes. Broken intervals will begin to change the embouchure (use 3rds, 4ths, and 5ths). You can also use tunes that "jump around" and that are articulated. You'll see that the embouchure will begin to set into a different position all by itself. Don't mention a thing to the student. Go slow at first so they can control it. Let them find their way and if they miss a note, it's not a big deal.

Detached articulation studies for certain kinds of changes are excellent. Lip slurs also work well if you want to stabilize the peripheries of the embouchure—i.e., the corners. You can develop a program that combines lip slurs and articulation. As you play varied music, you'll stabilize the musculatures in your face. Let your students play and become entertainers on the mouthpiece. You'll find that in two weeks, their embouchures will start to look differently.

Low Versus High Embouchure

Your sound is losing some of the brightness and gaining a little more roundness. The pressure volume relationships are moving in the right direction. What's happening is that your high range embouchure was tending to come down into the lower middle range and as a result the lip was too closed. Many players do this and it's perfectly all right. It's simply that it will tend to squeeze your embouchure a little bit. Your embouchure should open a little as you come down and closed as you go up, but it should not stay the same. In other words, the embouchure of a high register note—if you were to extrapolate from tuba to trumpet—is a small embouchure and the low note is protruded and long. There are many transitions between those two extremes. Now, we need a microscope to see the transition of the embouchure in a trumpet or a horn, but the principle stays the same. You can make some of these changes happen simply by practicing different tone colorations at home; more in a musical sense rather than in a technical sense.

Bringing the High Notes Down to the Low Register

You must learn to bring the high notes closer to the lower ones in terms of sound. Psychologically speaking, you are going to the high range too soon. Bring the upper octave down to the lower octave. Study the low notes. Let the low note be the teacher for the upper note.

Appendix F: Embouchure

Start building the ability of playing the upper notes in several different manners. Deliberately thinning them out might be one way. A thin sound in the upper register has its uses as well. However, playing with the thick sound in the high register will be much easier because you still have another octave to go. If you are struggling with this octave, you'll have a terrible time with the next one.

There is a phenomenon of doubling efforts. Five becomes ten and ten becomes 20. I don't have a hypothesis for this, but I know that if your 10 becomes 20 and you want easy high notes, make sure you have easy lower notes. I have seen this work out in my own studies. For several years, I did a study at the University of Chicago Medical School. Then I continued to do this research on my own and I found that, very consistently, if you start forcing in the lower range, you are going to have too much forcing in the upper range. If you want to match the qualities, make the low notes free and beautiful. Of course, you need to increase efforts in the upper range, as the doubling of efforts will still occur.

I want you to compare your octaves so you take three lower "A's" and you go up an octave. This way the lower note teaches the higher notes how to sound. Make sure you play the lower "A" freely so you gain the benefit of having that "A" as a good teacher. Your task is to find a beautiful lower "A." Study the lower "A" and learn its round and resonant sound. Then imitate it an octave higher.

The whole thing is to keep the same sense of vowel formation. If you simply change the pitch in your head, while keeping a constant "H," you'll minimize your problems. Make sure your notes don't climb up like a siren because that's when your tone cuts off and you feel the back pressure. We don't want acceleration of vibration sliding upward because when playing a brass instrument there are acoustic laws that have to be observed (i.e., the frequency of vibration has to match the correct length of tubing). You do all this by changing your thoughts and not by changing your embouchure. Make the changes by the control of sound as a concept in your brain and the biocomputer aspects of the brain will handle the tissue with much greater control and efficiency than you consciously could. When you allow the proper portion of the brain to take over, it will be so much easier for you to play. If you try to consciously control your embouchure, you'll feel back pressure from an embouchure that's giving you a much greater resistance because it's trying to climb up in pitch. Yet, the acoustical laws of the instrument won't permit it.

The main thing is to conceive what you want as a mental image. You must have the proper sound and the proper attack. Proper everything! Make sure the low note is the dominating note, not the high note. Don't go by the feel phenomena, but instead *sing* each note accurately in your head. As soon as you do that, the feel aspect will fade away.

Lateral Embouchure Length

If you can thicken up your air column, it will be easier for you to play. When you feel your sound thinning out a bit, stop and get organized. Strive to get that thick air column and the round sound again. The round sound will indicate a slightly longer embouchure. When the embouchure gets too small, you begin to lose control and it will be hard to find your pitches. When your embouchure is longer, there are more fibers for shaping the lips than when the embouchure is short. Actually, you'll feel a little more comfortable when you play with a longer embouchure. You lose the ease of the sustained high *tessitura* as the embouchure gets a little longer, but the up and down maneuvering gets a little easier because there are more protractors and retractors involved. You'll find that your general playing is always better with a slightly longer embouchure.

Controlling Your Embouchure

Don't blow your embouchure into position by using air pressure. I want the psychology of forming the note to form the embouchure. I want you to be able to have a responsive embouchure. Don't depend on the strength of the breath.

I want you to get away from thinking about your embouchure. Control your thoughts about your music instead. This is the key of great brass playing. Stop trying to control the muscles and start controlling the music. It will happen very quickly if you have enough air in the lungs. Think of a great singer on stage. Keep this concept alive and don't stop the *singing* in your head.

The idea is to hear soft playing in your head. You must base the tools you use in brass playing on simplicity. Don't let any joker complicate your thinking! Your physical development is already set. In other words, you have many tools right now. You have well-established reflexes. What you need is an artistic approach to your playing and not somebody telling you about your embouchure or brass methodologies. That's not necessary. If you need to achieve an altered sound, you can go at it as an artist (by imitating) and not as a student by trying to control your embouchure.

APPENDIX F: EMBOUCHURE

Play some etudes loud and beautiful (like Walter Smith's *Top Tones* No. 13). This is specialized work I want you to do for now. I am not going to have you be the loudest player in the business. This type of loud practice is just for now because you need it. You are not used to playing very full in the high range. As a result, you have under developed muscle tissue. The muscle tissue will start developing and responding to this challenge. The challenge can be some heroic type of music in the high range or some nice ballad played an octave higher.

Walter Smith
Top Tones No. 13

You are a good player, but I've got to get you playing in wider dynamics so the challenges become extremely soft, extremely loud, extremely high, and extremely low. We also need to practice *the norms*. Just take J.B. Arban's *Carnaval of Venice* and it play louder. Then play it even louder and see how it holds together. Perhaps play it softer as well. How well can you whisper?

The Psychology of Buzzing

Don't let the tongue have anything to do with tone production. You should use your air for buzzing. All the tongue can do is get in or out of the way of the column of air. In brass playing, don't do anything that doesn't involve the buzzing of the lip. Instant vibration! Instant buzz!

The spitting sound some players get when attacking a buzzed note comes from connecting the air and the tongue instead of connecting the air and the embouchure. To remedy this, do some short *staccato* notes on your rim. You have to put a magnifying glass on your buzz and not on your tongue. The amount of air that can get to the embouchure increases dramatically when you work this way.

I want you to separate your air from your tongue. When you blow while pronouncing the syllable "KEEH," you are making the tongue antagonist to the air. I want the embouchure to be antagonist to the air instead so it becomes much easier for you to buzz. There is no sound with air and tongue; it's always silence.

However, don't eliminate the tongue while playing. That doesn't correct anything; it just delays the problem. The closer you get to speech, the better the tongue will be. Say, "It's ten 'till two." Where is your tongue when you say that? Do this daily and your embouchure will gain a sense of freedom.

Mouthpiece Buzzing

When buzzing the mouthpiece, be careful with your pitch interpretation. Decide what you want to play and with great authority go for it. You should always carry a pitch source (pitch pipe) with you to challenge yourself. Don't rely on your mental recall. You'll find that your relative pitch will get better and your absolute pitch will relax. Absolute pitch is not important. As long as you have a pitch source, your recall will improve. When I am testing you for pitch recall, I always do it away from your instrument. I want my student's pitch recall to be superior.

Drop the lower jaw and practice the following vowels: "AH, OH, OOH" and keep that openness when you play the mouthpiece. It doesn't mean that you are going to use that openness on the job all the time. In other words, you are going to have a variety of tone colorations that you'll use because they are in your repertoire. All of those tone qualities are legitimate. You are the artist, so you decide. However, I want you to always keep the open one.

Give yourself three to four minutes of continuous mouthpiece playing. Play a movement from a concerto or an excerpt. You must become aware of how easy your tone production is once your air column is thick.

There are usually no bad habits on the mouthpiece because it's all new and very strange. You are already an advanced player so you have embouchure functions based on reflex response to proper stimuli. You'll automatically begin to open up your airways and thicken up your air column to the point where tone production becomes comfortable. Then you have to copy that and take it back to your instrument. Make sure you don't force while playing the mouthpiece. Go for less resistance. Try to connect your lips and your air. Remember the sound of good mouthpiece buzzing and not the feel of it. Even in the high register, make sure you stay, up to a high "C," away from forcing. In extreme piccolo playing, it's another story. Sing some tunes first and then imitate them on the piccolo. Other times, reverse the method. I want you to build a connection between buzzing and singing. I want to make sure your singing is accurate.

The main thing when you go back to playing your instrument is to make sure your tongue is the same as it was on the mouthpiece. Go into the show business

Appendix F: Embouchure

profession when you play the mouthpiece. Think you forgot your instrument at home and you have to play a concert with your mouthpiece. Run around the room playing tunes on the mouthpiece and you'll see that all sorts of body tensions will begin to fade away.

The only difference between playing the mouthpiece and playing your instrument is that on your instrument, the stupid tongue wants to get in the way. I have been fighting the tongue and the diaphragm as two focal points in my teaching for over 40 years—I have been trying to get around them. The larynx is another focal point. I can't call too much attention to them because there is a lack of recognition from the student's part. However, you can get around them when you play your mouthpiece.

For specialized training, you should do about an hour a day (in ten minute increments) on the mouthpiece and you'll see that it will pay off big. Do it all on music you have memorized because I want it all from pitch recall. We want to see what kind of a musician you are without the aid of the acoustical device [brass instrument]. We want accuracy to the extreme. Make a big fetish out of being exactly in pitch.

Adolph Herseth and I used to play duets in the back seat of Schilke's Cadillac when we were traveling with the Chicago Symphony Brass Quintet. We played Walter Smith's *Top Tones* No. 15 an octave apart. All of my life I have been a mouthpiece specialist. Often, people in universities used to put me down for mentioning things like these in lectures.

The principle of mouthpiece playing is to introduce the strangeness that will permit the source of stimuli to take over in the brain. Your conditioned reflexes will follow. By playing on the mouthpiece, you are enhancing the connection between your thoughts and your tissue's ability to respond to thought. We need the strangeness of removing your instrument because as soon as you play your instrument, you'll have all sorts of conditioned reflexes (good and bad) come right back.

When you are fooling around the house or driving the car, you can buzz the mouthpiece and get some training. You can sing and play all sorts of tunes. This will keep your brain and tissue connection very strong. It's also a good substitute when you can't get to your instrument. The idea is to take the increased pitch accuracy you gained when playing the mouthpiece back to the instrument. This way, you'll amplify your pitches properly.

Advanced Mouthpiece Buzzing

Your pitches slide out of tune when you play intervals on your mouthpiece. If you buzz like that into the horn, you'll get into an acoustical "clash" to the point where your horn won't resonate. As soon as you do that, your sound will cut down in terms of resonance. Your ear—which wants to hear loudness—immediately picks up on that lack of resonance and as a result, you put effort into your playing giving you a forced tone production. You get much better tone production if you play in perfect pitch. Can you further refine your mouthpiece playing so it's perfectly in pitch? Just add another challenge to your playing. You'll feel more secure as a result.

It's fascinating when I work on mentalization with my students and I hear their improvement. The students, however, won't feel any changes (or at least anything tangible). They might recognize the security of finding the note, but in the sense of having a physical feeling, there is almost none. You have to perfect your tone production without an instrument. You do this by working on ear training. You'll wind up with an above average tone recognition.

Mouthpiece Buzzing and Intonation

I want your ear training to be developed to such point that you won't miss intonation details in your mouthpiece buzzing. The intonation has to be impeccable on each note. You can do simple intonation exercises with the tuner or the keyboard for a few minutes every day. This will make a big difference in your playing.

I remember Bud Herseth being very conscious of the concentration required to play. That's why he didn't want to do any teaching. He didn't want to have anything interfere with his concentration. He would say, "I need to concentrate, I need to concentrate." Every day you should do about one or two sets (fifteen minutes long) of concentrated intonation practice.

Practice mouthpiece buzzing with intervals of thirds, fourths, and fifths. You can use the intervals in Pasquale Bona's *Complete Method for Rhythmical Articulation*. Just pick a scale and get around the different intervals within that scale. Make sure every note is in tune.

APPENDIX F: EMBOUCHURE

***Buzz It* and the BERP**

The problem with the buzz aids I tried at first was that there was too much back pressure. That's what they wanted and I didn't. I don't want a lot of back pressure from mouthpiece buzzing. The advantage of using some of these tools is apparent when teaching students who are dependent on their fingering. In other words, by the fact that they are holding the horn, they recall the pitch—similar to using Jack Holland's *Buzz It*. They sent me a BERP now with two holes instead of one so there is less back pressure. The fact is that the finger reflexes you have developed over the years become associated with pitch. As a result, when you finger while buzzing, you become much more accurate. Jack Holland's *Buzz It* is different because I noticed that when I tried it, I sensed more stability and more of a sense of stimuli. Just holding the *Buzz It* in your hand brings the feel of playing your instrument while buzzing the mouthpiece. That's what I want.

High Note Hypertrophy

High note development requires playing up there without too much fatigue. Reserve some time to play many high notes with long periods of rest. You'll soon find that your lip will get used to it. Treat your high range as you would elementary tunes. I play lots of melodic material up there to work on my high register. Also, slur your high solos from time to time just for practice. You want to develop a great sounding high register.

You can depend on long tones for developing your high register abilities. For instance, you can use J.B. Arban's *Complete Conservatory Method for Trumpet* exercise number one on page one an octave or a fifth higher. It's four beats to each note. To develop a note, it always takes sustaining that note for more than four beats.

There will be hypertrophy in the various muscle groups—which gradually strengthen to give you the shaping processes—you need for particular pitches. You must handle your high register with kid's gloves. In other words, don't bully it.

You have to consider yourself elementary when you begin to study your high range. Don't worry if you are successful or not. However, in your brain you have to be successful. Your high range comes from playing up there. Just make sure it doesn't deteriorate your normal playing. When you finish playing the piccolo, make sure you open up your airways as you come back to the larger instrument.

If you consider yourself elementary in the extreme upper register, you have to recognize that all you've got to do is play enough up high for the muscle tissues to develop, strengthen a bit, and properly connect with the brain. Once you complete this process, you'll be able to play anything. You can do that easily on the mouthpiece or on your instrument.

Spend some time sounding good in the high range playing ballads or lyrical tunes. There is a great tendency among brass players to sound forced and strained in the high register. People get uncomfortable listening to that. Maybe playing high is difficult, but the trick is to make it sound easy and comfortable. You might only find a few people who can play beautifully in the high register, but if one person can do it, everybody can. Remember that whenever you lose your sound, you also lose your endurance.

High Note Methodology

High notes have to be developed. Don't forget that you've formed many habits from years of trying to reach your high notes. You've got methodologies already in your brain developed to play high. Now, some are not very good methodologies. What I want you to do now is to try this new methodology. As an artist, when you start going up, make it as simple and childlike as you can. Play folk tunes or simple ballads up there and sound good.

Whenever you develop a high note, hold it for four to eight seconds. Let the tone develop based on its length and never its attack. If your high long tones don't sound good, you must improve them in your brain first and don't worry of the sound coming out the bell. Soon, that sound will match what's in your brain. Your brain always comes first, and the lip will follow.

In the high register, you are dealing with an extreme. That means that you are dealing with a lack of development where you are extremely elementary–like you used to be many years ago in the middle range. Give the high register a chance to develop. Then I would like many more long tones in the high range. You've got to play up in the high register every day. Your lip will find out its way in almost any mouthpiece.

When I wanted to bring my high range back, after I was done with cancer, I was playing *Taps* in many keys. I went as high as I wanted. I still do it. I also use all sorts of ballads and bugle calls I knew from when I was a kid. As you arrange your tissue, it will get easier to play up there. You should have at least a perfect fifth above the top note you have to play in a concerto or excerpt.

Extreme High Register

To play in the extreme high register, you've got first to set the mouthpiece where you know is going to vibrate, blow like hell, and *sing*. Frankly, playing in the extreme high register for too long harms your playing. Even high piccolo playing will do some harm to your playing, but in this profession you've got to learn how to recover from it. When you play under high air pressure, your body automatically begins to reduce your airways. Consequently, you'll further increase the air pressure. This happens once you've played high for a while, but remains once you go back to the big instrument. Suddenly you'll find that there are many notes in the big instrument that are hard to play. The problem then is not in your embouchure, but it's in your airways. If you open up your airways, your problem will disappear right away.

Playing High Notes

Don't reach for a high note to suddenly to find it's not there. Avoid that by having the high note first in your brain. Make sure it's psychomotor. In other words, you must have that note in your head first right before you play it. Your high notes must have the same clear sound you get in the lower octave.

You must always motivate the buzz so blowing is secondary to buzzing. Remember, you can blow without buzzing, but it's impossible to buzz without blowing. In other words, you don't have to worry about blowing, but instead worry about buzzing.

Let the lower octave teach the upper octave. Always play with a lot of vibration. Practice with a buzzing rim an octave lower. You'll often find that your lip is not too tired because the buzzing of the rim suddenly freshens it up. The lip simply gets out of adjustment and yours depends too much on the blowing of the air to function. Air is secondary to buzzing. When you motivate the buzz, you are getting the air with it.

Buzzing Extreme High Notes

For buzzing the high range on a mouthpiece, you can try cutting off the mouthpiece stem (to lose the bugle effect) so you can play all the high notes on it. In the regular mouthpiece, you'll always have a gap between the high partials, but in the cut off mouthpiece, you won't have that. The sound waves in the high register are so short and the tube (stem) of a regular mouthpiece so long, that you get the bugle effect.

Use a "high mouthpiece" for your general playing and see what the results are after your embouchure is used to that mouthpiece. Don't only use the mouthpiece to see if you can get the high notes right away. The "high mouthpiece" has to be functional in the middle and lower range as well.

Buzz and Tongue

Always find the rhythm of your music in the buzz and not in the tongue. If your buzz and mind are connected, your sense of authority in music will increase right away. Years ago I had a gauge—which had a tube connected to the player's mouth—mounted on the music stand. This gauge produced a read out of the player's attacks. Often, in troubled players, the gauge indicated air pressure first followed by the player's tone. I deducted that the brain was satisfied that the first note was in rhythm because the tongue was on time even though the tone was late. You can avoid this problem if you simply *sing* the pitch in your head first before you play.

Can we make sure that we play by wind and buzz rather than by wind and tongue? Buzz! Your lips are always supposed to vibrate. Open a little space in between the lips so the air goes between them instead of pushing them apart. The air has to go between just like it does in an oboe reed.

Your breath is not used to working quite the way it should because it's gotten used to feeding the tongue and not the embouchure. You have tended to use your breath as pressure just as the violin bow stands on a string pushing down without moving.

Using your imagination, you have to pretend you can feel and see the lips vibrating for each note you play. Do this from time to time to activate your lips. Your imagination will affect your physiology, but it's up to you to use it for your own good.

Negative Effects of Mouthpiece Pressure

You have to recognize that when you play high and loud, your mouthpiece pressure will exceed the pressure in your lip's arteries. That means that in about ten seconds you'll feel a bit fatigued. That comes from the accumulation of lactic acid in the tissues. If you can release the mouthpiece pressure ever so slightly as you breathe in, you'll avoid some of the lactic acid accumulation.

When you breathe, don't remove the mouthpiece, but instead release the pressure a little bit. If you hold a continuous mouthpiece pressure, your playing is going to begin to deteriorate because of the lack of blood circulation to the lip. You might get a little swelling as well. The accumulation of lactic acid in the lip region doesn't permit the same flow of neurological messages down the seventh cranial nerve. In other words, the lactic acid interferes with the transmission of your artistic message.

There is very legitimate work effort when you play in the high range. The muscle contractions are rather severe staying up there all the time. There is simply some hard work up there.

You can begin to develop your high range by simply practicing some sustained notes to develop sustaining power. While you sustain up there, you come close to the work efforts required to playing in the high range. Can you come closer to the sound of your long tones when you play your high excerpts? You'll see that your excerpts will sound better.

Setting Up Mouthpiece Pressure

Make sure you have the same contact in the lower lip than you have in the upper lip. In other words, make sure you don't have more pressure in the upper lip so when you are going for the upper notes you press too hard against it. All you have to do is isolate the lower lip. This is not about mouthpiece placement, but rather this has to do with mouthpiece pressure against the lip.

What you have to do to keep your muscles healthy, is simply stop and rest when you are tired. That's all! There won't be any damage if you stop playing. Damage comes when you are tired and you keep playing. Even then, the damage is temporary. You'll have to play concerts when tired, but you'll learn how to deal with that.

Maniacal Strength

In muscle physiology, strength comes from how many fibers you innervate. When you stimulate a single muscle fiber electronically, you'll have maximal contraction. You base the degrees of strength on the muscle's ability to have more or less contractions. Incidents of maniacal strength (the classic example is that of a mother whose child in pinned under a *Volkswagen* and she picks it up) can happen when the electrical outputs in the brain fire massive amounts of muscle fibers. You have safeguards so when everything contracts you don't break a bone or rip tendons.

Dynamics in the Practice Room

With an instrument whose amplifying potential is up to 45 decibels, you want to play right in the middle of that potential. Regular practice should be always half way between the minimum and the maximum of your dynamic potential. In other words, the development of your playing won't happen in the *fortissimo* or *pianissimo* levels. Instead, find excellence in the *mezzo forte* level and take that excellence to the extremes. Always practice from the center and make your way outwards.

The embouchure has to learn to respond to the dynamics you play. Just because you add more air, it doesn't mean that the embouchure has to respond to that air stream. Instead, you might meet resistance. Make sure your embouchure is comfortable in all your dynamics.

Rest as Much as You Play

Don't try to follow a strict formula for resting. Fatigued muscles accumulate lactic acid and the neural transmissions are impaired as soon as that happens. If your muscles are not accumulating lactic acid, then it doesn't matter. You are playing it safe by resting as much as you play, but you can generally go by how the lip feels. What I am saying is that you can guide yourself very much by how your lip feels and by how you sound.

Don't become dependent on a "resting formula" because you might get into situations where you can't rest and you'll still need to play. In your practice, gradually reduce the rest periods and see how the lip feels. If there is real fatigue, then you stop and see how you do. In the professional sense, you don't always have the opportunity to rest. It's like other types of physical exercise in which your muscles pick up strength as they are challenged. The principle in building strong muscles is to have certain amounts of contractions followed by rest periods. You can contract your muscles from repeating drills or from heavy stress while playing solos or excerpts.

In weight lifting, after some of the heavy lifts, it takes 72 hours or so for the muscles to recover. If you continue to train on a daily basis, you'll show lack of strength. However, if you have the periods of rests, you'll have increasing strength.

What I am suggesting is to use your head. If the lip feels great when you are playing, then don't stop. If the lip doesn't feel great, then you stop. Eventually you'll learn a little bit more about yourself as a player. When you formalize your practice by resting as much as you play, you are following a pattern that's habit forming in itself. Your lip can even get used to that and you can start to become dependent. If you feel that your lip is deteriorating, then stop. I rather you become dependent on resting than on abusing your lip.

It's OK for your lip to hurt a bit. However, if it starts to swell, that's another thing. Then we have to cool down. Take some time off. However, don't worry about your lips, but instead worry about your thoughts. Lips are like vocal chords in that you are not even aware of them. Think of all the times you have played big difficult pieces in an ensemble and you don't even think of your lips. Instead, you hear the music and you play it.

There is effort involved in playing, but you need to apply it properly. Besides, what effort does it take to vibrate a pair of chops? The body is designed for strenuous activities like wrestling and running, but in brass playing we don't need that kind of muscular activity. We deal with small muscles groups . The conservation of energy dictates the principle of getting excellent end results with the least amount of effort. That should be our goal in brass playing.

There are players who complain of early signs fatigue when doing jobs. This is not good in our profession. As you go out on a job and your lip gets tired, always play a little bit softer and more musical. In other words, don't fight the tiredness by increasing your energy. Don't do that. Just go along with it and give a little more music—more pretty, more vibrant! Take plenty of air and don't worry about it.

I don't like to fuss with the embouchure trying to build endurance for endurance's sake. Instead, I like to develop endurance in a musical way. For example, in Walter Smith's *Top Tones* etude No. 13 stays in the moderate *tessitura* and not in the extreme. That's where you should build your strength first. This is what we call the money register. This etude does the developmental job for you. You want to play this etude with a healthy *forte* with a good quality of tone. It does keep your lip's strength up.

APPENDIX G

TONGUE AND VOWEL FORMS

Preview

- *Music is always a combination of air and a buzzing embouchure. Air and lip makes music. Not air and tongue!*
- *The tongue does belong in the music making equation, but it's on a very small basis. In a graph, the use of the tongue would show as a small line when compared to the importance of air and buzz.*
- *When tonguing, the vowel has to be dominant over the consonant.*
- *Always build the attack upon the downward stroke of the tongue and not upon the upward stroke of the tongue.*
- *It's the connection between air and embouchure that's important, not air and tongue.*
- *You want to play down much of the tongue's interference. Your job is to connect the air with the lip.*
- *To thicken up your sound, you don't have to play louder. You simply have to get your tongue out of the way.*
- *The first attack of a phrase needs to be "success or failure" in terms of tone production by the first subdivision of a 32nd note.*
- *Sometimes the mouthpiece is not on firmly on your lips because you take the mouthpiece pressure off as you breathe. As a result, you might miss your entry note. You must also have a tight enough control in the mind.*

Tongue Physiology

When tonguing, the vowel has to be dominant over the consonant. The vowel is always open, and the consonant is always closed. In other words, if you analyze the consonant "T," you notice that it will have, for a moment, no air getting through. The consonant "T" simply acts as a barrier between the breath coming from the lungs and your lip. These are the lower branches of the Genio-hyo-glossus muscular group that protrudes your tongue. Biologically, when you put your tongue forward, that forward movement is initiated down in that muscle region. What frequently happens is that those muscles, instead of being innervated off and on, remain innervated and the tongue gets clumsy. You can't feel these things. It's like a tug of war between muscle groups. You can't even be aware they exist because you won't get any feedback or sensations of their motor activity.

As soon as your tongue starts to move forward, the brain will innervate the intrinsic and extrinsic musculatures—those muscles that help the tongue move around—but often the tongue becomes stiff. When the tongue moves forward, it has more power. I mean, it becomes more isometric within itself. If you start this combination in fast tonguing and you start to stutter, you know that's a problem down in the genio-glossus group and not a problem with the tip of your tongue. That's why you can't stop practicing single tonguing. When you practice your double and triple tongue, don't neglect your single tongue.

Teaching Tonguing

One of my biggest problems as a teacher is in establishing the correct relationship between tongue and air. With so many players, the brain very frequently tends to make the tongue the dominating part for controlling the breath. The needs of the embouchure is what predicates the use of the breath.

The tongue is a villain in many ways and you have to make sure of its downward stroke as you tongue an entry note. You have to emphasize the vowel rather than the consonant [e.g., when pronouncing 'TOH' you emphasize the 'OH' instead of the consonant 'T']. Always use a good vowel when you play. You must play down the nuisance value of the tongue. The problem is that the brain will start to accept your tongue as the regulator of the breath and it will send signals based on what your tongue needs and not on what your embouchure needs.

Neurologically, you must handle the tongue by specific stimuli to fire up your conditioned reflexes. As you learn these concepts, use your voice often in your practice of different vowels (such as 'TOH' or 'TOO'). You have to get into the spirit of tonguing based on the vowel and not based on the consonant. If the tongue stays in total closure while pronouncing the consonant, there is no way you can get air through it. The tongue has to swiftly pronounce the consonant and learn to get out of the way of the wind by moving to its vowel form right away.

You have to make sure that you minimize the tongue. The two main problems in brass playing are the use of the tongue and the diaphragm. Those two have tremendous relationships in the larynx. I don't have to teach the larynx directly because all you have to do is make sure of your airflow and nature will take care of the rest. The tongue seems to be easily trained to get in the way of the air. Soon, the conditioned reflexes develop based on the position of the tongue and not on the needs of the embouchure.

The Use of the Tongue

You must emphasize the connection between embouchure vibration and breath. These are the tools we use to produce a basic sound on a brass instrument. The tongue, however, is not a musical tool for creating sound. To produce a basic sound, use "thick air" and lots of vibration. Put more importance on the vibrating lip than on the breath. Always think, *Buzz, Buzz, Buzz, Buzz* and not *Blow, Blow, Blow, Blow!* Simply, put more attention on the buzzing than on the blowing.

Your old habit of connecting the breath and the tongue is starving your embouchure. Your embouchure needs the breath to function properly. In other words, the tongue is deciding what gets to the lip and that has you all screwed up. Psychologically, you must move the air to the lip and not to the tongue. Your first note has to be your best. Prepare for it! *Sing* in your head and blow!

Setting Up Resistance at the Tongue

You don't want to set up a pattern of pushing [blowing] against the resistance of the tongue. It's the connection between air and embouchure that's important, not air and tongue. Tongue is important as far as speech and language goes [as in the pronunciation of a clear consonant], but you create a basic sound by the buzzing of your lips. The air has to be at the lip and not stuck behind the tongue. Think, "*Buzz, Buzz, Buzz, Buzz*" as you play. Always stress the buzzing of the lip rather than the blowing. Remember that if you buzz, you'll get the air as a bi-product, but if you just blow, you might or might not get the buzz as a bi-product.

After coming back from playing the piccolo, you want to make sure the middle range of your bigger instrument has little resistance from the tongue. Your tongue wants to get in the way and block the air that has to go to the lip because you just came back from playing the piccolo and the tongue wants to still be up high. It has to be thick air at the lip—not thin air. Can you go even more into the open vowels "OOH" or "AHH"? Drop your jaw and rub the floor of the mouth with your tongue. Now say this, "AH-LAH, TAH." The idea is for you to first get this open vowel concept as an exaggeration so you can later transfer that to *the norms* (normal playing). Don't think of your tongue merely as a muscle, but rather think for its potential as when used in speech.

Building Up Air Pressure Behind the Tongue

You don't want to build up the air pressure behind the tongue. It's air and lip that plays music. Use the "rim" [visualizer] to put the focus back on the relationship between air and lip. Of course, it will feel differently when you play your instrument, but you pretend it feels the same. Air and lip, not air and tongue. Psychologically, the air should be at the outer part of your lip and not inside of your mouth.

Controlling the Air with the Tongue

Be careful so your low register has the same standard of sound as your middle register. After a while, you start to control the air with your tongue [while playing the low notes] and we don't want that. You are using your tongue like a clutch in an automobile. The embouchure always needs air so it can vibrate. Don't let the tongue set the need for air by blocking its way to the embouchure.

Taking the Tongue Out of Tone Production

Can you play down your tongue a little bit so the buzz of the lip creates the *staccato*? You know how the buzz would be like on the rim [visualizer]. Right now your brain wants to connect the movements of the breath, the tongue, and the lips to buzz. That's wrong. I want the connection to be breath and lips only. Then you simply use the tongue as when you use it in speech—so you use it for timing and diction purposes. Music is always a combination of air and a buzzing embouchure.

Even a short note is a short buzz. You have to use the tongue, but basic tone production is air and buzz. You are giving the tongue too much emphasis to the point where the brain is beginning to accept the tongue as a control factor in tone production. For that reason, your brain is accepting the tongue as part of the musical equation with more importance than it deserves. The tongue does belong in the music making equation, but it's on a very small basis. In a graph, the use of the tongue would show as a small line when compared to the importance of air and buzz.

When you buzz the rim, you'll feel the lips as well as your tongue. Can you forget about the feel of the tongue and instead put a magnifying glass on the feel of the lips? When you go back to your instrument, you won't be able to feel the lips, but you have to pretend you do. Simply, remember the feel of the lips vibrating. Somewhere along the line, this has to become a learned function because it is very basic to your playing. You can't unlearn something that has been already learned and has reached a "habit form." You simply have to add and develop this new tool by using the rim for a few minutes twice a day and frequently touching your lips where they vibrate so you sensitize the feel of the buzz.

You want to play down much of the tongue's interference. Your job is to connect the air with the lip. There will be manipulation of the air column caused by various movements of the tongue, but keep that to a minimum. The tongue will want to take over. To avoid that from happening, play your tongued passages slurred. Notice the ease of playing and blowing. Take some of that ease to the tongued passage. Always look for the lack of back pressure.

Nothing has to be perfect when you start. At home, you can play simple tunes on the mouthpiece or the rim. Feel through the skin where the vibration is actually happening. It doesn't have to be exact, but it's simply that the brain is now concentrating on providing the motor activity while feeling the same motor activity. Can you make a study of connecting the vibration of the lip and the air so the tongue is almost like an accessory that works going up and down like a valve in an automobile? The tongue is important, but it's not the whole engine.

I want you to have the dominance in *Song* and embouchure so you are motivating your buzz. When you look at string bass players, they move their bows across the strings and you can actually see the strings vibrating. Well, in the tuba mouthpiece rim [visualizer] you can see the lips vibrating. You must concentrate on that lip vibration.

To improve the buzzing of the lip, be more mental in your playing. Record everything you play and listen to it from the standpoint of an audition committee. This way you'll also improve your aural skills. At your present stage of development, the more you imitate somebody, the better you'll play because your thoughts will become more creative and less analytical.

Some teachers teach their students to think in an analytical way. Try to avoid that. Great players should teach music because they are great musicians, but they also have to be good teachers. Fortunately, I was a fine player and a well-developed teacher (I have been teaching for sixty years). Teachers get in trouble when they teach a subject they don't know well. In brass playing that subject is physiology. They also get in a lot of trouble when they teach the methodology of muscles. As a student, you want to brush off those thoughts of physiology and muscles as soon as you can. You don't want those analytical teachers to turn you inward with self-analysis. Your playing is of a high order now and what you need is to learn the variety of styles so you can compete with great artists.

The Study of Vowels Forms

Don't fight an old habit because you are not going to win. Instead, add a new habit to replace the old one. It's just common sense. Instead of working with the small vowel forms, go back to the open vowel forms. For now, go for the oversized or the extreme. There is nothing wrong with the pure "EH" vowel form in brass playing, but if you get to "EEH," you might begin to have trouble with your chops. The "EEH" vowel is used for a very special purpose and when you use it, you should still have air at the lips. Use the study of the vowels as a "home teacher." [Exercises that reinforce the training of concepts learned in the lesson]. With students, you have them feel their trachea and if they have a tight throat, you don't have them use the "EH" or "EEH" vowels. You always want to have soft muscles in the throat area because then you'll have a relaxed throat. A relaxed throat is an open throat.

Go to "KEEH, EEH, and TEEH," so you emphasize the back, middle and front of your tongue. Inhale and exhale while you practice those vowels. With "KEEH," you'll feel your tongue staying at the top of your mouth and you will also feel tremendous pressure. Now, go to the other extreme. Try "AH, OH, OOH" and inhale and exhale. Now, go back to your instrument and try to feel that open oral "cavern." Studying the vowel forms this way is an exaggeration, but I want the exaggeration for your own recognition. Later—once you have the recognition of the vowel forms—you can find the tongue level as well as the tone production you want. I want you to be able to function with a closed or an open oral cavity. It doesn't have to feel good, but it has to sound good.

You should use precise language to control your tongue. For example, there is a specific shape for each vowel. If you modify them or mix them, you won't get the results you need. You need to perfect your vowel forms because it will help your playing. If you need to play with the "OOH" vowel, make sure it's "TOOH-KOOH-TOOH-KOOH" and not "TE-KE-TE-KE." Your tongue will shape differently for each of the vowels making it easier or harder to get the air to the lip.

Your tongue might be too forward and too close to the lips. Can you get it closer to the "AH" vowel? We need to get more of the language and the diction of speech. We need more of the "AH," "OH," and "OOH." You are not pronouncing the vowel forms clearly enough. Say "TOH," "TAH," "TEH," "TEEH," "TOH." Keep your diction pure.

If you would use more precise vowel forms, I could hear the difference in your sound. I hear for the student's precise diction. I hear it in the sound when players go "EEH" or they move into modifications. Many students don't use the tongue with proper language. They go to pseudo-syllables while they are playing. That is, they gradually go from "TA-LA-LA-LA" to "TO-LO-LO-LO." The whole thing is about diction. Feel your tongue when you go "OOH" and breathe in. The big problems often occur during inhalation. The shape that I want will happen during inhalation. In other words, the learning experience of the vowel forms will come when you breathe in. That's the one you have to learn.

Remedial Vowel Work

You have to emphasize the vowel so the tongue gets out of the way. Emphasize the vowels "AH-LAH-TAH" and rub the bottom of your mouth. You'll notice your tongue stays low in your mouth.

As you tongue, your tongue moves up and down. The down needs to be stressed because your tongue will want to start holding its upward position and you'll find it harder to proceed. Get the tongue out of the way by using the psychology of playing and not the physiology of playing.

You have to move your tongue out of the way. Say, "A-LAH." Is it possible for you to tongue where you say "LAH"? If you do this, the air will come out easily because it will be closer to the slur. Many people like to tongue right behind the lip, some others like the "T" to touch the lip, but it's not so important where you place the "T" compared to where the tongue withdraws. If you go "AH-LAH-LAH," your tongue becomes very flexible. You can also go "EH-LEH-LEH." When you do that, it becomes very easy to tongue, but it feels strange as hell. If you think of it almost as a slur, it becomes easy. What I am trying to do is separate the distance between the tongue and the lip. I am being somewhat experimental with this.

Your embouchure might be getting too small to play the lower notes partly because it's reacting to a thin column of air. That's why you are getting a thin sound in the low notes. That's similar to playing a bassoon with a small oboe reed. You don't have to do a thing about your embouchure, but instead you have to do something about your airways. First, drop your jaw, go "AH," and rub your tongue against the bottom of your mouth. Say "AH – LAH – LAH." Now play.

The answer is in the training of the tongue and not in the training of the embouchure. Your tongue has to be trained more towards the low vowel forms (AH, OH, OOH) and not the high vowels forms (EEH- KEEH-TEEH). The high vowel forms are imprinted in your brain as conditioned reflexes so you simply have to add the lower vowel forms as new stimuli every day.

As your embouchure gets smaller, you'll find that you lose the control of the lower notes. However, there are several ways of getting more air to your embouchure. First, you must make sure that your tongue is not too long. Say, "DOH" and "A-LAH" and you'll find that the tongue gets shorter. Now say "KEEH" and "OH." "OH" is the smaller tongue (either 'OH' or 'AH'). The study of vowel forms I just mentioned should become a daily airway study for months or years to come.

There is a continuity of procedures and we must start with the tongue. First of all, start with taking a deep breath because the shallow breath will have the brain assign a priority of closures in the mouth area (the tongue included) and it will closed no matter what you do. This occurs simply because you don't have enough air coming up the trachea. Take plenty of air and then play with a small tongue (lowering your jaw).

Appendix G: Tongue and Vowel Forms

Thickening Up Your Tone

To thicken up your sound, you don't have to play louder. You simply have to get your tongue out of the way. You do that by simply saying "TOH" as you play and avoid using your tongue as a roadblock—so the air can get to the embouchure. Once your tongue is out of the way, your tone will thicken up right away.

You can also memorize your sound under more favorable conditions (such as when you play selected studies from Max Schlossberg's *Daily Drills*). Don't memorize the feel, but instead memorize the tone itself. To help you maintain good tone production, you can divide long etudes into smaller sections so you can achieve good playing throughout.

You must constantly copy your good playing. Don't let bad notes go by. If you put in your head an excellent tone, you'll get an excellent tone in your instrument. On the other hand, if you go by the meat [lip] and its chain of commands, it's going to be difficult to play.

Attacks

The attack is always built upon the downward stroke of the tongue and not upon the upward stroke of the tongue. You have to blow your attacks as you would if you were blowing a candle or a bowl of soup—not like the air pressure of an "escape valve." When blowing like a escape valve, your tongue waits for a building up of air pressure and then releases it. Don't do that! Always motivate the attack with the lips vibrating and not simply by attacking with a hard stroke of the tongue. Don't motivate your attacks by using the tongue like a spring—i.e., springing forward. Instead, motivate your attacks by the buzzing of your lip.

The first attack of a phrase needs to be success or failure—in terms of tone production—by the first subdivision of a 32nd note. Play some single tongue exercise out of the Arban's method book—e.g., No. 19 on page 28—by first having the right sound in your head as you begin to blow. That means the dynamic and the tone color so your brain is flooded with the right sound. You want to make sure the quality of your performance doesn't deteriorate. Begin to memorize the music so your standards are memorized in the brain.

Tonguing in Accordance to the Art Form

You have to keep your tonguing functional one way or another. When I first retired from the symphony, the first thing to go was my single tonguing. I still have trouble tonguing today compared to where I was years ago. This is due to the reflexes that come into play when the air pressure increases when forcing the air out of the lungs. As soon as that happens, I involuntarily activate the muscles that have to do with throat closures. Of course, those closures slow down my tongue right away. I know that's simply due to insufficient air volumes. Keep in mind that my lung volumes are smaller now.

I have analyzed my playing and I know what's causing my slow tonguing. By now, I have overcome some of it already. The point is that you can't let your single tongue go. What I do, for instance, is work on Walter Smith's *Top Tones* (e.g., the double tongue *Etude* No. 22 in single tongue as well as in double tongue). I play all sorts of music with a variety of articulation.

Anything that keeps the tongue musically functional and strong in the art form is good material to practice. Not only talk about tonguing. Instead, play a great deal of tongued music under a variety of circumstances.

You have to create new forms of stimuli to form new tonguing habits. You do this over time by playing new music using the proper motivation. Of course, some professional players spend a considerable amount of time working on their tonguing because of the pressures involved in their jobs.

Find materials to develop a fast triple tongue as well as slow triple tongue. You must have a fast single tongue and a slow double tongue so you have a cross over rather than a break point where they might separate. That's how you can manage pieces like the trumpet solo in the Maurice Ravel's *Piano Concerto in G*.

High Note Entrances

You must prepare your embouchure and your air—not your tongue and your air—to play a high entry note. Try to imagine you are in the orchestra and [Sergei] Koussevitzky is there ready to give you a downbeat. You take a breath, wait four seconds [at zero pressure], and connect your embouchure and air to play. Hold the high entry note for four seconds and then come down the scale. This way, you'll soon get used to coming in on a high note.

Always base your playing on buzzing and not on blowing. Remember that you can blow without buzzing, but it's impossible to buzz without blowing. Make sure the music you play stabilizes your embouchure and not the other way around—that is, stabilizing your embouchure to stabilize your music. When you take a breath, don't go by connecting the breath and the tongue because you'll be unprotected and vulnerable to missing the entry note. If the sound comes right away, you are fine, but if the sound doesn't come right away, you'll be in trouble.

While you are holding your air at zero pressure, I need you to play the music in your head. You'll find that you'll come in with perfect preparation. Don't become distracted with peripheral thoughts—like preparing the tongue and the air—but instead prepare the embouchure and the air by mentalizing the entry note. This is the missing element in the playing of many brass players.

Bad Entrances

Sometimes the mouthpiece is not set firmly on your lips because you take the mouthpiece pressure off as you breathe. As a result, you might miss your entry note. We don't want that to happen. You must also have a tight enough control in the mind as well as the contact between your mouthpiece rim and your lip. Sometimes, soft entrances printed on the page create vagueness in the mentalizations of developing brass players. Even when your music printed *piano*, you should *sing* it loudly in your head. Make sure you put the notes into the cup of the mouthpiece. As soon as you put lyrics to a tune, you bring in accuracy to each pitch. You'll find that singing aloud and in tune before you play will help your soft entrances.

Playing *Staccato* Notes

Short *staccato* notes are short buzzed notes. They have to be perfect little sounds. Play them on the rim [visualizer] as short little notes. The lip has to want to vibrate. The ability of the lips to buzz is more important than the ability of the wind to push. Your airflow line has to be high and your air pressure line has to be low. You always lose when you force. As you are playing, it's hard to feel your lip buzzing, but if you use your imagination you can. Think, "*buzz, buzz, buzz.*"

The "H" Consonant

You should blow your *staccati* notes with an "H" consonant to give them their maximum sound. In your practice, I would like you to overdo the "H" consonant to get used to it; especially in the high register. Then your high notes will sound easy. As your playing improves, you'll find small details that will help you sound better. The "H" consonant is one of those details.

Without the "H" consonant, you find that every attack weakens the breath. In other words, there will be a reduction in the breath. However, you'll hear the change of sound right away if you use the "H" consonant. At this point in your musical development, it's up to you and your sense of interpretation. I'll teach you about it, but you'll decide if the use of the "H" consonant is useful in your musical interpretations.

Light Tonguing

Can you play the tongued passages so the notes are buoyant and light? You have to move towards the direction of more airflow and less back pressure. Also, you should give more of the characteristic of the sound you get in the sustained notes to the articulated notes. Play with a full tank of air. Don't be a shallow breather. Temporarily, go into massive inhalation and then make great music.

Triple Tongue

Don't make a big issue out of triple tonguing or you might make its application too severe. In other words, triple tongue is a light movement of the tongue. Say "TA-TA-KA-TA" and say "LAH-LAH-LAH-LAH." Can you have your "TA-TA-KA-TA" sound more like your "LAH-LAH-LAH-LAH"? Make sure your "AH" vowel stays equal throughout. Can you get the tone "AH" to be equal in quality throughout the entire passage? Match the tonal quality. You need a tonal triple tongue. Say "LAH-TAH" and match the tone of the vowel. I don't care what type of "AH" vowel you use as long as the vowel form matches throughout the entire passage. Any tonal changes happen because of shape differences in the tongue. As you triple tongue—because it goes so fast—you usually change the shape of the vowel form resulting in a change of tone. It's maybe getting a little harder, a little less accurate, or a little more severe.

In other words, right now there are tonal differences of which you are not in charge, but you should be in charge.

While triple tonguing, how close can you get to the pure sound that you produce in your long tones? Nine out of ten brass players will allow their tone to deteriorate when triple tonguing. That's not necessary.

Most people are not aware of this deterioration. In other words, it's not a disaster performance, but when you can achieve excellence, why have mediocrity? That's the challenge. You do the passage under the most favorable conditions to get the tone [e.g., slurring the entire passage to get a pure sound] and then you do triple tongue without allowing the deterioration of tone to come in.

Fast Tonguing

You must make sure you are completely relaxed. Usually when people tongue fast, they practice in short bursts [short phrases] and later they add length. In other words, you must develop fast tonguing by gradually practicing short passages and increasing their lengths. The phrases should be little pulses at first so you gain coordination. Don't play loud at first because everything will tense up (including the contraction of the tongue). You should isolate the function region of the tongue. You are going to feel all sorts of muscular sensations and it's going to indeed take more muscular activity. I have lost what I once had since I have not played in the orchestra for ten years. Now, I would get it back by practicing short units of tongued passages.

Continuous Triple Tonguing

Even during continuous tonguing, you have to find good qualities of tone. You have to find an excellent tone first in the sustained or slow playing and then you imitate that quality in your fast tonguing. Now, the tone changes shape as the air column gets thicker. Your air is thinning with all this tonguing because your tongue is not at the same place as when you play *legato*.

If the tongue would stay in the same place, you would get the same sound. The air column should be just as thick as when you are continuously tonguing. Most brass players settle for a lesser tone when they triple tongue. It might be expedient, but it's not the best brass playing.

Vowel Forms as Conceptual Thoughts

Open your oral cavity and make sure your tongue is not blocking. You do that by saying "AH" or "OH." Use your imagination and go "TAH" like a singer. Sing "EEH – AH." Play the horn and conceptualize those syllables like a singer would. Don't think of the mechanics, but think of the sound. Listen for an "EEH-AH" coming out the bell. If you are honest and you are thinking like a singer, there will be change in your sound. If you are thinking of it as an abstract thought and your habits are such that you are playing by feel, it won't happen and you won't hear any changes.

You'll do some of vowel changes at subconscious levels anyway. There are physiological changes that will tend to initiate these changes based on air pressures. For example, when you play a piccolo instrument *forte*, much of the reductions in the airways happen by themselves. The thing I worry about is that the changes in your playing come in too soon as you ascend into the high register. In other words, you are blocking your airways. I don't want a wide-open oral cavity when you are playing the piccolo in the extreme high register. That's not what I mean. I just want you not to close it in the lower register or to the point where you starve your embouchure. This won't work if you are used to playing by feel.

Using *Vibrato*

To avoid closing your airways prematurely as you ascend into the high register, I want you to occasionally use *vibrato* because of its pitch averaging. The tone floats more with it. It's not appropriate to use *vibrato* in all music, but it helps your over all tone production. To compete with the great players, you have to hit the center of the partial. With the *vibrato*, the pitch will go up and down, averaging dynamics and pitch. Acoustically, it will throw you towards the center of the channel where the easiest tone production is.

Index

A

Abdominal
    area, 120, 126, 223, 228
    muscles, 26, 40, 42, 112, 119, 120, 222, 224
    wall 40, 44, 46, 112, 116, 117
Absolute pitch, 95, 244
Acoustics, 5, 6, 69, 71, 74, 142, 146, 152
    device, 55, 60, 70. 137, 150, 173, 245
    laws, 6, 9, 69, 71, 152, 157, 241
Acting, 75, 132, 155, 170
Accuracy, 172, 245, 265
Adelstein, Bernard, 89
Aging, 144, 159
    breathing capacity, 48
    process, 33, 41, 48, 49, 84, 145
    psychological factors, 49
Air
    airways, 45, 62, 63, 83, 84, 119, 122, 129, 139, 202, 210, 211, 227, 230, 244, 248, 249, 262, 268
    feeding the tongue, 81, 227, 250
    pressure, 42-47, 54, 62, 66, 79
    thick air, 52-55, 62, 77, 84, 85, 116, 135, 164, 198, 200-202, 216, 227, 228-230, 242, 244, 257, 267
Alexander, Matthias
    Alexander Method (technique), 125, 223
America the Beautiful, 96, 181
Arban, Jean Baptiste, 2, 62, 67, 188, 203, 206, 211, 243, 247
Audition preparation, 94, 195
Auer, Leopold, 98
    The Spanish Hour, 37, 159
Authority, 37, 80, 87, 94, 95, 97, 159, 174, 184, 187, 203, 209, 244, 250

B

Bach, Johann Sebastian, 16, 62, 66, 196, 211-212, 231
    Cantata No. 51, 16
    Brandenburg Concerto No. 2, 62, 66, 196, 211-212, 231
Bach, Vincent, 70, 142
Back pressure, 56, 79-80, 138, 211, 241, 247, 259, 266

Bell's Palsy, 65
Bell, William (Bill), 193
Bernoulli, Daniel
    Bernoulli principle, 16
BERP, 247
Big bravuras, 226
Biocomputer, 4, 20, 36, 105, 148, 150, 153, 155, 158, 165, 167, 188, 202, 241
    programming 106, 108, 165, 181, 205, 222, 225
Biological science, 122, 214
Bjorling, Jussi, 22
Body and Soul, 185
Body types, 114
Bona, Paquale
    Complete Method for Rhythmical Articulation, 37, 98, 101, 160, 246
Boyle, Robert
    Boyle's law, 16, 84, 131
Brain, 4, 5, 7, 10-11, 17-21, 28-29, 34-36, 38, 40, 47, 49, 56, 61, 64, 76-77, 79
    as a tool, 160-162
    attacks, 263
    conceptualization, 74
    embouchure damage, 64
    fatigue, 67-68
    insecurity, 94
    round sounds, 91
    saturation, 218
    singing, 90
    study of vowels, 262
Brandt, Wassily
    34 Etudes, 64, 101, 216
Breath builder, 44, 46, 116-117
Breathing
    bag, 45-47, 115, 118, 226
    bellows, 40-43, 112-113, 117, 121, 126, 130, 221, 223
    blueprints, 40-43, 112-113, 116
    curves, 16, 47, 115, 119, 124, 127-129, 144, 225-226
    exercises, 44, 46-48, 116-118, 122-124
    gadgets, 46
    isometrics, 103, 113, 140
    modifications, 50-51
    physiology, 40, 112, 118, 123
    pressurization, 44-45, 82, 121, 231
    refinements, 50
    regional, 43, 114-115

surplus, 84, 94, 144, 185
tension, 46, 116-119, 224, 229
zero pressure, 44-45, 81, 122, 128-129, 225, 229-230, 264-265
Bronchial trees, 44, 116, 232
Bruckner, Anton
   Symphony No. 4, 73
   Symphony No. 8, 141
Buzz
   double, 135
   instant, 3, 236, 243
   mouthpiece, 55, 58, 60, 62, 69, 80, 95, 134, 135, 149, 192, 212, 237-239, 244, 246-247, 250
   psychology, 52, 243
   rim, 54, 79, 134, 137-138

C

Carnaval of Venice (Arban), 188, 206, 216, 243
Casio keyboard, 171
Challenges, 21, 41, 82, 110, 120, 132, 150, 158, 162, 166, 169, 170, 177, 196-197, 206, 213, 215, 220
Charlier, Theo,
   Trente-Six Études Transcendantes, 68, 101, 200, 201, 204-205, 216, 219, 227
Chicago Symphony Orchestra, 9, 11, 71, 74, 84, 98, 114, 176, 177, 189, 193, 196, 235, 277
Chicago Symphony Orchestra Brass Quintet, 142, 220, 245
Childlike approach, 18, 122, 148, 248
Christian Science Church, 10, 147
Clarke, Herbert Lincoln, 77, 101, 186, 215, 216
Clevenger, Dale, 35, 160, 217
Commercial music, 185, 216
Concentration, 10, 16, 20, 67, 108, 116, 132, 147, 176, 188, 211, 218, 246
Confidence, 34, 95, 150, 174, 176, 217
Consistency, 176, 198
Cornet solos, 110, 206, 215
Cranial nerves, 35
   fifth, 39, 56, 135
   seventh, 7, 39, 57-59, 135, 149, 153, 161, 190, 237, 251
Curtis Institute of Music, 8, 37, 73, 95, 96, 98, 154, 159, 180, 183
Cvejanovich, John, 16, 21, 28, 50-51, 77

D

Development
   challenges, 21, 162, 171

ear training, 37, 40, 149, 161
embouchure, 52, 60-61, 71, 131, 142, 150
endurance, 33, 36, 66-67
high levels (stages), 68, 170, 177, 206, 217, 260
high range, 62, 248
Jacobs's teaching, 10, 25, 28, 30
levels, 12
muscular, 61, 110
musical, 131, 266
physical, 242
process, 106
self, 98
tissue, 18, 148, 243
Diaphragm, 40, 43, 45, 48, 112, 115, 122, 125-127, 222, 245, 257
Discomfort, 58, 156, 225
Dixieland Jazz, 109, 219
Dockshizer, Timofei, 22-23, 98, 194
Double sound, 36, 150
Drills, 28, 34, 61, 111, 195, 202, 206, 213, 253

E

Ear training, 33-37, 149-150, 160-161, 169, 171-172, 203, 246
Effector, 38-39, 107-108, 163
Entry notes, 37-38, 111, 183, 229, 233, 255-256, 264-265
Embouchure
   air starvation, 83, 85
   as vocal chords, 4
   control, 18, 91
   damage, 33, 64-67, 251
   development, 60-64
   endurance, 33, 67-68, 210-211, 253
   handling, 7
   lateral length, 242
   pulls and balances, 20, 53
   reflexes, 12
   vibration, 56, 131
Emotions, 20, 110, 116-118, 169, 175, 177, 185
   study, 109
Ensemble playing, 75, 170, 177-178, 192, 232, 253
Excerpts, 61-62, 96, 137, 151, 164, 167, 181, 188, 199, 203-204, 211, 215-220, 251, 253,

F

False fingering, 63
Fatigue
   mental, 61, 67, 167

pseudo, 61, 68
Ferguson, Maynard, 71, 89, 142, 154
Fifth cranial nerve, 39, 56, 135
Focal points, 187-188, 206-207, 245,
Folk songs, 209, 213, 248
Friedman, Jay, 35, 160, 217

G

Galwey, Timothy, 138
Generations of musicians, 2, 30, 169
Getting back in shape, 55, 72, 134, 213,

H

Habits
    bad, 5, 154, 244
    biocomputer, 153
    breathing, 41, 49, 121, 130, 234
    forming, 152, 162, 248
    old, 35, 160, 173, 175, 217
    positive, 177
    sound production, 60
    tonguing, 264
Hanson, Harold, 117
Hasselman, Ron, 89
Haydn, Franz Joseph, 184
Heifetz, Jascha, 137, 220
Herseth, Adolph (Bud), 10, 15, 21-23, 35, 48, 63, 66, 68-69, 73, 84, 87, 89, 91, 94, 96, 101, 120, 132, 138, 146-147, 150-151, 154-155, 160, 162, 169-170, 175-177, 179-180, 184-186, 189, 192, 194-196, 199, 204, 216-219, 230-232, 245-246
Hiccup, 131
High register
    airways, 63, 198, 227-229, 232
    buzzing, 250
    development, 62
    extreme, 164, 249
    lips, 54
    practicing, 208
    rim buzzing, 55, 138
    round sound, 97, 230
    tessitura, 211
    tonguing, 83
Holland, Jack
    Buzz it, 247
Hypertrophy, 62, 67, 88, 104, 120, 138, 143, 208, 211, 239, 247, 272
Hyperventilation, 46-47, 118, 124-125, 272

I

Imagination, 10, 81, 86, 88-90, 93, 103, 105

110-111, 119, 147, 165, 167-171, 173, 186, 189, 219, 237, 250, 265, 268
Intercostal muscles, 40, 112, 118-119, 272
Intonation, 63, 142, 190-191, 207, 246
Intuition, 137, 168
Instrument makers, 70, 142

J

Jazz, 33, 66, 185, 209, 219,
    ballads, 209

L

Lactic acid, 60-61, 68, 210, 251-252, 272
Ladder of improvement, 32, 160, 170
Laryngeal nerve, 7, 57, 149
Laureano, Manny, 18, 22, 29, 39, 81, 92, 215, 272
Learning
    process, 88, 97, 195, 199, 234
Leather lips, 67
Lip
    buzzing, 29, 52, 58, 60, 134, 228
    changes, 2
    effector, 39
    embouchure, 53, 131
    fatigue, 67, 167
    feeling, 61, 229, 253
    lipping up/down, 63-64
    mind connection, 164
    resistance, 42, 103, 114
    singing, 5
    stiff, 129
    swelling, 66
    vibration, 3, 12, 33, 52, 54, 56, 77, 152, 231, 260
    vocal chords, 6, 133, 135-136, 146
Long Beach Municipal Band, 186
Lyric Opera of Chicago, 22, 64

M

Mahler, Gustav
    Symphony No. 2, 71, 142
    Symphony No. 3, 151, 203-204, 220
    Symphony No. 5, 220, 226
    Symphony No. 6, 96, 180
Maltz, Maxwell, 27, 138
Maniacal strength, 120, 252
Marsalis, Wynton, 206
Mentalis, 52, 131
Mental fatigue, 61, 67, 167
Mentalization, 2-5, 7-8, 68, 87, 94, 98, 150

INDEX

152, 156, 165, 167, 175, 185-186, 218, 46, 265
Mind over matter, 10, 147
Minimal motors, 42, 46, 114, 117, 119, 121, 224
Missed notes, 172
Minneapolis Symphony Orchestra, 89
Motivation, 11, 18, 136, 171, 182, 189, 263-264
    study, 109, 144
Motor nerves, 38-39, 107-108, 166
Mouthpiece
    acoustical laws, 6, 9, 69, 71, 152
    adjustable cup, 71, 141-142
    bugle effect, 250
    flat rim, 71, 142
    placement, 239
    pressure, 52, 68, 134, 251, 255, 265
    rounded rim, 71, 142
    thin wall, 142
Muscle
    fatigue, 212, 252
    fibers, 53, 55, 60, 67-68, 117, 119-120, 122, 134, 190, 224, 252
    innervation, 223
    rest, 60-62, 67, 212, 247, 251-252
Music Minus One, 196, 218

N

Nagel, Robert, 200
Neck
    bulging, 139
Nervous system, 4, 6, 38, 57, 94, 107, 148, 155, 175, 206
Neural inhibition, 119
Neural pathways, 36, 167, 199
New York Philharmonic, 106, 193

O

Obicularis oris, 52-53, 134
Orchestral repertoire, 8, 71, 142, 151, 154, 180, 199, 202, 205, 207, 215, 219, 220
Oscilloscope, 73
Over pressurization, 231

P

Paralysis by analysis, 132
Parton, Dolly, 225
Pavarotti, Luciano, 155
Perfect pitch, 9, 246
Performance consistency, 176

Personality types, 170
Philadelphia Orchestra, 183, 197
Phrasing
    building by individual notes, 181
    class, 96
    nuances, 162, 184
    practice, 181, 183, 188
Piccolo instruments, 186, 209-210
Pitch
    absolute, 95, 244
    pipe, 95, 176, 203, 244
    recall, 33-34, 40, 95, 110, 112, 147, 150, 161, 163, 171-172, 183, 188, 191, 244-245, 247
    relative, 95, 244
Positive attitude, 87, 95, 138, 174-175
Posture, 117, 126, 223
Practice, 8, 30
    breathing habits, 41, 45-47, 117, 121-124, 234
    dynamics, 74-75, 135, 189, 195, 197, 252
    high range, 63, 84, 110, 205, 208-209, 247
    materials, 50, 196, 198, 202-206, 217-218, 227, 264
    mouthpiece buzzing, 58, 246
    multiple tongue, 77, 83-84, 256
    phrasing, 181, 183, 188
    pitch recall, 171
    reflex development, 36, 106, 150, 188
    repetitions, 34, 199
    schedule, 60-61, 68-69, 202
    singing and playing, 35, 161
    slow, 207
    tone, 200, 212, 214-216
    vowel forms, 76, 78, 244, 257, 260, 266
    warm up, 65, 155
Prokofiev, Sergei, 217
Protractors, 52-54, 71, 134, 142, 242
Pseudo-functions, 55, 119, 123, 134
Psycho cybernetics, 27, 138
Psychodynamics, 11, 147
Psychokinesis, 10, 98

R

Recital preparation, 94, 184, 218, 220
Reiner, Fritz, 8, 22, 154, 183, 193, 214
Regional breathing, 43, 114-115
Relative pitch, 95, 244
Relaxation pressure, 118, 127, 225-226
Respighi, Ottorino
    The Pines of Rome, 203

Respirometer, 26, 126
Retractors, 52-54, 71, 134, 142, 242
Rhythm, 35, 80-81, 160, 163, 168, 178-179,
    182-183, 187, 196, 199, 207, 234
    blowing, 233
    buzz, 250
    pulses, 186
    stabilizing, 188
Rim, 47, 52, 54-56, 72, 79-80, 123, 134, 138,
    142, 165, 237-238, 243, 249,
    258-260, 265
Rochut, Joannes, 101, 110, 205
Rodzinski, Artur, 193
Round sound, 19, 53, 64, 73, 88, 91-93, 97,
    186, 191, 200, 210, 227, 230, 233,
    238, 240-242

S

Scarlett, William, 9, 15, 21, 26, 42, 48, 92,
    114
Schilke, Renold, 25-27, 70-71, 142, 245
Schlossberg, Max
    *Daily Drills and Technical Studies
    for the Trumpet,* 101, 177, 199, 202-
    203, 205, 215, 227, 263
Schwartz, Gerard, 200
Self-analysis, 132, 137, 168, 260
Seventh cranial nerve, 7, 35, 39, 56-59, 135,
    149, 153, 161, 190, 237, 251
Severinsen, Doc, 89, 154
Shallow breathers, 16, 26, 33, 41-42, 49, 78,
    119, 121, 141, 212, 262, 266
Singing approach, 5, 8, 10, 98
Shew, Robert (Bobby), 51
Short notes, 191, 233, 243, 265
Sight reading, 178, 193
Smith, Philip, 106
Smith, Walter
    Top Tones, 68, 101, 197, 200, 204-
    205-206, 216, 219, 227, 243, 245,
    253, 264
Solfège, 7, 9, 33-35, 40, 110, 150, 153, 157,
    159-160, 163, 171-172, 237
Solti, Georg, 96, 180, 193, 235
Song and wind, 2-5, 8, 15-16, 18, 20, 56-57,
    87, 98, 104, 108, 116, 120, 148,
    152, 162, 168, 207, 221-223, 229,
    234, 277
Soprano arias, 187
Sound
    big, 75, 137, 189
    loud, 2, 12, 26, 61, 67, 74-75, 113,
    125, 137, 139, 141, 189-190, 196-
    197, 203, 209, 224, 232, 243, 251,
    263, 267

    thin, 230, 241, 262
Spirometer, 48
Staccato, 79, 192, 243, 258, 265
Stardust, 185
Static pressure, 45, 54, 122, 197, 221, 229,
    234
Stiff players, 187
Strobo-tuner, 191
Storytelling, 22, 58, 87, 93, 93, 97, 132, 136,
    179, 186
Strauss, Richard, 217
    Also Sprach Zarathustra, 219
Stravinsky, Igor
    Petroushka, 220
Stress, 60-61, 74, 213-214, 253
Summit Brass, 22, 194

T

Tabuteau, Marcel, 73, 95, 183-184, 233
Teaching
    fatigue, 29, 163
    schedule, 163
    teaching hat, 132
The Inner Game of Tennis, 138
Test lung, 45, 47, 115, 124
Thick air, 52-55, 62, 77, 84, 85, 116,
    135, 164, 198, 200-202, 216, 227,
    228-230, 242, 244, 257, 267
Thin air, 77, 164, 198, 202, 228, 258
Thoracic breathing, 222, 235
Tone
    deaf, 161, 169
    edgy, 33, 54, 56
Top Tones
    Walter Smith, 68, 101, 197, 200,
    204-206, 216, 219, 227, 243,
    245, 253, 264
Tomasi, Henri, 226
Tongue
    attacks, 40, 43-44, 81, 113, 121, 140,
    183, 210, 241, 248,
    255, 263, 266
    bad entrances, 265
    controlling the air, 258
    continuous triple tongue, 267
    fast, 82, 256, 264, 267
    high note entrances, 264
    multiple, 77, 82-84, 256
    physiology, 85, 256
    setting up resistance, 257
    staccato, 79, 192, 243, 258, 265
    study of vowels, 78, 85, 210, 260-
    262
    teaching problems, 76
Torchinsky, Abe, 197

Trills, 212
Triple tongue
    tonal, 82, 266-267
Trumpet player blackout, 232-233
Turns, 212

U

Unfocused thinking, 212
University of Chicago
    Medical School, 232, 241

V

Valsalva, Antonio Maria
    Valsalva maneuver (reflex), 17, 20, 79
Veil *pianissimo,* 59, 136
Velocity development, 199, 206-207
Ventilin, 115
Verdi, Guiseppe
    Simon Boccanegra, 158
Visualizer, 54, 59, 79, 136-137, 164, 238, 258, 260, 265
Vowels
    conceptual thought, 268
    open forms, 210, 260-261

W

Warm air, 52, 77
Warm up, 65-66, 110, 120, 219
Wedge breathing, 51
Williams, Ernest, 164
Wind
    patterns, 51
    thick, 51, 77, 228

Y

Young mind
    teaching, 88, 107

Z

Zero pressure, 44-45, 81, 122, 128-129, 225, 229-230, 264-265

Biographical Information

Arnold Jacobs

Arnold Jacobs is considered by many musicians to be one of the most influential brass pedagogues of the Twentieth Century. This is evident in the number of players who studied with him and in the various books and articles published as tribute to his work. Jacobs's teaching principles were summarized by the expression *Song and Wind*. In general, the word *Song* summarizes the psychological aspects involved in music performance while the word *Wind* summarizes the physiological aspects.

Jacobs was born in 1915 in Philadelphia but was raised in the small desert town of Willowbrook, California. He played the trumpet from a young age, switched to trombone, and later to tuba. At the age of 15 he became a student at the Curtis Institute of Music in Philadelphia and later played with the Indianapolis and Pittsburgh Symphony Orchestras. He toured with Leopold Stokowski and the All-American Youth Orchestra before joining the Chicago Symphony Orchestra in 1944. He performed as principal tubist of that orchestra until 1988. Jacobs passed away on October 7, 1998.

Luis E. Loubriel, D.M.A.

Luis E. Loubriel is a trumpeter, music teacher, and researcher who has performed with the Minnesota Orchestra, The Canadian Brass Quintet, and the Artie Shaw Orchestra, among others. He currently serves as Director of the Department of Music and Assistant Professor of Music at Benedictine University in Lisle, IL. He earned a B.M. and M.M. in Trumpet Performance from Northwestern University in Evanston, IL and a D.M.A. in Trumpet Performance and Literature from the University of Illinois at Urbana-Champaign.

He has published articles with the *International Trumpet Guild Journal*, and the peer-reviewed journals *Forum on Public Policy Journal* and *The Journal of Integral Theory and Practice* (distributed by SUNY Press). He has given lectures on the subject of brass pedagogy and performance at Carnegie Mellon University; Harris Manchester College in Oxford, England; University of Texas at Austin; Western Illinois University; and the University of Illinois at Urbana-Champaign. He is the author of the book titled *Back to Basics for Trumpeters: The Teaching of Vincent Cichowicz* published in 2010 by Scholar Publications.

Also available by
Luis E. Loubriel

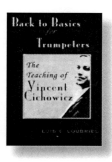

"A **MUST READ** FOR ANY AMBITIOUS TRUMPETER."
—*Frank Kaderabek*

"AN ENGAGING, CLEAR, AND INSPIRING READ."
—*The Brass Herald*

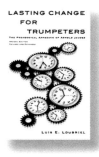

SECOND EDITION
UPDATED AND EXPANDED

Available at www.scholarpublications.com or at our fine re-sellers